1950s-1960s Fable

TODD M. DALEY

Word Art Publishing
9350 Wilshire Blvd
Suite 203, Beverly Hills, CA 90212
www.wordartpublishing.com
Phone: 1 (888) 614 - 1370

© 2021 Todd M. Daley. All rights reserved.

No part of this book may be reproduced, stored in a retrieval system, or transmitted by any means without the written permission of the author.

Published by Word Art Publishing

ISBN: 9781955070065 (paperback)
ISBN: 9781955070089 (ebook)

Any people depicted in stock imagery provided by Shutterstock are models, and such images are being used for illustrative purposes only.

Certain stock imagery © Shutterstock.

Because of the dynamic nature of the Internet, any web addresses or links contained in this book may have changed since publication and may no longer be valid. The views expressed in this work are solely those of the author and do not necessarily reflect the views of the publisher, and the publisher hereby disclaims any responsibility for them. The opinions expressed in this manuscript are solely the opinions of the author and do not represent the opinions or thoughts of the publisher. The author has represented and warranted full ownership and/or legal right to publish all the materials in this book.

Kierkegaard: "Life can only be understood backwards; but it must be lived forwards."

CONTENTS

Chapter 1 - Loose Pigs 1
Chapter 2 - School Days 11
Chapter 3 - Going to Church 17
Chapter 4 - Little Mommy 24
Chapter 5 - Holidays with the Smiths 30
Chapter 6 - Summer Days 36
Chapter 7 - Planting and Harvesting 44
Chapter 8 - Cold Wars 51
Chapter 9 - Black and White 58
Chapter 10 - A Letter from Little Mommy 62
Chapter 11 - Clove Lakes Park 70
Chapter 12 - Acting Up on the Farm 73
Chapter 13 - Day if Departure 88
Chapter 14 - A New Life on Staten Island 91
Chapter 15 - P.S 21 101
Chapter 16 - The Drinking Dads of Elm Park 105
Chapter 17 - Poetry Recital 119
Chapter 18 - Church Issues 128
Chapter 19 - Return to the Farm 135
Chapter 20 - The Space Race. 141
Chapter 21 - Basketball Tournament 146
Chapter 22 - The Return of Thomas Haley 148
Chapter 23 - Newspaper Route 152
Chapter 24 - Marxism vs. Capitalism 163
Chapter 25 - Thomas Haley in Trouble 169
Chapter 26 - Thomas Haley at Rest 174
Chapter 27 - Port Richmond High School 178
Chapter 28 - A Serious Student 178
Chapter 29 - Latin and Science 194
Chapter 30 - John Kennedy at the Ferry 200
Chapter 31 - An Offer by the Coach 206
Chapter 32 - The Scholarship Class 216
Chapter 33 - Union Issues 223
Chapter 34 - Nervous Breakdown 228
Chapter 35 - Prom Night 238
Chapter 36 - Rites of Spring 242
Chapter 37 - Friendly Competition 245
Chapter 38 - Joanie Gardello 250

Chapter 39 - PRHS Graduation 257
Chapter 40 - Fun City 261
Chapter 41 - Summer of Love 267
Chapter 42 - The Worst News 273
Chapter 43 - Helen to the Rescue 276
Chapter 44 - A Game of Stick Ball.. 280

About The Author 283

CHAPTER 1

Loose Pigs

The sun rose over the pale blue eastern sky—visible from the kitchen window of the Smith's narrow six-room house. Through this kitchen window much of their 12-acre farm could be seen. There were fields planted neatly with rows of corn plus the many kinds of vegetables of Mom's truck garden. To the right was a winding narrow road that led to a chicken coop, pigpens, and a large enclosed turkey pen. The Smith farm was bounded by pine trees to the left, a long shallow creek, Hunt's Creek, to the right, and a broken wooden fence at the far end of the property—not visible from the kitchen window. Suddenly the eerie quiet of the mild spring morning was interrupted by pigs squealing and snorting in the backyard.

"The pigs are loose!" shouted Mom. Soon everybody was on the move—Mom, Dad, and Harry, and Helen, the Smith's teenagers, plus the two youngsters, Tom and Cara—tossing off blankets and dressing quickly. In a few minutes, all hands were outside—running, shooing, yelling, chasing, and even laughing at the errant pigs. The escaped pigs were in Mom's truck garden munching on her tomatoes, lettuce, and tasty melons. Though wide in girth and clumsy in their movements, pigs can be quick on their feet and slippery skinned from rolling in the mud. Tom giggled when the biggest pig, a 300-pound sow, eluded Harry's grasp as he slipped on some loose topsoil. The pigs, enjoying their short-lived freedom, squealed and squirmed when caught.

Eventually, the big pigs were shooed back with brooms and rakes, while the piglets were grabbed by their back feet and carried back to their smelly pig-pen. When all six pigs were accounted for, the four Smith kids were driven to school by Dad, having missed the school bus. The excuse for their tardiness—a familiar Smith alibi: "The pigs were loose."

The Smith family was dominated by Mrs. Smith, a stocky hard-working woman, who combined the job of mother, farm wife, and factory worker in one energetic package. Mrs. Smith would occasionally dream that something was awry on the farm—the pigs were loose, the chickens had fled the chicken coop, or the turkeys were dying of a disease. Waking up in a fright, she would discover that her nightmare was actually happening. Mr. Smith had a slightly more limited role because of polio-inflicted handicap—limited mobility and restricted use of his hands—though he also worked in the same factory and did much around the farm. Thus the Smith family had shared responsibility and a balanced power structure— somewhat unusual in the 1950's.

The four Smith children were so unique and individual that it was hard to believe that they belonged to the same family. The eldest child was Helen, a smart, resourceful, and pretty young woman who entertained her two youngest siblings with stories about God, good versus evil, and the origins of the world. She could convert mundane household and outdoor chores into magical games. Naturally, Helen was adored by her two youngest siblings, Tom and Cara. The second oldest child was Harry, an ambitious, hard-working, soft-spoken teenager, who got up early every day before school to work for the Geratty poultry farm—feeding and tending its hundreds of egg laying and fryer chickens. The youngest child was Cara, a moody, dreamy eyed girl who was an artist-in-making. She would spend hours drawing pictures of flowers, animals, and cartoon figures with uncanny accuracy and movement. Cara, wise beyond her years, would jump on the backyard swing when the pigs got loose. The younger boy, Tom was Cara's senior by one year. He was an introverted boy who liked to make things, play baseball, and read books. The older Smith kids would affectionately tease their younger siblings—called Cara "Miss Pencil" and Tom "Uncle Sam."

In the 1950's, New Jersey—especially the south-western part—was truly the "Garden State." There were farms all around the town of Bloomington—as far as the eye could see. Across the road, Eden Avenue, was a big apple orchard. In the late summer, the neighborhood kids would cross the road to grab an apple from the ground for a quick tasty snack. Snatching one from a tree was frowned upon in those days. The humming sound of tractors plowing the area's vast fields was commonplace during the spring. And the stirring sight of a piper plane spraying the crops with DDT was a customary phenomenon during those innocent times.

The sights, sounds and odors of 1950's farm life were pleasantly familiar. The food—home-grown corn, tomatoes, potatoes, carrots, green beans, peppers, strawberries, watermelons, fresh eggs, chicken, turkey, and even the occasional rabbit—was plentiful and delicious. However, much of family farming consisted of nitty-gritty chores like planting crops, weeding and watering the garden, and feeding the pigs, chickens, and turkeys. Repairing pig-pens, turkey-pens, and cleaning the chicken coop had to be fitted into a busy schedule of factory work, school, homework, and play. During the 1950s, corporations were viewed as benevolent providers of jobs and goods for working people. Charles Wilson, the head of General Motors, had said: "What is good for General Motors, is good for America."

Weeding Mom's truck garden was a tedious job for the younger Smith kids. Yet, there was something special about the feel and smell of the rich South Jersey soil from which so many things grew abundantly. Tom and Cara were drafted into weeding duty by Mom on hot summer mornings. Older sister Helen made a game of it—singing "Tip-toe Through the Tulips", pointing out various insects—lady bugs, beetles and spiders. Helen had them race to see who finished his row first. In their rush to be first, one of the kids mistakenly pulled up a carrot or string bean, instead of a weed. Then Helen sent them packing— "Scram! Go play in the yard."

Tom was his dad's helper for various farm repair jobs—broken fences, ripped pigpens and torn turkey cages. Dad, hampered by childhood polio, was surprisingly adept with a hammer and saw. Since Harry often worked for the Geratty farm, Tom was Dad's willing apprentice. The boy liked to make things out of discarded wooden planks, two-by-fours, and other discarded materials found on the 12-acre farm. He built a wooden shack near the chicken coop, complete with a tar-paper roof, a door, and a window space. He would go to the shack to read his adventure books and play with his baseball cards. One day, a thunderstorm appeared suddenly while Tom was hanging out in his shack. Though scared by mother nature's fury, Tom thought he'd wait out the storm inside his cozy shack. But Mom dispatched Harry to fetch the younger boy as the storm raged with pounding rain, roaring wind, streaking lightning, and booming thunder. Harry, none too happy, brought his younger brother back sopping wet, after cursing him for his brazen stupidity.

On the way back to the house, they ran past a big weeping willow tree, which bent under the wind. Moments later, a lightning bolt severed a huge branch from the tree. Timing is everything in life!

Tom also built a go-cart out of wooden planks attached to baby carriage wheels. He constructed a square passenger compartment where the driver sat, a clear plastic windshield, and a circular cardboard steering wheel. The cart was painted black inside and outside like his dad's 1954 Plymouth sedan. Unfortunately, the boy chose to sit in the cart seat before the paint had completely dried so his overalls were stained black in the rear. Harry chided his brother about his black-painted backside: "Somebody is gonna kick your black ass!" Nevertheless, the Smith's dad was a wonderful role model for Tom, who even adopted his father's awkward shambling gate—another grim result of Mr. Smith's childhood polio.

The Smith farm had in addition to the six pigs, twenty egg-laying chickens housed in the chicken coop, and some ducks who wandered freely around the farm, plus approximately sixty turkeys kept in a large fenced-in turkey cage which was raised four feet above the ground. Turkeys, the Smith's "cash crop", were raised from March to November and sold to co-workers for holiday dinners. Initially, the turkeys were dispatched by placing the hapless bird's head on a wooden block and chopping it off with a hatchet. Mom was the executioner because neither Dad nor Harry had the stomach to decapitate the big birds. It was unnerving to see the headless, bleeding turkey wander about aimlessly in their short dance of death. Later on, Mom became more adept at this gruesome job—slitting the bird's throat and holding it at arm's length as the frantic turkey flapped its wings and bled to death. Anyone within a few feet of the flailing turkey was spattered with blood.

1950s-1960s Fable

Then, the moribund bird was tossed in a big pot of boiling water to be de-feathered—another unpleasant job in which the entire family, including Tom and Cara, was drafted. The kids hated this gruesome job, which left them with scalded fingers and with smelly turkey feathers covering their clothes.

Tom was also struck by the idea that a lot of animals must die in order for people to eat.

Tom didn't spend all his time working on the Smith farm—playing baseball was a new passion. The wide-open fields afforded the opportunity for pick-up games with kids from neighboring farms. Tom made up with enthusiasm what he lacked in talent. Not good enough for the little league, he played on the farm team. In his first game, Tom was chosen to pitch because of his strong arm. He started the game throwing over-hand but when his arm tired, Tom switched to side-armed pitches. Either way, he had trouble getting the ball over the plate for a strike. After three walk-filled innings, the coach replaced Tom with a chubby kid who threw the ball with an awkward flinging motion, similar to that of a girl. Yet this unconventional novice had good control—so the game progressed.

Wild and erratic as a pitcher, clumsy-handed as an infielder as ground balls skirted beneath his glove, Tom was banished to the quiet expanses of the outfield. Despite occasionally misjudging fly balls, Tom possessed a centerfielder's assets of foot speed and a strong arm. However, he played too deep in center field. The thought of a ball sailing over his head was a constant fear. At bat, he was a wild swinger— seldom taking a strike and hitting the ball (when he made contact) to right field because he was a chronic late swinger. When time permitted, big brother Harry would take a break from his chores at the Geratty farm to play catch with Tom or pitch batting practice to the boy.

A muscular teenager, Harry could have been a baseball star at Bloomington High School had he not spent long hours working for Mr. Geratty. Despite his inauspicious start, Tom loved baseball—the sizzling sound of a fast ball zooming by the batter, the sharp explosion of wooden bat hitting the ball, the pop of a thrown baseball snagged by a leather glove, the dusty grittiness of the infield, the sweet smell of outfield grass, the wonderful symmetry of the diamond-shaped infield, the parabolic path of a fly ball, the magic of an infielder scooping up a ground ball and throwing out the runner by a half step—captivated the impressionable boy. Across the road (Eden Avenue) were an apple orchard and vast stretches of wheat fields tended by migrant farm workers—Puerto Rican men wearing sleeveless undershirts and straw hats. Mom warned the kids not to talk to "the PRs", who scrupulously avoided the local people and spoke to each other in Spanish. On Saturday nights they would dress up and head into town to do whatever working people do to blow off steam.

One day, Tom was playing catch with Cara when one of her errant tosses flew across Eden Avenue into the apple orchard. Before Tom could cross the road, a muscular brown-skinned man jumped down from a tree-propped ladder, grabbed the ball, and tossed it back to Tom. For no reason in particular, the boy threw it back to the man, who then tossed the ball to Cara, who caught it smartly with her baseball mitt. Soon a game of toss and catch ensued between the unlikely threesome. However, the appearance of a red-faced overseer brought the impromptu game to a halt. The two kids waved good-by to the Puerto Rican farm worker, who quickly climbed up the ladder and resumed picking apples.

The Smiths were frugal hardworking people—managing their twelve-acre farm along with working at the nearby Bloomington canning factory. A by-product of their assembly line work was an abundant supply of canned goods—soup, pork and beans, spaghetti and meat balls, and various canned vegetables for their kitchen table. Dad went to the A & P to pick up discarded produce to be fed to the pigs. The Smith's also made long trips to a farming supplies store, where they bought 50-pound bags of chicken and turkey feed at a good price. During supper, the Smith children were urged to clean their plates, an order which was readily obeyed, because Korean children often went to bed hungry. Yet the Smiths would often invite family and friends from Jersey

City for holiday weekends and summer breaks. The small six-room house would be filled with "city people" sleeping on mattresses in the living room, attic, and pantry. Mom would cook spaghetti, turkey, chicken, potatoes, corn, and other vegetables in huge pots in her small, steamy, odor-filled kitchen. Card games, board games, TV watching, back-yard picnics, and tours of the farm provided the entertainment for the city folks.

June 25, 1950

North Korea invaded South Korea, crossing the 38th parallel with thousands of troops and hundreds of tanks. The U.S. responded by deploying troops, tanks, ships, and planes into the Korean peninsula—gradually pushing the North Koreans back to the 38th parallel and recapturing Seoul, the capital of South Korea. Approximately 40,000 American and 8,000 South Korean troops under General MacArthur landed at Incheon, South Korea— pushing northward and threatening to trap the North Korean army near Seoul. As the Americans, British, French, and South Korean forces (under United Nations command) pushed well beyond the 38th parallel into North Korea, Red China began massing its troops near the North Korean border.

By November 1950, 200,000 Red Chinese troops pushed the U.N. forces towards South Korea. After advances and retreats on both

sides, the Korean War turned into a bloody stalemate with huge losses of soldiers and civilians for all combatants – including the destruction of Seoul. Following many months of arduous negotiations, an armistice agreement was signed by the U.N., North Korea, and Red China in July 1953. A demilitarized zone was established just north of the 38th parallel. The U.S. suffered more than 44,000 battle deaths (including 8,000 MIA), North Korea lost approximately 500,000 men, and Red China lost roughly 400,000 men. Total civilian casualties were estimated at 2,000,000 with Seoul, South Korea, decimated as well as most North Korean cities destroyed by U.N. bombing.

During the war, General Douglas MacArthur was relieved of his command by President Harry Truman for insubordination. General MacArthur had wanted to use nuclear weapons against Red China without authorization from the President. A popular criticism of MacArthur was that he never spent a night in Korea and directed the war from the safety of Tokyo. In submitting his resignation to Congress, General MacArthur said, "Old soldiers never die, they just fade away."

One Jersey City relative, Uncle Eddie, liked to watch baseball on TV which broadcast the games of local favorite – the Philadelphia Phillies, whom Eddie referred to as the "Whiz Kids." He talked about baseball stars like Robin Roberts, Stan Musial, Ted Williams, Jackie Robinson, Yogi Berra, and Pee Ree Reese. As a result, Tom began to read the sports pages – studying box scores, the major league standings, and other baseball statistics. The ups and downs of the Phillies reminded the boy of everyday life, which had its good days and bad days. Aside from baseball, Uncle Eddie had little interest in looking at farm animals or walking through Mom's truck garden. When the other Jersey City visitors left for the grand tour of the Smith's twelve-acre farm, he hung around with the kids – Tom and Cara.

1950s-1960s Fable

Tom soon tired of watching TV and ran over to the Hunt's farm to play catch with a friend. When everyone returned, Cara was in her room taking a nap, while Uncle Eddie watched a baseball game. She told Mom that she didn't feel good. Upon waking, the little girl was upset about something, but wouldn't say why.

Everybody assumed that Cara was having one of her "moody days"—a common affliction for "Miss Pencil." After the visitors had left for Jersey City, Tom noticed Helen whispering to Mom who frowned and looked troubled. From that day onward, Uncle Eddie did not return to the Smith farm for many years.

CHAPTER 2

School Days

Starting out in the early grades as a below-average reader, Tom progressed to the point where he was placed into the top reading group by the third grade. The reason for this steady improvement was the boy's discovery of an old book case in the Smith's cellar. The wooden book case contained approximately fifty books of every type. There were picture books, dictionaries, encyclopedias, animal books, science books, and history books. Most importantly, there were his favorites—adventure stories about pirates, cowboys and Indians, detectives, and jungle boys. In addition to be becoming a good reader and speller, Tom became proficient in arithmetic—quickly learning his time tables, addition and subtraction facts, and the intricacies of fractions and decimals.

He did his class work diligently and quickly—leaving himself ample time to talk to his pals and tease the girls sitting near him. Eventually, his rambunctiousness was drilled out of him as a result of after-school sessions writing "Silence is golden" five hundred times. The boy had a zany sense of humor that amused his teachers. "Tom is a bird!" exclaimed Mrs. Fisher, his strict fourth-grade teacher. Despite her no-nonsense approach to pupil conduct, Mrs. Fisher had a heart of gold. One day she was complaining about a boy's behavior in her class to his mom. The parent angrily responded that she would beat Johnny when they got home.

1950s-1960s Fable

Appalled, Mrs. Fisher responded: "Oh no, Mrs. Bosco! Johnny is really a good boy. Please don't hit him. "Like most school children, Tom's favorite class was recess — when he could burn his pent-up energy.

Bloomington Elementary School had a big triangular-shaped playground, bounded by an old wooden fence and filled with oak trees, a big sand box, seesaws, monkey bars, and swings. The fenced-in playground was not far from some railroad tracks. Whenever a train passed by, the children would wave to it — resulting in an occasional toot in response. Most of the kids played with their classmates remaining in one area, but Tom liked to roam around the entire playground — especially the extreme apex of the triangle where there were huge oak trees and big boulders for climbing. He struck up a friendship with an older "colored boy" named Earl, who enjoyed the sand box.

One day, Tom threw a tin sand bucket over his head without looking — striking Earl in the head. Tom ran over to his friend — apologizing and rubbing the growing bump on his scalp. Earl told him to scram, "I'm going to get you for this!" For weeks whenever Tom approached Earl, he would shove the younger boy away — threatening to beat him up. Desperate to renew their friendship, Tom brought Earl a peace offering hidden in a paper bag — a chopped-off turkey head. Mollified, Earl allowed the younger boy to hang out with him as the two explored the triangle-vertex area — far away from the other kids and the patrolling teachers. The boys found an old wooden box which they converted into a rabbit trap complete with a carrot tied to a string. The box was propped open with a stick that was supposed to give way when the carrot was yanked by a hungry hare. The only animal they ever trapped was an alley cat who scratched Tom's hand when he reached into the wooden box. Occasionally the children's rollicking recess time was interrupted by an elderly white-uniformed nurse who corralled them for a visit to the school's dental clinic. A fully-equipped dental office was housed in a large gray trailer parked near the playground. Tom was drafted by the severe-looking nurse for a terrifying ordeal, the repair of his first cavity, performed by a balding dentist with a brusque, heavy-handed manner. Like his classmates, Tom was frightened to be yanked from the joyful anarchy of recess to the torments of the dental chair. The tiny dental office was marked by its medicinal odors and the terrifying array of metallic instruments. The uncanny quiet of the office was punctuated by the buzzing sound of the snakelike dental drill. The boy was placed in the dental chair with little explanation and told to open his mouth wide. Apparently, his cavity was a deep one because Tom's lower jaw was numbed by Novocain. It felt like there was a chicken bone stock in his mouth. The boy endured the experience with no complaints, though he shook visibly. Accordingly, the mean-spirited dentist named him "Nerves" and dispatched the shaken boy with the command: "Now don't bite your tongue!"

The 1950's was an era when people did not cross racial, religious, and ethnic barriers. The Smiths were honest, hardworking, and good people. Yet, they held the prevailing view about ethnic minorities—Italians, Jews, Puerto Ricans, and Afro-Americans. They espoused the typical stereotypes for these ethnic groups: Italians spoke funny and had peculiar old-world ways; Jews were shrewd with regard to money; Puerto Ricans carried knives and kidnapped children; Afro-Americans (colored people) were lazy and ignorant. When the Smith's got word about Tom's friendship with Earl, they weren't happy. The message was: "Play with your own kind." The same message was given to Cara who had befriended a colored girl named Susie Jackson. Towards Jews, the Smith's had ambivalent views combining admiration and hostility. On the one hand, they admired TV and movie stars who were Jewish: Jerry Lewis, Sid Caesar, Milton Berle, Jack Benny, Jack Webb, and others.

On the other hand, they decried the presence of so many Jews in America's elite circles. Tom, brimming with childhood idealism, would respond that a person's background shouldn't matter because "all men are created equal."

May 17, 1954

The United States Supreme Court under Chief Justice Earl Warren unanimously (9-0) decided that "separate educational facilities are inherently unequal." The Topeka Board of Education, under an 1879 Kansas law, had been maintaining separate elementary schools for black and white children. Oliver Brown, an Afro-American welder, had to send his daughter to an all-black elementary school one mile away, instead of a white elementary school seven blocks from his home. The Court said that even if segregated black and white schools were of equal quality, segregation was harmful to black students and therefore unconstitutional. Overturning Plessy v. Ferguson (1896) which supported the doctrine of "separate but equal," the Supreme Court asserted that de jure racial segregation violated the equal protection clause of the 14th Amendment of the Constitution.

In a follow-up decision (Brown II) in 1955, the U.S. Supreme Court stated that public schools in the South must desegregate "with all deliberate speed." Many southern school officials interpreted this phrase by resisting, delaying, and avoiding integration of schools for many years. For example, some southern school districts closed down their public schools and used state money to fund segregated private schools. Opposed by most southern governors and congressmen at the time, this landmark decision sparked a prolonged battle aimed at ending racial segregation and inequality throughout the United States.

At the Bloomington canning factory to bolster worker morale, management held a minstrel show each summer. Participants would wear outlandish, bright-colored costumes, cover their faces with black makeup, and paint their lips white—creating a caricature of Afro-Americans.

The song-and-dance routines expressed the most blatant racist stereotypes associated with "colored people." Mom was an enthusiastic member of these minstrel shows—even adopting a "colored accent." Though amused by his mother's clowning, Tom felt uncomfortable with this race baiting. After the show, Mom would keep the black-face makeup on and go around knocking on neighbors' doors as a prank: "Hello, do you know where the Jackson's live?" The startled neighbor would start to close her door in fright before realizing she had been tricked by an imposter. Tom wondered if colored people held white minstrel shows depicting white people in unkind ways. Perhaps children could put on a minstrel show mimicking grownups with their dumb rules for kids and their constant worry about money. Yet Tom and Cara realized they were fortunate compared to some of their poorer classmates, both white and black, who wore raggedy clothes to school and were subject to nasty remarks by their classmates. There was a part of Bloomington, called "colored town," consisting of ramshackle houses with cluttered yards and broken windows, which made Tom and Cara feel bad for the people living there.

Though loving parents, the Smiths were old-fashioned in their approach to disciplining children. Mom had a leather cat-of-nine tails which hung ominously on a hook by the kitchen sink.

She merely had to grab it and the youngsters Tom and Cara would cease their shenanigans. But if the kids were especially rambunctious, a stinging slap on the butt or legs would quickly restore order.

Of her four children, Mom claimed that Tom was physically punished the least. He seemed to know the point beyond which his behavior should not stray. Also the boy had a way of pleading for mercy with his hands extended towards his parent—"Oh please, please don't hit me! I'll be good!" Usually, a menacing wave of the feared leather strap would magically restore peace and quiet to the Smith household.

CHAPTER 3

Going to Church

The 1950's was an era of strong authority in the American institutions of government, the military, business, schools, and churches. People obeyed the laws, paid their taxes, went to school, worked hard in their jobs, served in the armed forces, and attended church regularly. Although the Smiths seldom went to church, they made sure their children attended the local Catholic church, St. Teresa's, where they received communion and confirmation. The church was a formidable place for Tom because of its strict doctrine of sin and punishment, and the severe demeanor of the nuns and the priest. In catechism, Tom learned a long list of mortal sins for which the consequence was an eternity in hell. One sharp-featured nun exclaimed grimly that every day we were getting closer and closer to our death. When the priest stopped by to lecture the candidates for conformation, Tom could smell the liquor on his breath. Father Sullivan had a beet-red complexion with a distracted manner. Yet he spoke passionately when dwelling on the terrible suffering of Jesus on the cross—his hands nailed to the wooden beams—because of the sins of mankind.

Then, there was that awful Sunday in June, when his friend Earl walked into St. Teresa's church. Father Sullivan had been talking about the church's patron saint, St. Teresa, who would beat herself with a wooden stick in order to achieve ecstatic visions of Christ. Whenever the priest spoke about St. Teresa, he would work himself into a frenzy. Upon seeing the colored boy walk down the aisle, the priest went berserk. Dashing down towards the boy, Father Sullivan grabbed Earl by the scruff of his neck, shouting racial epithets and cursing like a sailor, he tossed him out of the church. The appalled congregation sat in stunned silence. With hardly a missed beat, the red-faced priest resumed his sermon about St. Teresa and her pain-induced raptures. After that incident, Tom no longer felt the presence of God when he entered St. Teresa's—instead he felt an uneasy dread. When the boy looked at the billowing clouds on a sunny day, or the twinkling stars on a clear night, or a pink-and-gold sunset in the evening, then the presence of God was palpable.

November 1950

After visiting President Harry Truman in the oval office, the Reverend Billy Graham told reporters that he had urged the President to attack the Red Chinese, who had just invaded North Korea. President Truman was furious with Reverend Graham for talking to the press—calling him a "counterfeit evangelist who has gone off his beam." Known for his radio and TV sermons, and his big revival meetings in the 1940s and 50s, Graham asserted that salvation could occur only through the acceptance of Jesus Christ as our personal savior. A graduate of Wheaton College (1943) with a degree in anthropology, Graham had no formal training in theology. He opposed communism, homosexuality, and racial integration (at first). Newspaper mogul William Randolph Hearst supported Reverend Graham for his patriotism and family values.

In addition to President Truman, Billy Graham advised presidents Eisenhower, Johnson, Nixon, Ford, Carter, and Reagan as "pastor to the presidents." Graham once apologized for remarks made in agreeing with President Nixon that Jews control American media. A church spokesman said that Reverend Graham was not an anti-Semite and had been a long-time supporter of Israel.

In the early years, Graham's revival meetings were segregated, but in the late 1950's, he dramatically tore down ropes separating blacks from whites to signal his acceptance of racial integration. Billy Graham once told a southern white audience.

"We have been proud and thought we were better than any other race . . . but we are going to stumble to hell because of our pride."

The favorite summer time beverage of Tom and Cara was Kool-Aid — a super sweet drink made from powdered fruit-flavor, a cup of sugar, and a half-gallon of water. It tasted as good as soda at a fraction of the price. One hot summer day, Tom and Cara decided to set up a Kool-Aid stand by the road. The problem was that there was very little traffic on Eden Avenue — especially on summer days. On a small wooden table, the kids placed two quart-sized containers of Kool-Aid — one grape and the other strawberry, along with a bowl of ice cubes, some paper cups, and a sign stating the price: 10 cents per cup. There were only a handful of customers — some grownups driving by in cars, a few Puerto Rican workers on foot, and some children riding their bikes.

About to close their Kool-Aid stand, the two youngsters noticed a shabbily-dressed man walking down the road. Approaching them, the man asked for two cups of Kool-Aid — one strawberry and one grape. He handed over a quarter and told them to "keep the change." Happy to get his business, the kids poured two cups of Kool-Aid, which the man drank in a few big gulps. Then he sat down on the grass and told the two children to join him because he was going to play a game with them. As soon as Tom and Cara sat down next to the stranger, he exposed himself. Stunned by his bizarre behavior, the kids stared incredulously at his displayed private parts.

1950s-1960s Fable

Cara began to back away from the man, but Tom could not because he had grabbed the boy's hand — touching it to his penis. Tom withdrew his hand quickly — as if from a hot stove. At the same time, the stranger was talking to the boy softly.

Tom could hear his mother calling her children — telling them to come into the house. Out of the corner of his eye, he saw his big brother Harry zoom by him on his bicycle — heading down Eden Avenue towards the town. Suddenly, there was a clamor from the house and big sister Helen marched towards them carrying a big kitchen knife and yelling at the stranger: "I'm going to cut it off! Get off my property you son of a bitch!" The stranger seemed to be afraid of the young woman, abruptly stood up, zipping up his fly and heading down the road. Later on, the children heard that the stranger, a former convict, had been arrested by the Bloomington sheriff and deputies.

Once a month, the Smiths went to a colorful farmer's market in a nearby town. The market was housed in a long pavilion with booths selling freshly baked breads, pies, and cakes, homemade jellies and canned vegetables, hand-sewn quilts and knitted sweaters, and handmade wooden furniture. Last year, Mr. Smith had rescued two boys from a swamp behind the pavilion — pulling them out of the quick-sand with a big branch. Mr. Smith was rewarded by the boys' father with a big bag of pastries and sweet rolls, whenever they visited the market. Mrs. Smith was happy to accept the gift in appreciation of her husband's good deed, referring to him as "my hero." Tom wondered how the baker equated the lives of his two sons with a bag of bakery goodies. Had the father been a hardware store owner, would the Smiths have received a monthly box of screws and nails? Had the father been a banker, would the Smiths have received a sack of dollar bills?

Nevertheless, the bag of bakery items was appreciated by the Smith's as a tasty treat and as a nice token of their dad's benevolent actions.

There were lots of strange sights at the farmer's market that captivated the children's interest: An old man with a wooden leg selling his hand-carved wooden knickknacks, a blind man playing a violin who took coin donations in a big brass bowl, an exotic gypsy woman with a shiny red jewel in her forehead who did palm readings, a colorful group of American Indians who did a rain dance to end a local drought, and a strong man lifting a huge barbell selling bottles of liquid vitamins. And there was a familiar looking man taking pictures of people with various scenic backdrops — a barren desert, a lush jungle, a medieval castle, a Wild West town, and a city street background. Tom did a double take because he recognized the man as the stranger who had exposed himself on the Smith's front lawn. Cara started to say something, but her brother nudged her to keep quiet. The man winked and smiled at the children, signaling them that the unfortunate episode of the past few weeks should remain their secret. Which it did, as the two youngsters remained calm and composed. Wise beyond their years, Tom and Cara, understood that certain happenings in life are best kept secret.

Mom and Dad worked different shifts at the Bloomington canning factory — the 8 AM to 4 PM day shift, the 4 PM to midnight evening shift, and the 12 midnight to 8 AM night shift. Consequently, big sister Helen was baby sitter and acting parent to the youngsters Tom and Cara, while Mr. and Mrs. Smith toiled at the factory over the long night hours. Whimsical and imaginative, Helen could transform the nitty-gritty chores of everyday life into fun-filled activities. For example, washing dishes was organized into a factory assembly line. Helen would wash a single dish and hand it to Cara for towel drying.

1950s-1960s Fable

Then Cara gave the dish to Tom, who climbed a chair to put it in the dish cupboard. Naturally, this step-by-step process took longer than regular dish washing and drying, but it was more fun for the kids. Helen was the family member who had showed Tom the cellar bookcase and encouraged him to read books that were beyond his reading level. Helen made Cara sketch pads cutting loose-leaf paper and stapling it to cardboard. In another era, Helen would have made a great elementary school teacher, but her destiny would likely be the housewife to a farmer or factory worker Tucking the youngster into bed at night, Helen would regale them with her wonderful stories about God and the origins of the universe. God started the world's clock about one million years ago, when he created the angels, his helpers, much like Santa's helpers, the elves. God and his angels worked very hard to create a perfect world filled with beauty and goodness—the sun, the earth, the moon, the other planets, and the stars. This beautiful world was the Garden of Eden, in which there was plenty of food and summer time all over the earth. Fruit grew abundantly on trees and vegetables grew everywhere without weeds. No one ever got sick or died in this perfect world. But one of God's angels, Satan, did not like following God's orders so he rebelled. Satan began spreading evil throughout the world: the earth had floods, severe droughts, and cold weather. He created scary jungles filled with fierce beasts like lions, tigers, and giant snakes and barren deserts where nothing could exist but cactus plants, scorpions, and rattle snakes.

When the first human beings, Adam and Eve, disobeyed God by eating the forbidden fruit, the apple, God cast them out of the Garden of Eden. From that point on, life became difficult for people all over the world—they had to work hard for their food. Furthermore, people would get sick and die.

"But when does Jesus come into the story?" asked Cara. Helen explained that God felt bad about people having to die and not live eternally like himself and the angels. Therefore, God sent his son Jesus to the earth to teach people how to live righteously.

Continuing, Helen asserted, "Remember the Sermon on the Mount? Jesus blessed all the good people on the earth—the meek, the poor, the merciful, the pure in heart—who will enter heaven. Jesus said that rich people, and those who hurt others or do evil things will go to Hell." Tom interrupted Helen's wonderful sermon about God and the Creation— "If the meek will inherit the earth, why do grownups worry about money so much?" Exacerbated, Helen replied, "You know what kids? It's time to go to sleep!"

CHAPTER 4

Little Mommy

Every few months the Smith family had a visitor from the city — "Little Mommy" — the birthmother of Tom and Cara. In the early years, the two youngsters couldn't quite grasp their relationship to Little Mommy because she seemed more like a friendly aunt than their real mother. But unlike the Smith's relatives from Jersey City, Little Mommy always brought a big shopping bag of gifts for the children — practical stuff like shirts, trousers, dresses, socks, and hats. It was uncanny that the new clothes fit them well — much better than the hand-me-downs from their older siblings that Tom and Cara often wore. Little Mommy differed from the Smith's Jersey City guests in other ways. She always arrived by cab from the town's bus stop. An energetic, compact woman, Little Mommy was a native New Yorker with a rapid manner of speaking. She had only a passing interest in the farm or its animals, and the Smith's weren't particularly warm in welcoming her to their home.

Whenever Little Mommy visited the Smith family, the two youngsters were taken outside by Helen while Mr. and Mrs. Smith conferred with their mother. The children felt a certain tension in the air when they returned to the house. Usually, the Smiths were outwardly friendly to Little Mommy during her weekend visits to their farm, but when she left there were some unflattering comments about her: She was a fancy-dressing city slicker; she wore too much makeup;

she had strange political views; she always carried a book with her; she didn't know how to take care of children; she wasn't married; and worst of all — she was Jewish. One of the best things about Little Mommy was her pure joy and enthusiasm when she greeted her children, whom she referred to as "my babies." Tom and Cara were always greeted with hard and prolonged hugs and squeezes and kisses that left them breathless and dizzy. Then she would always take them for a walk around the Smith farm to see the chickens, turkeys, pigs, the corn fields, and Mom's truck garden.

One day, Tom and Cara decided to take Little Mommy on a walk following the school bus route though the eastern farm section of Bloomington. On the school bus it was a 20-minute ride along three miles of country road which eventually looped back to the Smith farm on Eden Avenue. It was a mild summer day with a gentle breeze — a perfect summer day for a long walk. The two children bounced along, chattering about friends, school, and day-to-day events on the Smith farm — barely keeping pace with their fast-walking, fast-talking mother. After Cara questioned her mother about her heavy makeup, Little Mommy laughed, "It's my war paint. It covers the mess some butcher of a doctor made of my face years ago."

Truth be told, the high-strung woman had a disfigured, asymmetrical face — the result of radium burns on the right side of her face. Little Mommy, who had a good singing voice, began singing the Tennessee Waltz: "I was dancing with my darling to the Tennessee Waltz when an old friend I happened to see . . . and while they were dancing my friend stole my sweet heart from me." Tom and Cara stopped by the side of the road to pick some wild flowers. The children told their mother about God and the Garden of Eden, where it was always summertime and nobody had to work for food and people never got sick or died.

They talked about Jesus's Sermon on the Mount in which he blessed the poor and the meek and the pure in heart. Little Mommy smiled sadly, "Well sweetie, we live in a world of rich and poor and never the twain shall meet. But capitalism contains the seeds of its own destruction and someday we will all be equal."

When they returned to the Smith farm an hour and a half later, Tom and Cara were in trouble. The Smiths had been looking all over for them — out in the corn fields, in the chicken coop, by the pigpen, by Hunt's Creek, and in the neighboring farms. "Where the hell were you?" shouted Mom glaring at Little Mommy, who kept her composure. Smiling at the red-faced Mrs. Smith and hugging her children, she replied "Why, we went for a walk along the school bus route. You have lovely farms out here." Then Tom stepped forward and gave Mrs. Smith the wild flowers they had gathered, "Here Mom this is for you." The latter smiled at the boy and tensions dissipated in the mild summer air.

April 6, 1949

Herbert Philbrick, advertising businessman, member of the Communist Party, and counter-spy for the FBI, testified against ten American Communists in the U.S. (Federal) District Court in Foley Square, New York City. The ten defendants, members of the American Communist Party, which included William Foster, Carl Winter, Ben Davis, John Williamson, Irving Potash, John Gates, Gil Green, and Gus Hall, were indicted under the Smith Act. Passed by Congress in 1940, the Smith Act makes the teaching and advocacy of the overthrow of the U.S. government a federal crime.

Philbrick, author of the book I Led Three Lives, had been an active member of the Communist Party and its associated front groups for nine years, while supporting his family (wife and six children) selling direct-mail advertising to various small businesses in the Boston area, and sending monthly type-written reports of his activities to the FBI. Initially, Herbert Philbrick was attracted to the Communist Party's support of the American war effort against the Nazis and the idealist nature of Marxism. In the 18th century Karl Marx had promised a bright new world without war, without poverty, without hunger. During the Great Depression, the economic status of American farmers, factory workers, and coal miners declined sharply. The American Communist Party was a strong advocate of the working class and ethnic minorities in its self-proclaimed role as "vanguard of the proletariat." During World War II, the Communist Party was a staunch opponent of Nazi Germany. After the war and with the advent of the Cold War, American Communists opposed American foreign policy. Domestically, they tried to infiltrate the labor unions of basic industries like coal, steel, rubber, auto, transportation, and electricity.

The Communists utilized Philbrick's advertising skills, his high standing in the Boston community, and his key role in the Baptist Church – training him in Marxist-Leninism and making him a card-carrying Communist in 1945. Disillusioned by the Communist Party's ideological zig-zags, its undermining of democratic values and advocacy of armed revolution against democratic governments, Mr. Philbrick began providing the FBI with inside information on its activities. The Court quoted Stalin's writings that the proletarian revolution is impossible without the total annihilation of the bourgeois state and its replacement with a dictatorship of the proletariat (workers). Consequently, federal judge Harold Medina ruled that the ten defendants were guilty of advancing the Marxist-Leninist agenda of violent overthrow of the U.S. government under the Smith Act – sentencing them to five years in prison and $10,000 in fines.

1950s-1960s Fable

The Smiths seldom talked about Tom and Cara's father, Mr. Haley, in front of the youngsters. A favorite expression of the Smiths was "little pictures have big ears." But from bits and pieces of surreptitious conversation detected over the years, the youngsters had some knowledge about their notorious parent: He was an incurable alcoholic; he used to pop up at the Smith's house in Jersey City demanding to see his children; he was an army deserter and drifter — traveling the country by jumping on freight trains; he was a talented artist; and he was one of the reasons that the Smith's moved from Jersey City to Bloomington, South Jersey. Another curious fact that the youngsters couldn't quite understand was the existence of several of their father's paintings in the Smith's house — hanging on the walls of the two bedrooms, another above the TV set in the living room, and a few more stacked in the attic. The pictures were "American primitives" — rustic scenes of lush meadows filled with wild flowers and trees, set off by a pond or meandering stream, with rolling green hills in the background.

The people were depicted as impressionist figures on an idyllic country holiday from all walks of life. The pictures were signed with such aliases as: Tom Haley, Joseph Healy, Jon Todd, etc.

The only Smith family member willing to talk freely to Tom and Cara about their father was Helen — during her nightly talks with the children covering topics ranging from the mundane to the philosophic. "Mr. Haley (She always referred to the kids' father as Mr. Haley.) must have been a good-looking man before he started drinking."

Helen described the youngsters' father as a husky six-footer with striking blue eyes and curly hair. She continually warned Tom not to fall victim to the bottle when he grew up.

The boy, who could not stand the smell or taste of beer, swore he would be a life-time tee-toller. Impressed by his paintings, Helen asserted Mr. Haley could have been a famous artist like Rembrandt or van Gogh — had he not taken to the bottle. Cara remarked that her teacher said that drinking was a disease like polio or cancer. Helen surmised that alcoholism was both a physical disease and a character disorder.

CHAPTER 5

Holidays with the Smiths

Christmas holidays were magical times at the Smith's house where efforts were unstinting to make the yuletide season special for the children. Their house was decorated inside and outside with colorful Christmas lights, batches of mistletoe and holly, and a pine-scented wreath hung on the front door. A seven-foot fir tree, chopped down from a nearby woods, was nicely decorated with shiny ornaments, flickering lights, striped candy canes, and strings of popcorn. The Christmas tree lights were the old-fashioned kind — series wired — so if one went out, they all went out. Of course, Christmas dinner featured the full array of Mom's truck garden vegetables, along with the obligatory turkey, which Tom recognized from his s-shaped neck as the dominant alpha turkey who continually pecked his pen-mates from morning to night.

The Smith's were extremely generous to Tom and Cara — lavishing them with toys, games, teddy bears, dolls, doll carriages, cowboy guns and holsters, baseball gloves and bats, plus two huge nylon stockings stuffed with crayons, coloring books, baseball cards, playing cards, candy, fruit, and chestnuts. All the children's gifts were neatly wrapped in colorful wrapping paper and strewn under the big, glowing Christmas tree.

Todd M. Daley

There were also some plainly-wrapped gifts from Little Mommy—practical things like clothes, shoes, coats, hats, scarves, books, and school supplies—which the youngsters opened last.

There was a festive atmosphere throughout the town of Bloomington where houses, stores, and government offices were all brightly decorated for the holidays. In the 1950's, mother nature usually cooperated with a late December snow storm—providing a story-book white Christmas. Even the no-nonsense Bloomington school system joined in the yuletide festivities with Christmas shows featuring traditional carols sung by the students. The blackboard in Tom's classroom had a big picture of Santa and his reindeer flying above a quaint, snow-covered village. And each child received a nicely-wrapped box of Christmas treats.

Gifts were opened at midnight on Christmas Eve, when Tom and Cara were awakened from their pretend sleeping states to view the bountiful toy land spread beneath the lighted tree. Both children believed in Santa Claus beyond the usual eight-year-old age of doubt. The dreamy-eyed Cara once told her brother that she saw Santa and his reindeer-pulled sleigh in the back yard next to Mom's truck garden. She described the gleaming gift-filled sleigh and skittish reindeer— harnessed to the sleigh with jingling red leather straps. Ever the artist, Cara's description was so vivid and compelling that Tom was a confirmed believer in St. Nicholas into his tenth year. The notion that Santa Claus maintained a huge book containing the names of all the children of the world—with naughty and nice sections—carried much weight with the children. As the holiday season approached, the Smith's emphasized the Christmas-gift consequences of bad behavior. Mom often told the story of big sister Helen getting black coal in her stocking (and nothing else) as a result of certain misdeeds committed by their well-behaved oldest sibling some years ago.

1950s-1960s Fable

The Smith's were experts at the carrot-and-stick approach to disciplining their children. Determined as the Smith's were to perpetuating the Santa Claus myth, certain events occurred which brought doubt into the youngsters' minds. One Christmas, the Smith's had

Angelo, a middle-aged burly Italian man from Jersey City, dress up as Santa Claus for the kids. Angelo would come to the farm on summer weekends to view the farm animals, walk around the corn fields, and make homemade lemon ice for the family. He spoke in a deep voice with a distinctive Italian accent and liked to walk through meadows and fields gathering wild mushrooms, which the Smith's refused to partake in. In any case, the children recognized Angelo's deep voice, his friendly face, and warm brown eyes under the white beard and red hat—undermining their naive belief in St. Nick.

Easter was another magical holiday at the Smith's house—marked by the miraculous appearance of two big Easter baskets brimming with cream-filled chocolate eggs, hollow chocolate bunnies, jelly beans of every color and flavor, plus dyed hard-boiled eggs (dyed by Helen and the kids the day before) that somehow found their way into their baskets. As the kids grew older, belief in the Easter Bunny was harder to maintain than that of Santa Claus. Neither child had ever observed the Easter Bunny making his early morning delivery of baskets to the Smith's house on Easter Sunday mornings. And the notion that a small brown rabbit could deliver big candy-filled Easter baskets to every child in the world from his secret hideout in the woods—stretched the children's credibility. And they simply couldn't connect the Easter Bunny with long-eared, cotton-tailed hares that regularly nibbled at and ran through Mom's truck garden. Furthermore, Mom's tongue-in-cheek choice of roasted rabbit (purchased from a nearby farmer who raised rabbits in pens as a cash crop) for an Easter

Sunday dinner—delivering the coup-de-grace to any lingering Easter Bunny beliefs on the part of the kids.

Because of their naivete, children are platonic in their understanding of the world around them. The ancient Greek philosopher Plato postulated the dual theory of reality—the world of ideas vs. the world of objects.
Like Plato, children believe that ultimate reality exists not in everyday objects like chairs, tables, and shoes, but in pure, eternal ideas—namely spirits, ghosts, and God. The notions of Santa Claus and the Easter Bunny, which belong to the latter class, possess a reality and meaning far greater than the mundane objects of the world. The effort put forth by the Smith's left Tom and Cara with a life-long appreciation of Christmas and Easter as special times of hope, joy, and love when day-to-day cares and concerns can be set aside. There was also the sense in both children that magical holidays like Christmas and Easter, preserved the special joy and innocence of childhood, shielding them against the awful dread of the grownup world with its worries about money, work, and an uncertain future.

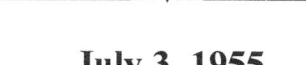

July 3, 1955

Alcoholics Anonymous was officially turned over by its founders, Bill Wilson and Dr. Robert Smith, to a group of elected representatives from various AA groups throughout the U.S. and Canada. Born in Vermont in 1895, Bill Wilson was raised by his maternal grandparents after his parents were divorced and his mother moved to Boston to study medicine (osteopathy). At age 18, Wilson suffered a nervous breakdown when his childhood sweet heart died from a botched surgery to remove a tumor. The Wilson family history of excessive drinking did not prevent Bill from taking his first drink at age twenty-two after enlisting in the Army as a heavy artillery officer.

1950s-1960s Fable

The magic of the first few drinks led him to an addiction to alcohol which plagued Wilson for the next 17 years of his life. He discovered that he loved drinking — especially in social situations.

After the war, Bill Wilson was a successful stock broker on Wall Street until the stock market crash of 1929. The 1920's was the era of Prohibition when the sale and use of liquor was illegal in America. A habitual drinker, Wilson found ways to get around the law — fermenting grapes at home to make his liquor or going to an after-hours speakeasy where bootleg whiskey was served. During the day on Wall Street, Wilson would abstain from drinking, but once the stock market closed at 3 PM, he would drink himself to a stupor — crawling home with no memory of where he'd been. Repeatedly Wilson wrote pledges (in the family Bible) to his long-suffering wife Lois, promising to give up drinking. Over the years, he lost many well-paid jobs and his reputation as a shrewd market analyst was eroded by his drinking problem. The investment company Wheeler and Winans forced Bill Wilson to sign a no-drinking contract before hiring him, which he soon violated.

Alcoholics are adept at hiding their addiction. They can pull themselves together, take long showers, act smarter, and be more alive than most people. There is a psychic energy to keeping their addiction secret. Nevertheless by 1934, Bill Wilson had hit rock bottom. Desperate, he exclaimed "If there be a God, let him show himself!" Suddenly his room blazed with an indescribable white light and he was seized with ecstasy: "You are a free man!" A profound change took place and he never drank again. Actually, Bill Wilson and a friend, Dr. Robert Smith, made the fundamental discovery that a group of alcoholics talking about their drinking problem was far more effective than the lone alcoholic, in a moment of remorse, promising never to drink again. Wilson realized that "he needed this alcoholic as much as he needed me." He also understood that each alcoholic has his own drinking story and his own road to sobriety.

Bill Wilson and Dr. Robert Smith founded Alcoholics Anonymous on June 10, 1935 — built on the concepts of group conscience, total honesty, anonymity (first names only), humility (no leaders), restitution (to family and friends), spirituality (seeking God's help), and service to fellow alcoholics. The two founders insisted that AA function as a network of autonomous AA groups with no leaders and no accumulation of money or power. The only requirement for membership to AA was the desire to stop drinking.

By the late 1960's after years of smoking, Bill Wilson's lungs were clogged with tar and he was dying of emphysema. He needed an oxygen tank to get through the day.

By the fall of 1970, Wilson had gone to bed permanently with round-the-clock nurses, plus his wife Lois attending him. A measure of the power of alcohol was illustrated through his death-bed request of three shots of whiskey. When turned down, Wilson became upset and belligerent. Most alcoholics never stop wanting to drink. They love to drink — it works for them. Bill Wilson believed that "Life is just a day in school." All our experiences are but lessons in some form or other which condition us to a larger destiny . . . it's a problem world. What matters, and what only matters is what we do with the problems."

CHAPTER 6

Summer Days

With the end of the school year, summer time was the best of times for Tom and Cara with its vast stretches of sunny days, blue skies, gentle breezes, and lots of free time to do whatever pleased their fancy. Up early with the rising sun, the youngsters would eat a hasty breakfast of corn flakes and fresh strawberries before dashing outside to roam the twelve-acre Smith farm and surrounding areas. Helen, the kids' guardian, companion, and teacher, would often accompany them on their meandering walks around the farm—usually done on bare feet. By the end of summer, the soles of their feet were so tough that the mid-day heat on the hot tar of Eden Avenue scarcely bothered the youngsters. Helen observed that if they walked in her shadow, the road would be a millionth of a degree cooler in the momentary shade. Visiting the pigs was always done with shoes on. While Cara remained outside, Tom would enter the pig pen with some lettuce, carrots, or apples to greet the mud-covered porkers, who liked being hand-fed. The biggest pig, the 300-pound sow, was particularly friendly to Tom—pushing her snout towards the boy's crotch—sniffing loudly like a dog. Pigs are intelligent animals and would make good pets were it not for their size and sloppiness. Once in a while the massive sow would inadvertently step on Tom's toe—ouch!

Often their summer walks led them to Hunt's Creek to look at the minnows swimming just beneath the surface, the hopping frogs with their pimpled skin, a green garden snake darting into the water, the occasional muskrat or beaver slinking among the tall grasses near the banks of the creek. A big metal pipe formed the mouth of the creek, which ran under Eden Avenue from the smaller stream that represented the southern boundary of the Smith farm. Tom and Cara liked to stand on this wide corrugated aluminum pipe to look at the fish and the tadpoles swimming in the creek. Though Hunt's Creek was a fast-moving stream, the youngsters were not permitted to wade into the creek's crystal-clear water. Polio was a major concern for parents in the 1950's before the break-through of the Salk vaccine. With the somber example of Mr. Smith's affliction, Mom was continually reminding the kids about the danger of the cesspool (There were no sewers in the farm areas of South Jersey.) and Hunt's Creek which were thought to harbor the polio virus. Little Mommy concurred, letting Tom and Cara know that they were lucky to be living in the country—far from Jersey City and New York where the polio epidemic raged during the summer months.

Running around bare-footed in the back yard and fields of the Smith farm had its hazards. Tom was stung by bees through the bottom of his toughened foot on a few occasions; Cara stepped on a board with a rusty nail; both children had cuts, scratches, and rashes from walking through fields covered with sharp rocks, thorny bushes, prickly weeds, and poison ivy. These occasional scrapes, bruises, and rashes failed to restrict the kids' wanderings over the vast fields and meadows adjoining the Smith farm. When thirsty, the youngsters would use the hand-pump from an underground well in the fields or open the garden hose nozzle for a quick drink of lukewarm water.

1950s-1960s Fable

And to answer the call of nature, the kids would use the outhouse a white-painted wooden outhouse. Tom often brought a book, whereas Cara brought her sketch pad, when doing their business. There was a colony of hornets nesting on the ceiling of the outhouse—necessitating shorter visits to the foul-smelling outhouse. The hornets may have been attracted to the outhouse because of its juxtaposition to a large rose bush. Fortunately, Helen always made sure there was a fly-swatter as well as toilet paper in the outhouse, and she badgered the kids to wash their hands with the garden hose before resuming their frolicking.

It was during the summer that the youngsters both learned to ride a bicycle. Tom mastered this deceptively easy task within a day with big brother Harry's help. The muscular teenager was holding on to the bike and running along as Tom peddled furiously along the side of Eden Avenue. Unawares to the boy, Harry had let go of the bicycle while Tom maintained his balance and rode off as a new two-wheel biker. Magically, the boy had quickly mastered the bike, including steering and braking. It was then incumbent on the boy to teach his sister how to ride a bike, since Harry had to go off to work. Cara, always the impractical, dreamy-eyed artist, insisted on riding her bicycle within the confines of the backyard—not on Eden Avenue where cars seldom traversed. Complying with his sister's wish, Tom ran along with her—holding the seat of the bike. After an hour of back and forth crossings of the yard from the dog wood tree near the edge of the road to the outhouse with its nearby rose bush, Cara hadn't quite gotten the hang of riding a two-wheeler. Exhausted, Tom pushed Cara's bike hard and ceased running besides her. The results—his accident-prone sister went headlong into the large rose bush—receiving scratches on her hands, arms, and legs, and entangling the bike in the thorn-filled rose bush.

It was just another busy day for Helen, wiping Cara's tears with her hanky and dressing the scratches with stinging red iodine before applying band-aids on her arms and legs. Tom was grounded for the afternoon, consigned to the cellar with its big book case of adventure books, history books, science books, and encyclopedias.

By the dog days of summer, Tom and Carrie were running out of things to do. Day-in, day-out, they walked the fields and meadows of the Smith farm and the adjoining farms, walked to Hunt's Creek, visited the mud-covered pigs, teased the turkeys with corn stalks, and fed the chickens in the hot chicken coop with handfuls of grain. Their requests to be taken to Wood's Lake for a day of swimming were denied — neither Helen nor Harry had a car to drive. But Harry had an ingenious idea. He constructed a make-shift shower by attaching a garden hose to a discarded sprinkler, which was nailed to the weeping willow tree in the back yard. Under the tree a big piece of sheet of plastic was placed — preventing mud puddles and allowing the kids to slide as they darted through the cascading cold water. The make-shift shower was a success, especially on ninety-degree days when the heat discouraged long walks through the stifling corn fields and the bug-infested meadows of late August. Helen permitted Tom and Cara to fill buckets, containers, and water guns so they could engage in prolonged water fights, with some neighborhood kids joining in the fun.

But when Mom was home, the rules governing back yard showers and water fights were tightened. Nevertheless, kids being kids, the water battles occasionally got out of hand. One hot August afternoon, a nasty water fight developed — the boys (Tom and his friend Larry Hunt) vs. the girls (Cara and two of her friends). The boys soon got the upper hand and the girls, thoroughly soaked with water, retreated into the house.

1950s-1960s Fable

Armed with water pistols and water-filled balloons, the boys pursued them into the house—splashing water on floors, walls, and table-tops.

At this point Mom's temper took over, yelling and grabbing the cat-of-nine-tails, she wacked Tom and Cara across the legs and told their friends to go home.

The kids spent the rest of the day mopping up the kitchen and dining room floors followed by a sweaty weed-pulling session in Mom's truck garden.

On cool summer afternoons, Helen and Harry would arrange a big softball game—gathering kids from the neighborhood on a fallow field where a chicken wire fence
served as a backstop, the sandy area represented the infield, and the surrounding grassy field provided a large outfield.

A flat shale rock was home plate and three wooden squares were the bases. There were enough kids to supply two teams of six players—including three willing and able girls. Helen pitched soft underhanded pitches to everybody, while Harry was the steadfast catcher. There were no balls or strikes, and the hitter remained at bat until he (she) hit the ball. It was always "Dodgers" vs. "Phillies" with Tom insisting that his team were the latter. Having grown up in Jersey City, both Helen and Harry were stalwart Dodger fans, which annoyed Tom to no end.

Helen was astonishingly knowledgeable about baseball fundamentals. A devotee of Pee Ree Reese and Jackie Robinson, Helen stressed fielding, bunting, and running the bases. She showed the kids how to hold the bat when bunting and how to put one knee on the ground so grounders don't slither under the fielder's glove.

Helen also showed the girls how to use the full length of their arms when tossing the ball, so they wouldn't throw like a girl. Harry showed the youngsters how to hold their glove— depending on whether the ball was thrown high or low, to the left or the right. And looking directly at his younger brother, he urged the kids not to swing at pitches over their heads or in the dirt. Harry told the youngsters to play fair and to play smart—not like the Phillies' Del Ennis who was prone to strike out in clutch situations or Robin Roberts who tended to give up late-inning home runs.

This irritated Tom who idolized Roberts, the Phillies workhorse 20-game winning pitcher. In any case, Cara was instrumental in winning the game for the Dodgers by beating out a bunt with her fast-running speed. Unusually fast for a girl, Carla often beat her older brother in foot races to the latter's great embarrassment. Nevertheless, these pickup soft ball games were great fun and having fun, rather than winning was the goal. After each game Helen would proclaim, "Who wins doesn't matter, it's how you play the game!"

October 1, 1950

The Philadelphia Phillies played the Brooklyn Dodgers on the last day of the season in a game which would determine the National League pennant. The Phillies, known as the "Whiz Kids" because of their youth, had squandered a nine-game lead over the Dodgers in ten days. Their slump was attributed to poor hitting, as well as the loss of key players like pitcher Curt Simmons (Army), plus outfielder Bill Nicholson and catcher Andy Seminick due to injuries. The opposing pitchers, the Phillies' Robin Roberts and the Dodgers' Don Newcombe, would oppose each other in hard-fought games throughout the 1950's. Roberts, who had pitched in three games in the preceding week, had difficulty getting loose before the game.

The game turned into a typical Roberts-Newcombe low-scoring pitching duel. Through the first eight innings, the score was tied 1-to-1. The Dodgers had scored on a Pee Ree Reese homerun, while the Phillies tied the game on a clutch single by Willie Jones. In the bottom of the ninth inning, the Dodgers had two men on base when Duke Snider lined one of Roberts' fast balls into center field. The Dodger base runner, Cal Abrams, attempting to score from second base, was thrown out at home plate by the Phillies center fielder, Richie Ashburn. In the top of the tenth inning, the Phillies scored three runs on Dick Sisler's home run off Don Newcombe. Consequently, the score was 4-to-1 in favor of the Phillies.

In the bottom of the tenth, Robin Roberts bore down and retired the Dodgers in order — copping the Phillies' first pennant in 35 years.

Robin Roberts, the durable hard-throwing Phillies' ace, won twenty games for six consecutive seasons — 1950 through 1955. Relying on just two pitches, a hopping fast ball and a sharp curve ball, Roberts had pin-point control of his pitches — locating them on the inside and outside corners of the plate. A workhorse, the Phillies' mainstay averaged 300 innings, 160 strike outs, and only 54 walks from 1950 to 1956.

In 1956 at age 30, Roberts won 19 games — failing to get his twentieth win on the last day of the season. Unable to straighten his right arm, Robin Roberts had lost some "pop" from his fast ball. He regularly pitched every fourth day for the weak-hitting Phillies, and was often called upon as a relief pitcher in between starts. As the Phillies' ace, Roberts was usually opposed by the top pitchers in the National League — Don Newcombe, Warren Spahn, Bob Friend, Sal Maglie, Johnny Antonelli, Lew Burdette, and Joe Nuxhall among others.

In 1962 Robin Roberts was traded to the Baltimore Orioles, where he was fairly successful — winning 52 games over the next four years. In 1966 at age 39, Roberts retired from baseball with a lifetime record of 286 wins and 245 losses in a nineteen-year major league career. Always a hard-nosed competitor, Roberts was at his best when the chips were down in crucial games. He had a fluid motion, using his legs, back, and arm to propel the ball forward. The fact that he could throw the ball hard with such efficiency was the secret of his longevity as a power pitcher. Robin Roberts loved the game of baseball, respected his competitors, and never forgot that it was a privilege to play major league baseball. Fellow pitcher Bob Lemon once offered to buy him a drink. Roberts said that he doesn't drink. Then Lemon offered him a cigarette. Roberts replied that he doesn't smoke. Lemon laughed, "No wonder you don't walk anyone."

1950s-1960s Fable

CHAPTER 7

Planting and Harvesting

Springtime, a time of planting corn and other vegetables, hatching chicks, ducks, and turkeys, and the birth of squealing piglets, was a miraculous season of birth, growth, and renewal. Suddenly, the unplanted fields and wooded wilderness would burst forth with tall green grasses, leafy trees, and wild flowers of rainbow colors. In the 1950's, the east coast weather with its cold, snowy winters, cool rainy springs, and hot sunny summers (marred by occasional thunder storms) — all contrived to enhance the vaunted fertility of the South Jersey farm region.

Spring was also the time when one of the Smith's cats would give birth to a litter of kittens. The unfortunate ones that were born defective were promptly drowned by Mom in a big tub of water. She also told the children to give notice in school that the other kittens were up for adoption. One day, Cara's colored friend, Susie Jackson, rode to the Smith farm on a bike and adopted one of the kittens — making the kids happy that one of the cats would have a good home. However, as soon as the little girl left with the kitten, Mom told Cara, "Don't you ever invite a colored person to this house!"

Before planting even began, Dad and Harry covered their twelve acres of land with powdery fertilizer — leaving the farm with a pervasive odor of cow manure.

Then the corn and vegetable planting would ensue—a joint family project with everybody participating—Harry, Helen, Tom, and Cara—under Mom's watchful eyes. Lugging two hundred feet of garden hose to water the newly planted seedlings, Dad was the irrigation engineer. Corn seeds were planted two feet apart, while tomatoes, lettuce, carrots, and cucumbers plants were set a foot apart. Water and honey dew melons, and cantaloupes were planted an intermediate distance of a foot and a half apart because of their size. The rich dark brown South Jersey topsoil had a wonderful earthy odor, velvety texture, and magical fertility that induced seeds to burst out of the ground as fast growing plants within a week or two. This fertile soil was suitable for every conceivable crop—from wheat to corn to soy to green and yellow vegetables of every type, to such fruit as berries, grapes, apples, peaches, and pears. Indeed, the southern tier of New Jersey was truly the "Garden State."

The youngsters, Tom and Cara, preferred the hopeful planting of spring time to the grinding weeding of summer time. The kids thought that the rich dark soil's ability to transform tiny seeds and plants into tall corn stalks, big ripe tomatoes and carrots, huge watermelons bursting with flavor, and hard green apples into juicy red apples—was nothing short of miraculous. Helen said that America was blessed by God with the richest soil and the best climate on earth.

"That's why we are so prosperous!" observed Tom. Momand Dad invariably attributed the country's prosperity to the American work ethic: "Money doesn't grow on trees." Then Tom would risk a smack on the butt by saying, "But apples do!" Even as a youngster, Tom believed that luck was a key ingredient to financial success.

1950s-1960s Fable

In a whimsical mood, Helen told the kids about special "farm fairies" native to New Jersey, who helped plants grow so fast and so big. The farm fairies were

Tinker Bell like creatures who spread magical dust on growing crops—causing them to grow into delicious vegetables and tasty fruits. When Tom and Cara suggested camping out at night to observe the farm fairies doing their miraculous work, Mom and Dad objected. Harry told his sister to stop filling youngsters' ears with silly fairy tales. "The secret to fast growing crops is this smelly fertilizer," he said, picking up some of the odiferous stuff from the ground and tossing it at Tom and Cara, who in turn threw some back at their big brother. At this point Mom intervened, "Do you want the strap? Cut it out!" Harry asked his mom if he would get the strap also. Turning tothe muscular teenager, she replied, "The last time I hit you I nearly broke my hand on your hard ass!"

As Tom and Cara grew older, they had more freedom to roam around the neighborhood by themselves. One summer afternoon, the two youngsters walked down to Hunt's Creek to capture a turtle for a pet. It was a boiling hot day so they trudged the three-quarter mile distance barefoot, carrying a wooden box and some string. Searching along the banks and wading in the creek, the kids observed water lilies, some tadpoles and minnows swimming in the water, plus a few frogs hopping around the tall grasses bordering the creek. After a while, a big black turtle was seen crawling along the bottom of the creek. The kids started after the large slow-moving turtle—hoping to catch it. At this moment, a man appeared suddenly through the tall grasses and cattails on the bank of the creek. He was the same swarthy Puerto Rican man who had played catch with them early in the spring.

Waving his hands, he yelled "That's a snapper. Don't touch it! Snappers can break your fingers when they bite."

The youngsters were more surprised by the man's good English than be his sudden appearance, because the creek adjoined the big farm which employed many of the

Puerto Rican farm workers. They wanted to know the difference between a snapper and an ordinary turtle. The man said that snappers were bigger, had pointy heads, longer necks, long sharp claws, and their shells were black or dark brown in color. Because of their aggressive nature, they don't make good pets, he observed. And unlike regular turtles, snappers don't eat plants. They are meat eaters—eating fish, frogs, rodents, and birds. Removing his shoes and wading through the creek, the man pushed the big snapper downstream with a tree branch. Looking around the creek, he grabbed a small green turtle and put it into the children's wooden box. "That will make a nice pet for you."

Then, a man's gruff voice was heard calling the farm worker. "Pedro, where the hell are you?" It was the red-faced overseer, a man who never smiled or talked to the kids. The friendly Puerto Rican jumped out of the creek and waved to Tom and Cara. "Good bye, amigos. Remember, don't mess with those big black snappers."

Autumn was harvest time at the Smith farm, where everyone pitched in with picking the crops—corn, tomatoes, lettuce, carrots, string beans, potatoes, strawberries, water melons, and cantaloupes. Injecting some fun for the kids undertaking this arduous task, Helen tried to make a contest out of crop picking. Tom and Cara each got their own "harvest basket" with their name inscribed on it. Helen would start them in a particular segment of Mom's truck garden—tomatoes, string beans, whatever.

Checking her watch, big sister would yell "Go!" And the two youngsters began their frenzied vegetable picking. Mom's strict rules required that corn had to be completely shucked of its leafy covering, string beans snapped right before the stem, potatoes and carrots pulled from the soil had to be dusted off, the green leaves carefully removed from strawberries, and melons piled neatly outside the garden without dropping them. At the end of a picking session,

the kids' baskets were weighed to determine the winner. First prize was an extra scoop of Mom's homemade peach ice cream, topped with fresh strawberries, chocolate syrup, and a squirt of whipped cream. Too prevent ill feelings, Helen (always the diplomat) awarded first prize to both children Corn picking, done in the late afternoon to avoid the sun's searing heat, was a challenge for the youngsters. The kids had to pull hard on the corn ears to wrest them from the stalks. The tall corn stalks created a mini-forest of shadows and buzzing insects — horseflies, mosquitoes, beetles, and hornets.

Pulling hard on the corn ear leaves to shuck them, the kids put them in a big bushel basket. One late September afternoon while Tom and Cara were busy picking corn in an isolated corn field, they got a big scare from big brother Harry. Wearing a gorilla mask, he snuck up on the kids, yelling "Boo!" Caught by surprise, Tom and Cara screamed, knocked over the big basket of corn, and ran all the way back to the house. Helen wasn't amused and Mom was furious at her older son: "That wasn't funny Harry. You wouldn't do that with Mr. Geratty. Stop acting like one of those crazy teenagers!"

Laughing, Helen exclaimed, "Mom he is a teenager. What do you expect?"

Often on summer days, Tom and Cara walked down the long winding road bounded by the tall corn stalks from the back yard to the chicken coop. On one side of the chicken coop was the noisy turkey cage—a side-and-top-fenced cage set four feet above ground to allow the turkey droppings to fall through the cage floor to the ground below. The two kids often stopped there to watch the turkeys gobbling, pecking, and fussing with each other. The large birds would peck at anything stuck through their cage—a blade of grass, a piece of wood, or a plastic spoon. The high-strung fowls exhibited an irritability unlike the complacent egg laying hens in the

chicken coop, whose job of providing eggs for the Smith household gave them old age security. Sometimes Harry would give the children a "fun" job like feeding the hens— scooping some grainy chicken feed from the flower-marked feed bags and tossing it on the concrete floor of the chicken coop for the chickens to peck at. In contrast to the mild mannered chickens, the agitated turkeys appeared to grasp their future fate—sitting on someone's dinner table as a crispy, roasted center piece.

One summer afternoon, Tom and Cara were playing with the ducks in a mini pond the two children had made by hollowing out a five feet by five feet square with some shovels and filling it with water from the garden hose. Harry was working in the nearby chicken coop sweeping out the many rooms and inoculating some newly hatched chicks against Newcastle disease.

The radio was playing some 1950's ballads like "The Tennessee Waltz," "Crying in the Chapel," "Unchained Melody," and Johnny Ray's "Cry." He had brought his 22-rifle with him in case there were any wandering wild deer daring enough to munch on the corn stalks or the vegetables in Mom's truck garden. There were only three kinds of wild animals which were considered "enemies" by the farmers of the region—foxes, raccoons, and deer.

1950s-1960s Fable

The former two species were threatening because they preyed on chickens, ducks, and turkeys—if they could get at them.

The deer, on occasion, would wander onto farms and eat whatever crop was available. Once Tom had outgrown his infatuation with cowboys liked Hop along Cassidy, Gene Autry, and Roy Rogers, he had ditched his six shooter and leather holster. Whether from Little Mommy's talk or Disney's "Bambi", Tom had unexpectedly developed a dislike of guns and hunting.
He even stopped playing with his BB gun, to the dismay of the Smiths.

Bored with the ducks, the two youngsters started walking through the corn fields towards the far end of the Smith farm, where the remnants of an old wooden fence marked the Smith's property line.

Tom and Cara had to be careful where they walked because Harry had set some muskrat traps in this region where a small stream ran through the woods. Often their big brother would bring home a rabbit caught in these powerful steel traps for dinner. Neither Cara nor Helen would partake of the roasted rabbit, but Tom was persuaded to eat some—finding it similar to chicken in taste—though gamier. Emerging from the tall corn stalks, they observed a baby deer trying to free itself from a piece of wire attached to the fence. Apparently, the fawn had one of his feet tangled in the wire. The kids saw a large doe, the fawn's mother, standing one hundred feet away in the grassy meadow beyond the fence. Watching out for their trigger-happy brother who would relish the chance to blast away at the two deer, the kids extricated the fawn from the fence. Steadying itself, the caramel-colored deer scampered over to its mother and the two animals quickly vanished in the nearby woods.

CHAPTER 8

Cold Wars

Lying awake one night, Tom overheard Mom, Dad, and Helen taking about a topic that interested him—politics. The Smith's were stalwart Republicans (unlike Democratic-leaning Little Mommy), who voted for the former World War II general Dwight Eisenhower both times he ran against Democrat Adlai Stevenson, the "egg head" governor from Illinois. With a teenaged son soon eligible for the draft, they were happy that President Eisenhower had ended the Korean War when he was first elected—just as he had promised. The Smiths trusted "Ike" to run the country frugally and keep the evil Russians at bay. Helen, who was old enough to remember FDR with fondness, had an independent streak with regard to political ideas. (Despite their Republican loyalties both Smiths had voted for Roosevelt before and during the Second World War.)

"Well Ike should stop testing atomic bombs. Radioactivity, in the form of strontium-90, has been found in milk and other foods," the teenager remarked. This made her parents uncomfortable—the idea of radioactive contamination of their food was alarming to them. On the TV news, the boy had learned that America had recently tested the hydrogen bomb in the Pacific Ocean, which was a thousand times more powerful than the atomic bomb dropped on Hiroshima.

1950s-1960s Fable

Tom also remembered a relative from Jersey City, an army veteran, talking about American bombers (B-52's) that flew around carrying atomic bombs. If war broke out between the two super powers, American B-52's would fly towards Russia to drop their atomic bombs, while Russian bombers, also carrying atomic bombs, would return the atomic favor on us. In school, they held air raid drills in which the children would crawl under their desks. These atomic drills were a welcome respite from tedious lessons on long division – providing the boys with the opportunity to peer at the girls' underpants peeking through their scrunched-up skirts. Whenever Tom heard an airplane flying overhead at night, he shuddered with fear at the thought it might be carrying atomic bombs.

November 4, 1952

Dwight David Eisenhower was elected the 34th President of the United States, serving during the Cold War years of 1953 to 1961. A five-star general, Eisenhower was the Supreme Commander of Allied Forces in Europe during World War II. In 1952, Dwight Eisenhower was nominated for President on the Republican ticket, along with vice-presidential candidate Richard Nixon, a notorious Communist hunter from California. The popular war hero defeated Democrat Adlai Stevenson of Illinois by a landslide. Eisenhower reflected the fiscally conservative, anti-communist, middle-of-the-road attitudes of the 1950's. Fulfilling a campaign promise, President Eisenhower went to Korea to obtain an armistice in that unpopular, stalemated war. Reportedly threatening the North Koreans and the Red Chinese with atomic bombs, Eisenhower effectively ended that bloody war. As President, Dwight Eisenhower reduced America's conventional armed forces by relying on a huge stockpile of approximately 5,000 to 7,000 nuclear weapons.

Todd M. Daley

The major domestic issues during the Eisenhower Administration were McCarthyism, school desegregation, and the building of an interstate highway system.

President Eisenhower refused to admonish Senator Joseph McCarthy for his Communist witch hunting, in which innocent people were labeled as traitors through guilt by association. After the 1954 Brown Supreme Court decision outlawing racial segregation in public schools, Eisenhower remained silent on this critical moral issue. The President did send federal troops to Little Rock, Arkansas when Governor Faubus tried to block the entry of black students to its Central High School.

In 1956, a world-wide ban on atmospheric and underground testing of atomic and hydrogen bombs became a major issue. President Eisenhower proposed a moratorium on all nuclear explosions, above-and-below ground, verified by on-site inspections stations in America and Russia. The paranoiac Russians balked at establishing inspection stations inside their borders. Both countries suspended nuclear testing for short time periods – only to resume atomic and hydrogen bomb testing again. In 1958 alone, the two super powers set off 81 nuclear explosions, resulting in worldwide protests as radioactivity levels increased in food and water across the globe. A 1959 summit conference between the U.S., Russia, England, and France to discuss nuclear disarmament and ban atomic weapons testing – was abruptly canceled by Russian dictator Nikita Khrushchev when an American U-2 spy plane was shot down in Russia.

President Dwight D. Eisenhower's greatest accomplishment was eight years of peace during the perilous Cold War, when nuclear saber rattling was practiced by both sides. Eisenhower rescued the Republican Party from isolationism and McCarthyism, while maintaining prosperity and balancing the federal budget. A moderate Republican, Dwight Eisenhower opposed hard-liners who wanted to spend millions on new weapons like the B-70 bomber. In his famous farewell address, President Eisenhower warned the nation about the increasing influence of the "military-industrial complex" which could endanger our freedom.

1950s-1960s Fable

The Cold War demanded the development of a huge armaments industry and extensive armed forces – which siphoned off scarce resources from other segments of the American economy. Leaving the Presidency as one of the most popular, beloved, and respected of the world's leaders, Eisenhower retired to his Gettysburg, Pennsylvania farm. In the 1950's

Americans expressed their fondness for Dwight D. Eisenhower in this simple phrase: "I likeIke."

Winters were pretty severe with lots of snow storms in South Jersey during the 1950's. The Smith's narrow six-room house was heated by a coal furnace in the cellar. Once a month, a big noisy truck delivered coal to the Smith's house. Rumbling up the driveway and stopping near a cellar window on the side of the house, the driver pulled out an eight-foot slide from the back of the truck. The cellar window opened to a dusty coal bin, where the coal was stored. After placing the slide through the open window, inclining the truck bed slightly and lifting the rear gate, a roaring stream of coal rolled down the slide into the coal bin below. Coal deliveries were noisy, dusty, and dirty – but fascinating to the children to watch.

A few times a day the coal had to be shoveled by Dad or Harry into the furnace to feed the roaring fire inside, thereby heating the entire house through floor grates in each room. One time, Tom left some plastic cars and trucks on the living room grates, only to find them badly distorted by the heat emanating from the grates. Once in a while, the kids played in the coal bin – climbing on the coal pile, throwing the shiny black nuggets at each other, and writing on the concrete cellar floor with the coal pieces.

Discovered in the coal bin by Mom covered with coal dust, Tom and Cara received a few cracks on their blackened legs with the cat-of-nine tails. One snowy week there was no coal delivery and the coal bin was empty.

The resourceful Smith's used an alternative fuel in the furnace—pine logs cut from a nearby woods. It seemed to work for a while, heating the house on a cold winter day, but the house was soon filled with pine smoke—irritating everyone's eyes. No matter how cold and snowy the weather was, Tom and Cara always wanted to play outside in the snow-covered back yard and surrounding fields. Helen bundled the kids and herself and they went outside. It is a truism that children do not feel the cold the way adults do. Unlike urban settings, the snow-covered fields never turned brown with street grime in the South Jersey farm region. On a sunny day, the trees, shrubs, and fields would glisten with reflected sunlight—created twelve acres of magical snow land. Helen told the children that weather conditions had to be just right for snow fall and God made each snowflake unique—in the same way that each person in the world is unique. Once outside, the first order of business was to make a big snow man—constructed of three huge snowballs, complete with tree branch arms, a corncob nose, two coal nugget eyes, a wooden stick mouth, topped off with an old cowboy hat and a frayed neck scarf.

Growing bored with their imposing snow man, the kids opted for a more ambitious project—an igloo-like snow house. Under Helen's supervision, Tom and Cara formed one-foot-by-one-foot snow blocks, which they arranged in a six-foot circle. Then, the children arranged the snow blocks in circular rows, one above the other, so the seams of the blocks were offset for maximum stability.

The circular wall attained a height of five feet without an enclosing roof. Tom hit upon the idea of a plywood roof, covered with a layer of snow. A door opening was left for entrance and exit into the snow house. The result, pleasing to both children and to Helen, was a quaint snow hut which was surprisingly warm inside. The kids wanted to bring blankets into their snow house and camp there overnight. To her good sense, Helen vetoed this idea — suggesting that their snow hut would make a good refuge for chipmunks, squirrels, rabbits, bears, and other neighborhood critters seeking a warm shelter during the long, cold winter night. But Tom wondered at this notion, "I thought animals like squirrels, rabbits, and bears hibernated during the winter?" Shaking her head, Helen replied: "Don't be a smart-aleck, Uncle Sam!"

One snowy day, Mom was working the 4 PM to midnight shift at the Bloomington canning factory, when Helen preparing dinner for the Smith family, discovered that they were out of milk, bread, and pasta. The kids volunteered to go with Dad to Miller's grocery store, which was in town — approximately 1 ½ miles from the Smith's farm. The roads had not yet been ploughed, but the black Plymouth sedan had chains on its tires so it could navigate in the snow. Slipping and sliding on the snow-and-ice-covered road, the Plymouth made it to Miller's and the necessary comestibles were purchased. The return trip didn't go as well — the Plymouth got stuck in a snow embankment roughly a mile from the farm. Fortunately, the youngsters and their father were suitably dressed for the snowy weather — hats, scarves, gloves, boots, and heavy winter coats. There was no alternative but to mush through the heavy snow.

Because of his polio-induced awkward gate, Dad was having difficulty walking through the deep snow. It was a bitterly cold day with a biting wind that stung their faces and froze their hands and feet.

Struggling and slowing down, Dad suggested that the children walk on by themselves, while he went back to their stalled car. But Tom and Cara would have none of that — they adamantly refused to abandon their father in that awful snow storm. Grasping each of his arms, the children supported their crippled father as they slowly trudged through the deep snow. A few more times, Dad became discouraged and told his kids to leave him by the side of the road. "No Dad, we're not walking home without you!" the children replied. Using a lesson once taught them by Helen, the kids understood that the big jobs in life consist of many little steps taken one at a time. Cara volunteered to count their steps — keeping up everyone's spirits. By the time they reached the Smith's front door, Cara had counted 4,356 steps.

Then Mom called Tom and Cara "my little heroes" — just as heroic as Dad who had been renamed "my hero" after rescuing the baker's two sons from the swampy quick sand behind the farmer's market.

Fall brought a new sport for Tom to apply his limited athletic skills on — football. The boy was never quite comfortable with America's autumn pastime — a missing knuckle on his right thumb prevented him from gripping and throwing the pigskin properly. His slender build was not suited for the position of lineman where bulk prevails. Though a fast runner, the boy was not adept at broken field running in which the running back would turn, stop, and start suddenly to avoid tacklers. On defense, Tom never mastered the proper tackling technique. His ineffective method was to grab the runner from behind by his shirt — sometimes ripping his shirt. In terms of natural attributes, the boy's speed, large hands, and knack for holding on to the football made him a fairly good pass-catching end.

1950s-1960s Fable

CHAPTER 9

Black and White

Like most small towns during the 1950's, the Bloomington high school football games were a big spectator sport for the town folk. The Bloomington Blue Jays played their home games Saturday nights in the high school stadium — on a large crab grass field enclosed by concrete stands on the home side and ramshackle wooden stands on the opponent's side. The outfitting of Bloomington Stadium with field lights, mounted on tall towers a few years prior, was a popular civic improvement for the town. Consequently, the major autumn social activity of the local townspeople was the Saturday night high school football game.

The blue-and-gold uniformed Bloomington football players always appeared smaller than their big town rivals. Despite their losing record, the Blue Jays usually played before a large enthusiastic crowd. Tonight, Bloomington's opponents were the Southfield Bears, an impressive team that dominated the Blue Jays in both size and athletic ability. After the first half, the Bloomington Blue Jays were behind by four touchdowns. With winning out of the question, Coach Kormen put in his younger players, including the sophomore running back Jimmy Jones, older brother of Tom's playground buddy — Earl Jones. To the home crowd's dismay, the Southfield fans began booing as soon as Jimmy entered the game.

Sitting with Cara and Helen, Tom asked his older sister why the Southfield crowd was booing Jimmy, who had just broken through the opponent's line— gaining 25 yards before being gang-tackled by a group of Southfield defenders. Shrugging her shoulders, Helen replied: "I guess the Southfield fans don't like colored players showing them up." Looking at both teams, the boy realized that Jimmy Jones was the only colored player on the field.

The fan's reaction perplexed Tom. Why does a person's skin color matter so much? Then, he remembers his teacher, Mrs. Fisher, talking about Abraham Lincoln and the Civil War—in which thousands of soldiers from the North and the South had died to free the slaves. She had said that some people from the South had never gotten over the Civil War. But New Jersey was a northern state, with no history of slavery. The boy loved it when Mrs. Fisher talked about American history—especially the Presidents.

He admired Lincoln and Washington the most— particularly the fact that both were known for their honesty. He once wrote a composition about his two favorite Presidents. As a young boy, Washington had admitted to his father that he had chopped down a cherry tree: "I cannot tell a lie." And Lincoln, known as "Honest Abe," was a backwoods lawyer who once walked miles to return a client's money he had overcharged. Lincoln, an animal lover, had saved a pig from a swamp—soiling his new suit. Mrs. Fisher also spoke about recent events in the South, where colored people were refusing to sit in the back of a public bus. Who would want to be forced to sit in the back of a bus?

Tom was amazed at the way grown-ups acted.

He felt that they could learn from kids, who played with everybody and seldom thought about a person's skin color.

December 1, 1955

Rosa Parks left her job at a Montgomery, Alabama department store around 6 o' clock and caught the Cleveland Avenue bus to go home. She sat down in one of the seats in the middle of the bus where blacks were permitted to sit – in addition to the seats in the back of the bus. When the bus began to fill with white people, the bus driver ordered Rosa to give up her seat and move to the back of the bus. Rosa Parks refused to give up her seat and the bus driver called the police to arrest her. Mrs. Parks said that she refused to move because she was tired of obeying the Jim Crow (segregationist) laws of the South. She was charged with a violation of chapter 6, section 11 segregation law of the Montgomery City code.

Working with the Montgomery chapter of the NAACP, Rosa Parks organized the Montgomery Bus Boycott, which involved the entire black community (40,000 people) of the city. Refusing to ride the public buses, the black people of Montgomery opted for car pools, black-operated cabs, and walking to work and school. The boycott lasted 381 days, severely damaging the bus company's finances and the Montgomery business community. The Montgomery bus boycott demonstrated the potential of nonviolent mass protests to successfully challenge racial segregation in the South. In 1956, the U.S. Supreme Court unanimously ruled that segregation in public transportation, and in public parks and playgrounds was unconstitutional. Dr. Martin Luther King said that the 1956 Supreme Court decision was "a victory for all mankind."

Mrs. Parks' refusal to move to the back of the bus has been viewed as the beginning of the civil rights movement of the 1960s. After her arrest, Rosa Parks suffered hardship – losing her job at the Montgomery department store. Eventually, she moved to Detroit and worked for Congressman John Conyers as a secretary and receptionist. When Rosa Parks died at the age of 92 in 2005, her coffin was placed in the Capitol Rotunda in Washington, D.C. – the first woman to be honored in that special way.

CHAPTER 10

A Letter from Little Mommy

It was a mild April morning with the sun shining and a gentle breeze stirring the trees' newly formed leaves.

Mom's truck garden was starting to sprout, the fields were marked with small corn stalks growing in straight rows, and pink apple blossoms had appeared on the apple trees across Eden Avenue. In the distant unplanted fields, wild flowers in colors of yellow, blue, and white had made their brilliant appearance. Tom had hooked up a makeshift basketball hoop out of a bushel basket attached to a wooden plank backboard, which was nailed to the backyard weeping willow tree. Starting to grow tall and lanky, the boy took a new interest in basketball, which was well suited to his slender build and meager athletic skills. He had quickly mastered the two-handed set shot, but the intricacies of dribbling and the banked layup shot eluded him. Cara, sitting on a lawn chair, was sketching a rustic scene of rabbits dashing amidst wild flowers and tall grasses.

Mom was off from work, while Dad worked the 8 AM to 4 PM day shift at the Bloomington canning factory. Harry was working extra hours at the Geratty poultry farm during his Easter break from school.

Helen was listening to the "Helen Trent" soap opera about a woman from a mining town trying to make a life as a newly wed in a big city, while washing the breakfast dishes. Cara got off the lawn chair to cross Eden Avenue and get a closer look at the apple blossoms. And Tom worked on a hook shot that Harry had taught him the day before. It was a pleasant peaceful day like so many others the children had known.

A U.S. mail truck pulled up in front of the house, and a gray-uniformed mailman deposited a stack of letters and bills in the metal mailbox near the old smoke tree in the front yard. Cara interrupted her sketching to retrieve the mail and throw it on the kitchen table for Mom to sort through. Then she walked down the long winding road to the chicken coop and nearby turkey and pig pens — presumably to do some more sketching. After a while, Mom called Tom into the house from the cellar door, where she had been doing a laundry. Using the old fashioned washer with its rotating rolls that squeezed the sopping wet clothes, she was putting them in a laundry basket before hanging the clothes on a clothes line in the backyard.

Mom's eyes were moist, apparently from crying, and she held a handwritten letter in her hand. "I have a letter from Little Mommy saying that she bought a house and wants you and your sister to live with her."

A wave of fear swept over the boy as he hugged his mother: "I don't want to live with her — you're my Mom! And I know Cara doesn't want to either." His mother replied that she would try to put it off for a year because they were too young to stay by themselves. Little Mommy worked long hours as a bookkeeper in New York City.

Apparently, the children's grandmother had died and left Little Mommy some money (along with some funds from her sister) — sufficient to purchase a house on Staten Island. Unfortunately, the law upheld parental rights above all other rights — as Tom and Cara would soon learn. The autonomy of children was restricted by society — purportedly for their own good.

Year later, Tom realized that Little Mommy's letter marked the end of his childhood. From that day onward, life took on a different meaning. The carefree days of living each moment of life as an endless series of happy times — was over. In that final year in South Jersey, the Smiths tried to cram as many activities into the youngsters as possible. Tom was enrolled in the Cub Scouts, while Cara was placed in the Brownies — neither of which pleased them. In addition to baseball, Tom was put on a soccer team, where he tended to be a spectator rather than a participant. He found the sport rather too random for his taste, preferring the symmetry and structure of baseball. Cara was given ballet and tap lessons at a dance school in town. An artsy free spirit, Cara preferred to roam the Smith farm fields when she felt the need to exercise. In a bad mood, Tom had torn down his wooden shack. Both children went along with this enrichment program, wondering what would happen at the end of the year.

Sometimes the two youngsters walked over to Hunt's Creek by themselves to talk about things. Some years before, Tom and Cara had spent a few weeks with Little Mommy on Staten Island. Their natural mother had a one-bedroom cold water flat in the Mariner's Harbor section of Staten Island, on a busy street called Richmond Terrace. The street faced an abandoned shipyard off the Kill Van Kull, where hulks of rotting ships could be seen from their second-floor window.

It took a while to get used to the noise emanating from the constant flow of traffic at night, when they were trying to fall asleep. But it was fascinating to watch the cargo ships and tugboats sail by on the Kill Van Kull day and night.

There was a "deli" right around the corner where Little Mommy bought ice cream and root beer soda. Then, while they watched TV in the evening, she made them a big ice cream soda—the highlight of their day. They went to Manhattan on the Staten Island Ferry, going past the Statue of Liberty, to gaze at the imposing skyscrapers and all the people walking on the city sidewalks. Everybody seemed to be in a hurry in New York City. They walked fast, talked fast, and made snap judgments about everything. Even the games were different. Instead of baseball, the kids played stickball in the streets with a broom stick and a rubber spalding ball, with no baseball gloves. Another thing about Staten Island that bothered the kids was that on every corner was a bar, where the strong odor of alcohol diffused into the outside air.

Little Mommy was an energetic walker and like most New Yorkers, she walked fast—forcing Tom and Cara to sometimes skip or trot to keep up with her. She took them on long walks along Richmond Terrace to gaze at the waterfront's abandoned shipyards—a hodgepodge of rotting warehouses, corroded ships, rusted anchors, and broken docks. Little Mommy said that the shipbuilding company Bethlehem Steel had been active in Mariners Harbor building war ships and freighters for the allied war effort. There were many factories in Mariners Harbor—including a bustling brewery where Ballentine beer was produced. Both Tom and Cara were World War II babies, so they had an instinctive curiosity about that era.

During the 1940s, Little Mommy had met the children's father and had fallen in love with that troubled alcoholic—conceiving Tom and Cara in successive years. It was clear to the children that their mother was sentimental about that war-torn era when she had come of age.

Living with Little Mommy on a day-to-day basis gave the kids a better grasp of her complex, lively personality. She was no longer the benign, cheerful bearer of gifts—the self-styled second mother to the children. Tom and Cara could not use the appellation "Little Mommy" on her turf. She had that big-city swiftness—quick to laugh, quick to joke, but also quick to get angry when the kids crossed her, which was seldom. Although she was on vacation from her bookkeeping job, Little Mommy still typed addresses on envelopes at night for extra money. The children were surprised to learn that she typed from 100 to 150 envelopes per week at five cents apiece. The meager amount paid for her lunch and bus fare for the work week. Like the Smiths, Little Mommy was a hard worker and careful about her finances.

Occasionally, their walks along Richmond Terrace took them in the opposite direction—towards the Bayonne Bridge, a beautiful arched bridge of grayish steel linking Staten Island with Bayonne, New Jersey. In addition to the choppy-watered Kill Van Kull, Staten Island was characterized by hills and valleys and close-set houses on busy streets. As they walked on streets that led away from the waterfront, the threesome trekked up some fairly steep hills. The children were amazed by the quaint names of the streets: Morningstar Road, Clove Road, Van Pelt, Van Name, and Pulaski Avenues, Targee and Van Duzer Streets, and Hylan Boulevard. Little Mommy told Tom and Cara that the Dutch had first settled on Staten Island in the 1600s, which was the reason for so many Dutch names—the Kill Van Kull, the Arthur Kill, Howland Hooke, among others.

In addition to the New York Ferry, there were ferries to Bayonne and Brooklyn. Observing the Manhattan skyscraper filled shoreline, watching the passing ships and tugboats, breathing in the salty sea breeze, and taking in the marvelous serenity of the open water, Tom and Cara enjoyed the ferry rides—especially the steamy hot dogs and sauerkraut.

With all the sight-seeing and new experiences, Tom and Cara looked back fondly on their two-week vacation with Little Mommy—with the exception of the last few days. They had spent a quiet evening with their mother sipping ice cream sodas and watching "Your Show of Shows" on TV. In this episode, Sid Caesar and Imogene Coca bumble along as a mismatched couple subject to the typical injustices of an indifferent world.

Not long after the children had fallen asleep on the two living room couches in the living room, they heard a loud banging on the front door of Little Mommy's second-floor apartment. It was the kids' notorious father, Thomas Haley, in an inebriated state. Pushing hard, he forced the door open against Little Mommy's opposition. Exasperated, Little Mommy shouted, "You're drunk! Get out or I'll call the cops!" The man muttered something about wanting to see his kids and sat down in the kitchen. Growing frantic, Little Mommy exclaimed, "Don't you touch my babies! I should never have left my mother!"

Then Mr. Haley asked for a drink—to which she replied that there was no beer or wine in her house. "Well, give me a couple of dollars and I'll leave you alone." Little Mommy went to her room and returned with some money, which she handed over to the man. Pocketing the money, he peeked into the living room—followed by the children's mother. By this time, the kids were wide awake but playing possum.

1950s-1960s Fable

Taking a deep breath, he whispered to the children, "I'll sober up and see you guys tomorrow." Then smiling in a grimace like manner, Mr. Haley nodded at Little Mommy and left the apartment.

The next morning, Tom and Cara vaguely recalled their father's visit the night before, along with the ensuing argument between their birth parents. Since the Smiths rarely argued, this was a new experience for the children. They were bothered by Little Mommy's regretful remarks about her predicament of being connected to Thomas Haley—consequent to leaving her own family. The initial impression made by their father had not been an auspicious one. But spurred by the bright sunshine and the dazzling blue sky of the new day, the kids were excited about the forthcoming events before them. Optimism is the natural proclivity of children.

Little Mommy was in a preoccupied state as she prepared the children's breakfast of sunny-side eggs and grapefruit sections. Tom and Cara liked to watch their birth mother go through her morning ritual of applying heavy pancake makeup and rouge to cover the purple scars on the right side of her face. She referred to makeup as her war paint. Their mother was vague about their plans for the day—mentioning a bus trip to Clove Lakes Park. "We will be seeing your father today. He has invited himself to accompany us on our day trip."

Cara asked if they could see their father's paintings today. "Helen told us that Mr. Haley was a gifted painter like Rembrandt and Van Gogh."

Snickering, Little Mommy indicated that most of his paintings had been sold or lost. Applying some white powdery makeup to her cheeks, their birth mother replied, "Your father has talent—that's for sure. But is he Rembrandt or Van Gogh? I wouldn't go that far.

1950s-1960s Fable

CHAPTER 11

Clove Lakes Park

Sure enough, as soon as Little Mommy and the two children walked to the bus stop, Mr. Haley appeared suddenly, as if by magic, to accompany them. To their mother's surprise, he appeared to be sober, which pleased her to no end. In addition, he was carrying a big notebook which aroused the children's curiosity. It was apparent to both kids that there was still a remnant of affection between their parents—although there were no hugs or kisses. Helen had described their father accurately: He was a tall, burly, pleasant-looking man with striking blue eyes, curly brown hair, and a hearty manner. He talked to his children as if he were thoroughly familiar with their habits, likes, and dislikes—surprising them with his knowledge of their everyday life in the South Jersey farm. He knew all the members of the Smith family and spoke highly of Helen.

He had a droll sense of humor—cracking jokes that brought smiles to the children and even to Little Mommy. However, there were two aspects of Mr. Haley which indicated that something was amiss: He smiled only with his lips while the rest of his face remained sad, and his brilliant blue eyes had an emptiness when observed closely.

At Clove Lakes Park, the newly-formed Haley family meandered about the extensive grounds, observing the greenish-blue lakes with their quacking ducks, yelling sea gulls, and skimming rowboats. After a while, they sat down on a blanket that Little Mommy had brought, along with a basket of sandwiches, fruit, cookies, and apple juice in a half-gallon jug. Mr. Haley opened his big notebook and began sketching the lake and the surrounding meadow and woods. He gave some paper and pencils to the children — telling them to sketch what they saw before them.

To no one's surprise, Tom's sketch was amateurish while Cara's was remarkable. But their father expressed pleasure with both drawings — putting them in his big notebook.

With the bright day beginning to darken into dusk, the foursome headed home via the same buses they had taken several hours earlier. Everyone was quite exhausted when they reached Little Mommy's second-floor apartment on Richmond Terrace. Mr. Haley offered to go to the deli and buy the children ice cream and soda. He just needed a few dollars. Reluctantly, Little Mommy gave him the money and he was on his merry way.

1950s-1960s Fable

Returning in a few minutes, the children's father delivered the goods as promised, plus a quart of beer for himself. Immediately, the pleasant mood of the family dissipated. Each time Mr. Haley took a swig of beer, Little Mommy would frown. Very quickly, he became drunk—his voice becoming a growl and his congenial manner turning to anger.

Growing irritated but trying to make light of the situation, the kids' mom observed, "You and your soda—always gulping soda." Tom and Cara looked at each other knowingly, as their father belched out loud. Suddenly furious, Little Mommy exclaimed, "You know what Mr. Haley? Get out or I'll call the cops!"

Grabbing his bottle, the kids' father headed for the door, "You never were any fun, Claire."

CHAPTER 12

Acting Up on the Farm

Back in the familiar environs of the twelve-acre Smith farm, Tom and Cara thought about their New York City experiences with a mixture of fondness and fear. There was a certain degree of excitement about Little Mommy's life on Staten Island—the colorful waterfront, the constant bustle on the hilly streets, the ferry ride to Manhattan, and the tumultuous encounters with their alcoholic father, Thomas Haley. Once Cara blurted out something about his love of beer and wine, only to be shushed by her brother. Tom felt such unpleasant family facts were best kept secret. A lingering impression remained with both children that they had little control over their own destiny. For children, there's no such thing as autonomy. The uncertainty about their future life led to feelings of anxiety and isolation in both kids. Their future, in terms of where they would live, go to school, what friends they would have, and whom they would call mom and dad—was up in the air.

This feeling of uncertainty lead to a certain rebelliousness on the part of both children. After Tom had taken apart his wooden shack, he stole some matches from the kitchen and tried to set fire to some bushes in the back yard. Fortunately, the bushes were located in the vicinity of the swampy cesspool—a section of the yard where the weeds and bushes were perpetually saturated with stagnant water.

1950s-1960s Fable

Even the docile Cara, the poster child of sweetness and obedience, got into Mom's makeup and lipstick, and began applying it liberally on her dolls and on herself. Never one to spare the rod and spoil the child, Mom applied the leather cat-of-nine tails generously to her rambunctious children. Helen wisely observed that it was good to see some normal feistiness in the two kids

One day at school Tom got an invitation from a classmate, Richie Reeman, inviting him to his birthday party. Tom was a bit surprised because birthday parties in the Smith family were strictly family affairs—no friends or classmates were invited. And since Tom and Cara's birthday fell in the same month of July (though Tom was older by one year), the Smiths traditionally had a joint birthday party for both children—inviting Little Mommy plus some Jersey City relatives. At first, Tom didn't want to attend because he was beginning to detach himself from his Bloomington school friends. In addition, the boy had found a new interest in science after discovering a high school science book in the cellar bookcase. He had set up a makeshift laboratory in an unused room of the chicken coop.

Using the discarded boards from the disassembled shack, Tom had built a laboratory bench. On the bench were jars of chemicals, fertilizer, animal and bird feed, flashlight batteries, wires, magnets, light bulbs, and an old electric motor. Cutting open the flashlight batteries, he put the chemicals in a big glass jar, added some vinegar for acid, and immersed iron and copper strips into the moist chemicals— creating a homemade battery. This homemade vinegar flashlight battery was strong enough to cause a 25-watt bulb to glow weakly.

He had also learned from this science book that our muscles are controlled by nerves carrying electrical currents. Replicating Italian scientist Luigi Galvani's experiment, Tom had captured a frog from Hunt's Creek with Cara's help—to observe the effects of electricity on frog legs. Tom wanted to sever the frog's legs to perform the famous Galvani experiment, but Cara objected—

mentioning cruelty to animals, one of God's cherished creatures. The boy thought about it and agreed to pass the current from the homemade battery on the frog's legs without amputation. Holding the frog down, they passed the electric current through his legs. The results? The frog jerked as if from a spasm, squirmed free, and with one big jump—leaped through the open chicken coop window. Laughing the two mischievous children then tried to the electric shock therapy on one of the egg-laying chickens from a nearby room in the chicken coop. The results were similar: the chicken squawked and shuddered—flapping its wings in a desperate attempt to escape its tormentors. At this point, Harry peeked into the room and told them in rather colorful language to leave the frigging chickens alone. Eying their lab setup with its various chemicals, batteries, wires, and magnets, Harry shook his head: "It looks like you're making a bomb here. Before you set it off, let me know—so I can run away!" Both kids often talked to big-sister Helen about personal concerns before broaching sensitive topics to Mom and Dad. Thus, Tom mentioned the birthday invitation in an off-hand manner expecting Helen to tell him to forget about—since there was plenty to do on the Smith farm. On the contrary, Helen told the boy to go to the party, "Look kid, your laboratory will still be here if you take an afternoon off to be with your school friends."

Arriving at Richie Reeman's house, Tom was surprised to find girls, as well as boys, among the party guests. Feeling awkward in the presence of mixed company, the boy gave his birthday gift to Richie. It was a wooden bird house that he had put together himself. Tom had screwed an eye hook in the roof with a string attached to it. The two boys went into the back yard where they

1950s-1960s Fable

hung the bird house from the branch of a large elm tree. Reluctant to return to the house, Tom went over to a leveled bare spot in the lawn, where some marbles were scattered. Picking up a stick, he inscribed a circle on the bare spot and began shooting the marble with his left hand.

Suddenly, a girl stood over him as played with the marbles. It was a classmate, Connie Mullen, a sandy-haired, freckled girl whose pig tails Tom used to pull in his early school years. Growing more reserved in recent years, the boy had ceased teasing and talking to his female classmates. Nevertheless, there was an implicit bond of affection between the two youngsters. A bit of a tomboy, Connie kneeled down and began firing the marbles herself. "I thought you were right-handed," she observed. The boy replied that he used his left hand to shoot marbles because his right thumb didn't work very well. Laughing, she cracked, "What happened? One of your pigs stepped on your thumb?"

The boy snorted, "Very funny. I have a missing knuckle, so it won't bend." He showed her the offending thumb. It was customary for Bloomington town folk, like Connie, to tease the farmers of their community, who had a mystique of their own.

They talked about their teacher, Miss Baird, a capable pedagogue with a distracted and preoccupied manner, who wasn't particularly warm to her students. Connie mentioned last week's spelling bee, which wound up in a tie between Tom and a spectacled girl named Francis. To the boy's dismay, Miss Baird gave first prize (a chocolate bar) to Francis because he had misspelled the word "elixir" right before she muffed it. Connie's older brother, William, a football player for Bloomington high school, was a friend of big brother Harry. "Tom, why is your last name different from your brother's?"

Tom just shrugged his shoulders and talked about his chicken coop laboratory where he trying to determine the effect of electricity on growing plants—especially corn. He wondered if he would have enough time to finish his scientific experiments before moving to New York City next year. Connie gasped, her eyes filling with tears. "Oh no! You can't leave. All your friends are here.

Besides you're a farm boy—you'll hate the big city." Abruptly seizing his hand, "I'll miss you, Tom." The boy started to shiver and he gasped for breath. "I'm just a kid. It ain't my decision." A big event in the Smith household was the purchase of a 12-inch black-and-white Motorola television. Immediately the entire family, with the exception of big brother Harry who worked long hours at the Geratty poultry farm, spent hours and hours gathered around the TV set. Especially for the youngsters, Tom and Cara, television watching became a fixed habit. Mom and Dad remarked that the kids had developed "television eyes" gazing at the flickering image on the tiny silver screen. The Smith family liked the classic shows of the 1950s—known as the "golden age of TV"—Sid Caesar's "Your Show of Shows", Milton Berle's "Texaco Comedy Hour", Arthur Godfrey's "Talent Scouts", Lucille Ball's "I Love Lucy", and Jack Webb's "Dragnet."

The kids even watched television extensively during the day, causing Helen to turn the set off—sending them outside to play. "What happened to your science laboratory, Tom?" And "What happened to your sketch pad, Cara?" The children would complain that it was too cold outside to play. But Helen would have none of their excuses. Bundling them up in winter coats, hats, scarves, gloves, and boots, she shooed them outside to roam the twelve acres of snow-covered fields in the frosty fresh air.

Once outside, the sparkling snow-covered fields seem to beckon the children to do what children have always done during winter time—go sledding. Grabbing an old wooden sled from beneath the back porch, they trudged up the winding road to the chicken coop. Just beyond the chicken coop was a broad flat field which declined slightly away from the chicken coop. It was ideal for sledding, which is exactly what Tom and Cara did—taking turns pushing each other on the sled down the gradually sloping hill.

After a while, the cold air had penetrated their hands and feet, so they went into the chicken coop. Tom had an idea. Working quickly with saw, hammer, and nails he built a large three-by-four-foot rectangular box—open at the top, with a large square window space in the front. He then nailed four large round washers on the front side—just below the square front window. Cara identified his project immediately—a make-believe TV. Working quickly, she made some hand puppets out of some old socks and drew some scenery boards on large pieces of cardboard. Soon they were engrossed in putting on clever puppet shows—complete with a hero, a heroine, and a villain enmeshed in an imaginative story line. The kids had discovered that activity and imagination were more fun than passive television watching—even on a cold winter day.

February 25, 1950

"Your Show of Shows" premiered on Saturday night at nine o'clock, beginning a three-year run for one of the most celebrated shows on television. The show featured Sid Caesar and Imogene Coca playing the "Hickenloopers"—reflecting the anxieties and frustrations of a married couple. The husband, Charlie, was much put upon by his high-strung wife, Doris. The authenticity of their domestic skits was based upon everyday experiences combining reality and humor.

Many of the sketches focused on common points of contention between husband and wife: hanging stockings on the towel rack, dropping cigar ashes on the rug, the wife counting brush strokes of her hair, the husband coming home with a blond hair on his jacket (from the dog), the wife starting a strict diet of shredded carrots, string beans, and yogurt. For example, there was a skit in which Charlie and Doris eat dinner at a fancy restaurant with an intimidating writer (Carl Reiner), who can't be satisfied with the tip – despite Charlie repeatedly peeling off bills from his bank roll, then tossing him his watch, and Doris throwing in her earrings. And still no reaction from the implacable waiter.

At last, the couple flees the restaurant with the mean waiter yelling "Cheapskate!" after them.

There was another memorable domestic skit in which Doris has smashed up their car. Ironically, Charlie has had a stressful day at the office and wants to go for a relaxing drive before dinner. Doris started hinting that there was something wrong with the car. After much hemming and hawing, she admits that she has totaled the car by smashing into a liquor store window. Gritting his teeth, Charlie mentions something about reminding Doris to send the check to the insurance company on time. "Did you send the check?" Doris grins and nods yes.

In another sketch Charlie comes home to find Doris smelling of perfume and kissing him passionately, as soon as he opens the door. Did she smash the car? He exclaims, "That was not a marriage kiss – that was a $300 kiss!" Doris had prepared a sumptuous meal of roast beef and mashed potatoes, plus lemon meringue pie for dessert. Then she comes out of the kitchen in a brand new mink coat. Charlie sees the mink coat and starts to cry, while Doris is talking on and on to him. There's a close shot of his face with the tears pouring down his cheeks, "I got no money lady." One memorable episode was a spoof of the 1950s TV show, "This Is Your Life." Carl Reiner, playing the host, goes into the audience to grab Al Duncey (Sid Caesar), who has to be dragged, kicking, faking, and running up to the stage. The first person from his past life was Uncle Goopy (Howard Morris), who kept on hugging and kissing Al – the two

1950s-1960s Fable

men cried and carried on as if there was no tomorrow. Each time another friend or relative was brought out, Al and Uncle Goopy would rush back into each other's arms — embracing and crying. At one point Uncle Goopy is clinging to Al's leg as he walks across the stage. The skit ends when a beautiful woman appears and starts kissing Al, who apparently doesn't even know her. "But it's alright with me!"

The secret of the success of "Your Show of Shows" was the ability of Sid Caesar and his great comedy writers, Carl Reiner, Neil Simon, Mel Brooks, Larry Gelbart, Mel Tolkin, and Woody Allen among others, to extract humor from everyday life and to combine comedy with pathos. The show's comedic sketches took real life situations and twisted them slightly — enabling the audience to see their own lives made fun of.

The domestic situations were commonplace events that occurred in the lives of all people. Sid Caesar said, "Comedy is a man in trouble." American audiences instinctively root for the underdog — the common man in over his head. Caesar went on to say that laughter and crying are two sides of the same coin: they both constitute the release of emotional stress. When the audience doesn't know whether to laugh or cry — that means the comedy is working. "Your Show of Shows" was ninety minutes of live television — no cue cards, no retakes, and only three commercials of one minute, ten seconds in length. If something went wrong, you had to take it in stride and ad lib. Sid Caesar played a wide variety of characters: Charlie Hickenlooper (every man), Professor Ludwig Spacebrain (physicist), Professor Ludwig von Henpecked (psychiatrist), and Kool Seas (jazz musician with coke bottle glasses).

At a personal level, Sid Caesar admired Albert Einstein, who believed that there was order and rhythm to the world. Einstein said "God does not play dice with the universe." Caesar, a talented saxophone player, linked music with comedy in that both are characterized by melody and rhythm. He also realized that you learn nothing from success — only failure teaches you about life.

The stress of weekly live TV shows did exact a heavy toll on the comedian who was plagued by alcoholism during the 1950s and 1960s. Nevertheless, Sid Caesar was able to conquer his demons by intensive self-analysis and by learning to make friends with himself. He adopted a very simple philosophy of life: "It's called living in the now."

Of course, there were times when Tom and Cara didn't get along so well. Like any kids, squabbles arose over toys, turf, and even treats. Once, Helen took the two youngsters for ice cream in her boyfriend Bill's car. They drove to the neighboring town of Vineland, which was bigger than Bloomington—similar to Staten Island with its closely set houses and stores along a wide main street. Helen bought them each a double-scoop chocolate ice cream cone, dipped with chocolate sprinkles. Unlike most kids, they seldom ate their treats quickly. For Tom and Cara, the race was to see who could make the treat last longer. On this occasion, Cara won the contest—outlasting her brother's forbearance, as she licked her fast-melting ice cream cone slowly while Tom devoured the sweet-tasting ice cream plus the crunchy cone in a matter of minutes. The Cara began eating her ice cream slowly in a taunting manner—making sounds of oohs and ahs. Reaching the end of his patience, the boy angrily pushed the cone into his sister's face, so the ice cream smeared on her face and fell into her lap and on the seat. Cara yelped and Helen uncharacteristically gave Tom a slap across his face, while her boyfriend fretted about the mess on the back seat. The unhappy kids were quickly driven home, where they were banished to the great outdoors of the Smith farm with the order to go their separate ways.

1950s-1960s Fable

The fresh air, open spaces, and the diversions of the pigs, chickens, and turkeys ended their sibling hostilities — permitting Helen to spend some time mending fences with her aggrieved boyfriend, Bill.

In their final year in the Smith household, sibling rivalry occurred more frequently between Tom and Cara, as each child noted the dwindling number of days left in the South Jersey farm. It appeared that the twelve acres of corn fields, vegetable gardens, pigpens, turkey pens, and chicken coop were not spacious enough for the two youngsters. One day, they were in the chicken coop room which housed Tom's science laboratory and workshop. Cara had taken some wood from the wood pile that had accumulated when the boy disassembled his wooden shack. Cara wanted to build an easel for her sketch pad, pencils, crayons, and paint brushes to paint outdoors. Tom objected and a short nasty fight ensued with the boy pushing his sister down so she hit her head on the concrete chicken coop floor.

Running out of the chicken coop in tears, she complained to big brother Harry who told Cara to get some ice for the bump on her head. He then administered a well-deserved smack on the boy's back side, which stung his hand more than the boy's bony butt. Tom was also sent back to the house to be banished to the cellar bookcase reading room. The consensus of the Smith family was that Tom was getting "too big for his britches." Interestingly enough, Cara proved to quite handy in making things and with Harry's help, she put together a homemade, portable easel which she toted around the farm with her sketching materials drawing clever pictures of the farm animals, fields, creek, and surrounding woods.

There were other times in this final year in Bloomington when Tom and Cara acted like old-fashioned bullies. As with adults, children who feel victimized can respond with cruelty towards their playmates. Two houses down from the Smith farm was the smaller Russel farm where Buddy lived, a boy two years younger than Tom. Most of the time, Tom and Cara got along famously with the clever Buddy, who invented imaginative games with plastic cowboys, soldiers, and Indians—called "guys." Like the Smiths, the Russels had a chicken coop, which housed twenty egg-laying chickens and four foul-smelling pigs.

One day, the threesome were playing in the chicken coop when Tom and Cara began tossing some dried pig poop at Buddy. He responded in kind, but when the two Smith kids got the upper hand, he ran to his mother. The fight capped a petulant, mean-spirited session in which Tom and Cara taunted Buddy about his mother—declaring his mom to be "lazy" since she didn't work at the Bloomington canning factory like their mom. She was just a stay-at-home mom who spoiled Buddy. When the boy's mother marched towards the chicken coop with an angry red face, the two kids knew they were in trouble. "I thought that you were nice children but I was wrong.

Get off my property and stay away from Buddy!" It took several weeks of coaxing plus a few severed turkey heads for the Smith kids to renew their friendship with the mild-mannered Buddy.

That final melancholy spring in South Jersey was a season of restlessness and rancor for the entire Smith household.

1950s-1960s Fable

Mom and Dad, whose relationship was usually harmonious and tranquil, appeared to bicker over such mundane matters as the number of turkeys they would raise, whether to plant corn or wheat next year, and what to do about the bothersome pigs. Big sister Helen, dating her high school boy friend Bill on a regular basis, wasn't around to spend time with the youngsters.

And big brother, Harry, was working extra hours at the Geratty poultry farm mornings, evenings, and weekends. Cara seemed to spend every free moment roaming the twelve-acre Smith farm and beyond with her easel and pencils. Occasionally, she would sit under the pine trees to the left of the Smith house and draw pictures. Her sketches had gotten better—remarkable likenesses of corn and vegetable fields, and the farm animals with a new somber quality not seen before in her pictures. Cara even spent time tutoring Buddy on her sketching techniques—as if she was designating him as the new artist-in-residence in her absence.

A few weeks before the children's departure for Staten Island, some of the Smith's relatives from Jersey City came down for a final visit. Uncle Eddie, who was among the visitors, asked Tom and Cara to show him the science lab and art display in the chicken coop. The two youngsters walked unwillingly down to the chicken coop with the strange man. However, Tom veered off towards the creek to get a look at some deer just beyond the Smith-farm property line. So the job of showing Uncle Eddie their work went to Cara by default.

After returning to the house, Cara looked particularly upset. But when she said something to Mrs. Smith (Helen wasn't around.), Cara was dispatched with a smack on her butt from the cat-of-nine tails.

Her brother Tom was not immune from the general malaise infecting the Smith household. His reaction was to clean up and dispose of everything he had been doing on the Smith farm in the last few years. After disassembling the wooden shack, which had served as his hideaway and personal reading room, he took apart the wooden go-cart. All the boards (with the nails carefully removed) were neatly stacked in a big wood pile outside the chicken coop. His science laboratory was taken apart, including the shelves and benches. Liquids and powders were put in the big iron barrel where the Smith family's trash was placed — to be incinerated by Harry from time to time. The science notebooks, where data on various experiments on the effects of electricity and chemicals on the growth of plants had been recorded, were given to Buddy who promised to take care of them and do similar experiments in the future.

Fearing the appearance of new needy children on the Smith farm in the future, Tom was reluctant to leave anything behind. Let them build their own wooden shacks and go-carts. Let them do their own science experiments in the chicken coop. Both he and his sister would be one hundred miles away on Staten Island. He began to spend time with his neighborhood friend, Larry Hunt, playing baseball. In an effort to improve his batting, fielding, and throwing skills, the two boys would take turns batting and pitching to each other. Tom figured he would be competing with those tough, fast-talking New York City boys on the diamonds of America's favorite pastime. Thus, his compulsive clearing the slate constituted a mood of deep despair — trying to impose order in an uncertain world.

Despite the distraction of the impending move to Staten Island, Tom did well at school — concentrating, answering questions, and doing his assignments — to maintain good grades.

Cara, always the dreamy-eyed artist, was less focused on her school work, but made satisfactory progress. Her art work did capture her teacher's attention and several of her farm animal sketches were displayed on the classroom bulletin board. Near the end of the school year, the school's principal Mr. Wood, talked to Tom and Cara about leaving Bloomington Elementary School. He had received a letter from Mrs. Smith stating that the children would be moving to attend a public school on Staten Island, where their birth mother lived. Mr. Wood had requested copies of their birth certificates to make sure the transfer was legal. In addition, he wanted to know how the children felt about this move to Staten Island, a place one hundred miles away and totally different from the farming town of Bloomington. The kids were nervous and frightened, wondering what they had done wrong to be summoned to the principal's office. Tom didn't know what to say, but Cara spoke up, "You mean that you can put a stop to the move and let us stay here?"

Mr. Wood shook his head, declaring he had no authority to revoke the transfer. "These papers (birth certificates) appear valid. Your foster parents, Mr. and Mrs. Smith, are wonderful people, but their hands are tied."

During recess, Tom had begun spending time with Connie Mullin, where they sat together talking things over on the big boulder of the triangle-apex area of the playground. Motivated by their impending separation, a blossoming puppy love had developed between the two youngsters in the final weeks of June. Tom talked about his brief visit to Staten Island a few years earlier — describing the waterfront area of defunct shipyards with decaying ships, rotting hulks, and broken docks, and the flow of ships, tugs, and barges on the Kill Van Kull.

He described the busy streets filled with cars, buses, and trucks, the neighboring delis, and the foul-smelling bars on every corner. He even mentioned his birth father's drinking habits and the arguments between his birth parents. The naïve country girl was appalled by these revelations, fearing something awful would happen to Tom and his sister.

Playing the role of big-city boy who knew how to take care of himself, Tom pooh-poohed everything he had experienced on Staten Island. He promised Connie that he would come back every summer, telling her all about his big-city adventures and teaching her to play baseball and throw like a boy. The sweet freckled-faced girl smiled and gave the boy a peck on the cheek.

CHAPTER 13

Day of Departure

At last the dreaded day of departure from the Smith family and their twelve-acre farm arrived—the abundant corn fields and vegetable garden, the chicken coop, the turkey cage, and the pig pen, and the surrounding woods and Hunt's Creek—the pastoral setting of so many childhood memories. All their belongings—clothes, toys, games, books, notebooks, and sketch books—were packed in suitcases and cardboard boxes. The Smith's had invited Little Mommy, babbling and smothering the kids with kisses and hugs, and Thomas Haley, appearing sober and smiling his empty smile, for some lunch. Turning their hosts down, the children's birth parents wanted to be back on the road shortly. Tom steeled himself to keep his emotions in check and urged Cara to do likewise—realizing that if she started to cry, he would surely follow. The boy now understood that each human being is alone in the world—especially when facing a crisis—illness, death, and separation from family and friends. The anguish and despair he felt was akin to what adults must feel as they make their way in an unfriendly world.

Everyone was on the front lawn, Mom, Dad, Helen, and Harry on one side, with Little Mommy and Thomas Haley on the opposite side, and Tom and Cara standing awkwardly in the middle—next to the stacked suitcases and boxes. For a moment there was a serene stillness, with only the sounds of singing birds and rustling trees wafting in the gentle summer breeze.

As if moved by some subliminal signal, Harry and Helen began carrying the suitcases and boxes to the trunk of the beat-up 1948 De Soto, just purchased by Thomas Haley. In a recent letter to the Smiths, Little Mommy said the children's birth father had gotten a job as a house painter and was helping her fix up the house. It was now ready for Tom and Cara to live in.

Tom looked across Eden Avenue to the apple orchard and saw the nice Puerto Rican man who had played catch with them and had showed them the difference between snapping turtles and harmless turtles. The swarthy man grasped the situation and crossed the street with a handful of apples which he gave to the kids. The adults didn't know what to make of his generosity, but Helen smiled and thanked the man who quickly returned to his apple picking. The boy thought about all the animals on the Smith farm he would miss—the chickens, the turkeys, the ducks, and most of all the smelly pigs wallowing in their muddy pig pen. He thought about his friends at Bloomington Elementary School, especially his sweet-heart Connie Mullen. Then he looked at his handicapped foster father, Mr. Smith. Who would be his number one helper in the many repair jobs around the farm? Little Mommy was talking rapidly in her usual frenetic manner on random topics—the weather, politics, her bookkeeping job—trying to fill up the awkward silent moments. Looking over at Mr. Smith, Thomas Haley inquired politely about his health. Mr. Smith, shifting his weight from one unsteady leg to the other, said he felt fine in an annoyed manner. Then he walked awkwardly over to Tom and Cara and gave them each a hug, which was unusual because Mr. Smith was not demonstrative in his affections. "Always remember.

1950s-1960s Fable

You are my son, Tom, and you are my daughter, Cara." At this point, Mrs. Smith joined her husband in embracing the children, "This is so hard for us!"

Attempting to break the tension, Thomas Haley smiled wanly at Helen, asking her how she was doing in school. Helen replied, "I'm doing fine and how are you doing with your drinking, Mr. Haley?" The Smiths tried to shush their oldest daughter but she persisted, "And if I find out that you're hitting the bottle, I will take those children away myself!"

Thomas Haley laughed, "You're a feisty girl. That's for sure!"

Somehow this exchange broke the stalemate. Quick, tear-filled good-byes were said and soon the children were zooming on the New Jersey Turnpike — heading north for
New York City. Daydreaming, the boy realized the elusive nature of time, which can only move forward. All those childhood experiences in the South Jersey farming town of Bloomington were in his past. Would he be able to recall them vividly? The past tends to fade over time. Somehow, he must hold the memories of this special time in his life or it was all for nothing.

CHAPTER 14

A New Life on Staten Island

Tom and Cara half expected to return to the second-floor apartment in Mariners Harbor with its view of the rotting ships, rusted hulks, and decaying docks of the derelict Kill Van Kull shipyards. Instead, they found themselves in the working-class neighborhood of Elm Park where the immense Wolstein factory could be seen, heard, and smelled around the clock. Their home was a two-family, flat-roofed, white stucco house with an enclosed sun porch and concrete front steps. Situated on a quiet narrow street, Pulaski Avenue, the house had a front view of some closely-set houses, one of which was perched above a junk yard with the sprawling Wolstein factory as a backdrop. The back yard was separated into two parts—a sunken concrete walkway followed by a small crab grass filled area bounded on two sides by concrete garages and rickety wooden fences on the other sides. There was a big mulberry tree in the far corner and an old pear tree on the opposite side, near the wooden fence.

Compared to the twelve-acre Smith farm, the back yard was meager. But there was a long four-foot wide cemented brick alley way, sufficient space for a game of catch-and-throw if you had control over your tosses.

1950s-1960s Fable

There was a cement-floor cellar which had seven-foot ceilings and nicely painted walls—courtesy of Thomas Haley. The house itself was a railroad flat of four rooms, a tiny bathroom, a long narrow hallway, and the sun porch with its own entrance from the front porch. The upstairs apartment, rented to a noisy, heavy-footed family of four, had a similar layout—except for the staircase in place of the long hallway.

There were other adjustments for Tom and Cara with regard to the tense climate in the Haley household. Their birth mother was stricter in terms of dos and don'ts for the children. Lacking experience with regard to day-by-day parenting of restless kids who were homesick for their South Jersey home, she imposed rules over their neighborhood wanderings—a few blocks in any direction. If a call to come home for supper wasn't answered, they were in trouble. A raised voice or hand scared the kids more than Mrs. Smith's cat-of-nine tails ever did. For children geography is autonomy and their mother's restrictions on the children's neighborhood wandering gave them a sense of being imprisoned.

Because of his sloppy handwriting (due in part to that malfunctioning right thumb), Tom had to practice his writing his letters and his numerals over the summer. And Cara had to practice her times table because of her occasional lapses in that area of arithmetic. In addition, both children were required to read one hour per day over the summer. The upshot was that Tom enjoyed reading less than he had in the past and Cara no longer carried her sketch book around with her as she had done on the farm. Where was Thomas Haley in all these rules and regulations? He was battling his own demons—consuming more root beer ice cream sodas to soothe his sweet tooth and hold off his growing thirst for alcohol.

Their birth parents began to argue more frequently and the kids, despite their homesickness, sensed a ticking time bomb would soon go off.

Initially Tom and Cara didn't mix well with the neighborhood children, who were hard-nosed fast-talking city kids — teasing them for their South Jersey accents. One boy, Joey Caprino, spent hours throwing a rubber spaldeen against his front steps and catching it on the rebound. This monotonous game was called stoop ball. Joey began playing with Tom — teaching him how to play stick ball in the streets. Using a chalked rectangular strike zone on a concrete wall, a broomstick bat, and the elusive high-bouncing spaldeen, the boys took turns batting and pitching to each other. Sometimes the neighborhood kids would play punch ball, in which the spaldeen was bounced to the batter who tried to punch the ball and then ran the bases. Joey was a loyal Brooklyn Dodger fan who snickered when Tom mentioned Robin Roberts and the Phillies, whom he labeled as losers.

Some of the older kids weren't very nice to the new kids on the block — causing Tom and Cara to feel isolated in their new Elm Park neighborhood. The leader of this unfriendly bunch was an impudent teenaged girl, named Joy Eggert, who liked to whisper and sneer whenever the two newcomers were in her vicinity. Cara did befriend a chubby girl next door, named Doris Schmidt, who had a shut-in mother and a peculiar grandmother with a habit of opening up her bedroom window to yell at the kids outside. Thus, their initiation to the Elm Park was not an easy one.

1950s-1960s Fable

Once Tom and Cara embarked on a long walk down Morningstar Road, heading towards Richmond Terrace, with the magnificent arching Bayonne Bridge on the right and the choppy blue-gray Kill Van Kull ahead of them.

They turned west on Richmond Terrace walking towards the old Victorian apartment building, the site of Little Mommy's second floor cold-water flat. Across the street was the abandoned World War II shipyard, with the decaying ships, corroded hulks, and broken docks, which the children never got tired of viewing. Wistfully, the kids looked across the water towards New Jersey, wondering how long would it take to walk to Bloomington, South Jersey. Tom suggested that he could build a wooden shack in the woods near the Smith farm where the two children could live — hunting, fishing, and stealing food from the neighboring farms to survive.

Both kids realized that this was a pipe-dream, and despite their homesickness and unhappiness — Staten Island was their new home and there was no going back to the farm.

Being resourceful, the children conceived of the idea of writing the Smiths in secret. They bought some envelopes and five-cent stamps at a nearby candy store on Morningstar Road. Their feverish letters were filed with the details of their day-to-day lives on Staten Island — including Little Mommy's strict rules and summer homework assignments, as well as Thomas Haley's drinking bouts as he jumped off and on the wagon. Their birth father would come home from his job as a house painter shouting at Little Mommy and reeking of alcohol. Their arguments were often scary and sometimes funny — especially when their birth mother flushed Mr. Haley's beer bottles down the toilet and he took a five-dollar bill from her pocket book to buy some wine, running out of the house.

The children did mention the new friends they had made on the block, as well as some the hassles they had with the older neighborhood kids who teased and taunted them about their South Jersey accents and their peculiar country ways. They also talked about the interesting sights on Staten Island, especially the waterfront on Richmond Terrace with its derelict shipyards and decaying old ships.

Through an exchange of letters, a secret meeting was arranged between the children and the Smiths at a school playground, a few blocks from their Pulaski Avenue house. The Smiths observed that both kids had grown over the summer months, while the latter noticed the deterioration in their foster father's health—his walking appeared more labored than in the past. The youngsters asked about Helen, who had encouraged Tom to read and Cara to sketch, and had taught them right from wrong, using Jesus's Sermon on the Mount. The Smiths said that Helen was engaged to her high school boyfriend, Bill, and told them that Harry was now working full-time at the Bloomington canning factory. Mrs. Smith had prepared Tom and Cara their favorite lunch—rye bread steak sandwiches, dill pickles, and cherry Kool-Aid. But the children were too emotionally overwrought to do more than nibble at the tasty sandwiches and sip the sweet Kool-Aid.

Talking rapidly, Tom and Cara told the Smiths about their latest doings in the Elm Park neighborhood, as well as their birth father's growing drinking habits and the havoc it created in the Haley household. Their foster parents listened sympathetically—but were unable to provide a remedy for this vexing problem. After a couple of hours, the Smiths said that they would have to be making the long drive home. The children's sadness was almost as overwhelming as their initial parting a few months earlier.

1950s-1960s Fable

The floodgates of tears flowed freely for both children, even for Tom who prided himself in keeping his feelings under wraps. He blurted out their secret plans for running away, which the Smiths strictly forbade: "You'll be kidnapped by bad people and we'll never see you again!" Unawares to the participants of this traumatic meeting, there was a witness — their neighborhood nemesis Joy Eggert, who quickly grasped the meaning of this strange encounter. To the vociferous teenager's credit, the teasing and taunting of the country newcomers diminished and they were accepted as star-crossed victims of some unknown family tragedy.

April 26, 1954

Dr. Thomas Francis of the Poliomyelitis Vaccine Evaluation Center announced the results of field tests on 1.8 million American children using Dr. Jonas Salk's polio vaccine. For Type I polio (causing paralysis) the vaccine was 68% effective, for Type II (asymptomatic) the vaccine was 100% effective, and for Type III (lethal form) the vaccine was 92% effective. In conclusion, Dr. Francis declared that the vaccine was safe, effective, and potent. After seven years of intensive work at the University of Pittsburgh, Dr. Salk and his team of researchers and technicians had developed a vaccine composed of killed polio virus, which could prevent polio. Salk's polio vaccine worked by stimulating the production of antibodies that fight all three types of polio virus. The vaccine was now approved by the National Foundation of Infantile Paralysis for nationwide use — to be manufactured by six drug companies, including Eli Lilly, Pittman-Moore, Wyeth, and Park-Davis.

Jonas Salk was born in New York City in 1916, a year known for a big polio outbreak, in which the city had half the polio cases of the entire country. At that time poliomyelitis had a mortality rate of 20%, leaving its victims with little use of their legs.

Todd M. Daley

Polio (infantile paralysis) struck mostly the young — infants and children — raging during the summer months and growing inside the nerve cells of muscle and brain tissue. Salk's mother kept young Jonas inside during hot summer afternoons and hung camphor from his neck. She rinsed his mouth with salt-water and washed his clothes in very hot water. Jonas Salk attended CCNY as an undergraduate and NYU medical school, where he took a keen interest in microbiology — opting for medical research.

After finishing his internship in 1942, Dr. Salk worked with Dr. Francis at the University of Michigan. Salk and Francis developed an innovative method of collecting influenza virus using red blood cells and washing, heating, and treating it with salt to concentrate the flu virus. Dr. Salt discovered the proper dilution of formalin (derivative of formaldehyde), the right temperature and time exposure to kill the flu virus. A flu vaccine composed of three strains of killed influenza virus was created by the two researchers.

At the University of Pittsburgh, Dr. Salk focused his research towards the goal of a polio vaccine. He discovered that there were three types of polio virus, with Type I — causing paralysis of the limbs as the most common form. It was also determined that 60% of nerve tissue must be destroyed for paralysis to appear. For his research, Dr. Salk realized that he would have to grow huge amounts of polio virus. In the 1940s it was learned that polio virus could be grown in various animal tissues — notjust nerve tissue. Consequently, Salk's Pittsburgh laboratory used Rhesus monkeys, chickens, rats, and mice to understand the behavior of polio virus. Dr. Salk perfected the tricky business of killing the polio virus with formalin. The process had to keep the outer coat of the polio virus intact in order to stimulate antibody production by the body — necessary for the development of immunity to the disease. After many years of hard work, the Salk team developed a safe, effective polio vaccine. During the 1940s and 1950s, there was an average of 35,000 annual polio cases in the U.S. — reaching a maximum of 57,876 cases in 1952. After the introduction of the Salk vaccine to America's children in 1955, the number of polio cases dropped to 15,150 in 1956 and 5,467 in 1957.

1950s-1960s Fable

By 1961, only 1,312 children contracted infantile paralysis — a 98% improvement from nine years earlier.

In his later years, Dr. Jonas Salk was involved in multiple sclerosis research and working to develop a vaccine against AIDS. The Salk Institute for Biological Studies, located in La Jolla, California, trains graduate and postdoctoral students to do medical research. Dr. Salk never won the Nobel Prize for his conquest of polio and his critics labeled his medical research as "kitchen science." He died in 1995 at the age of eighty from congestive heart failure.

Eventually, sentiments and thoughts about the children's early years in the South Jersey farm region began to recede. The day-to-day concerns of their new lives on Staten Island held sway over the melancholy remembrances of the past. Saying good-by to the Smiths after their recent secret encounter was so emotionally wrenching that their foster parents wisely refrained from seeing the kids again that summer. Adaptive and congenial, Tom and Cara made new friends on the block and adopted the pastimes and games of New York City kids — stick ball, punch ball, hard ball (baseball), hide-and-seek, ring-o-leerio, hopscotch, and jump rope. Along with Joey Caprino, Tom met the neighborhood stick ball champ, Mike Palermo — a gifted athlete who was equally adept at stick ball, hard ball, and basketball. Tom noticed that the city kids were very competitive and took losses in all street games very seriously.

Tom became a good stick ball pitcher — throwing a hard fast ball that tailed up or down, in or out — depending on the whims of air pressure and the irregularities on the spaldeen's surface. Hitting the dancing, fast-moving spaldeen was more of a problem for Tom — especially when thrown by the strong-armed Mike Palermo, who also had a good eye for hitting.

But the running bases form of stick ball, where the spaldeen was bounced slowly to the hitter, was easier for Tom to master. The hard impact of broomstick bat and spaldeen could drive the ball 250 feet—occasionally landing in a neighbor's living room after smashing through their window. The boy's enthusiastic and competent participation in these city-street games gained him acceptance into the tightly-knit group of neighborhood boys. After just one month of street games, Tom noticed that the soles of his sneakers were worn out—an occurrence that angered his birth mother but amused his birth father.

Cara also made new friends on the block—the chubby neighbor, Doris Schmidt and the feisty girl from the upstairs apartment, Elena Taglia. Cara, athletic in her own right, became adept at jump rope—one-strand and two-strand (double-Dutch). Doris and Elena would serenade Cara as she jumped rope tirelessly: "My boy friend's name is Fatty. He comes from Cincinnati. With a pimple on his nose and four black toes, that's the way my story goes."

Other sidewalk games that New York City girls played were hopscotch, jacks, and handball. Cara, a farm girl accustomed to roaming the twelve-acre Smith farm from morning to night, astounded the neighborhood girls with her speed and endurance. She could do a fast-paced jump rope for at least twenty minutes. In foot races, Cara easily beat all the girls and even gave the fastest boys (including Tom) a good run for their money. In fact, both Tom and Cara impressed the New York City kids with their hard earned, country-bred stamina and grittiness—often outlasting their city peers at street running games like ring-o-leerio. By the time autumn rolled along, both children were absorbed into the neighborhood boys-and-girls social groups.

1950s-1960s Fable

Meanwhile in the Haley household, things were beginning to run downhill. Thomas Haley was starting to miss work because of his drinking binges which grew longer and more intense. After a hard day's work painting houses, the kids' birth father would hit the neighborhood bars on prolonged drinking bouts that lasted well into the night. Consequently, the Haley family budget became tighter and the kids ate canned soup and crackers for supper — so unlike the meat and potatoes and garden vegetables that the Smith family regularly had for dinner.

Tom noticed that some of the neighborhood dads occasionally walked home in that shambling drunken manner — but such lapses were infrequent, usually occurring on pay days.

When Thomas Haley arrived at the white stucco house stinking drunk, a loud argument would ensue — punctuated by the crash of a thrown dish. The children's birth mother would yell and scream at her common-law husband, who answered her with a few curses and then collapsed into bed. Hearing the commotion while pretending to sleep, the kids were frightened by their parents' angry words and worried about the future.

CHAPTER 15

P.S. 21

Tom and Cara attended P.S. 21, a rectangular, red-brick school perched atop the Walker Street hill in Elm Park. The elementary school had narrow hallways, small classrooms, and a dungeon-like basement consisting of a small cafeteria, and some shop and cooking classes. There was a spacious fenced-in school yard, part grass and part concrete, with concrete wall handball courts, as well as nine-foot high basketball back boards. A small public school by New York City standards, P.S. 21 consisted of two classes for each grade level—ranging from kindergarten to eighth grade. The school offered the standard primary school curriculum consisting of the three Rs plus the major subjects of science and social studies, as well as the minor subjects of music, art, shop, cooking, and gym. Neither child received much homework from their teachers—leaving them ample time for television watching. One day the old black and white RCA TV broke down—its picture rolling continuously. Their smart mom refused to have the TV repaired: "Let it stay broken. Maybe you'll start reading books."

Well-grounded in the basics, neither child was challenged by this traditional curriculum and both of them displayed behavior problems. Cara became a nonstop talker and Tom acted out by showing off in front of his new classmates.

1950s-1960s Fable

The public schools of that era stressed arithmetic skills. To that end, Tom accumulated a big stack of yellow papers filled with multiplication and long division problems. He even told his teacher that his grade should be based on the weight of this stack of arithmetic computations. Tom's teacher, Mrs. Howard, was a pleasant woman with wire-frame glasses and short, curly hair, while Cara's teacher, Mr. Hays, was a tall man with huge hands and feet, and a congenial manner. For reasons unknown, the boy took pleasure in defying his teacher and making a general nuisance of himself in the class and on the playground. Once during recess, Tom chased a girl on the pavement—interrupting some eighth-graders playing hand ball. One of these big boys responded by giving the ex-farm boy a hard boot in his backside. The boy kept on running trying to appear unaffected by the rough rebuke. Both Tom and Cara brought a brown-bag lunch consisting of peanut butter and jelly sandwiches and an apple, which was gobbled down in the crowded cafeteria before dashing outside to play in the school yard. Lunch recess is the high point of the day for most school kids.

Academically, Tom did well enough to qualify for the honor roll each marking period. Every few months, the school held an honor assembly, where honor roll students were called to the stage by the principal Mrs. Stimp, to receive gold-embossed certificates with the student's name, grade, and date. At one point, Mrs. Howard told Tom that his behavior had become so problematic as to jeopardize his honor roll status. Since the honor assembly was only a few weeks away, the boy nervously waited for the shoe to drop and his mother to chastise him. Fortunately, his test grades were sufficiently high for him to qualify for the honor roll, but the warning curtailed his mischievousness—at least for a while. Cara's behavior never reached her brother's level of insubordination, but her constant chattering and day

dreaming in class impeded her academic progress.
More importantly, the dreamy-eyed young artist lost interest in drawing—a phenomenon which lasted for many months.

At one point, as Tom was coming back to his classroom late from shop where he was making a wooden lamp, he happened to run into Mrs. Howard on the staircase. She accosted the boy about his behavior:

"What happened you, Tom? Your behavior has become so bad. I'm at the end of my rope with you." His eyes filling with tears, the boy felt a surge of remorse. "I'm sorry, Mrs. Howard. It has nothing to do with you." For the first time in months, Tom looked at his actions at P.S. 21 and not liking what he saw, resolved to behave better.

One day, all the children of P.S. 21 were sent to the basement for polio vaccinations. The kids lined up in long rows, class by class and dutifully received their Salk polio vaccine inoculations via long shiny needles attached to liquid-filled syringes. The process went by smoothly with little incident except for a few tears from the younger pupils. However, one eighth grader, Vinnie Serio, the toughest kid in the school who had given Tom the thumping kick in the butt—passed out after getting his vaccination. It took many months of teasing and wise cracking for tough guy Vinnie to live down the needle-induced swoon. Observing this unexpected turn of events, Tom realized that we all have our Achilles heal.

The daily routines of the children's life on Staten Island were quite different from those in the farming region of South Jersey. The Smith's garbage was tossed into the big iron barrel in the back yard, and the contents were set ablaze every few weeks by either Harry or Mr. Smith. The unburned remnants, mostly tin cans and glass bottles, were thrown onto a big junk pile near the cesspool.

1950s-1960s Fable

Food wastes were deposited in a compost heap, which decayed and fermented over time—turning into excellent fertilizer for Mom's truck garden. At the dinner table, Harry once said that farmers and God are similar: "God turns coal into diamonds and farmers turn manure into food."

After his remarks, neither Tom nor Cara was very hungry. On Staten Island, the garbage was put into metal trash cans to be collected Monday, Wednesday, and Friday by big noisy sanitation trucks. Instead of a cesspool, Staten Island streets had an elaborate system of underground sewers. On every block was a heavy iron grate covering the concrete sewer canal, where periodically a batted or thrown spaldeen would wind up. Attempts at retrieving the spaldeen from the five-foot deep sewer with a broom stick or rake often failed. Handy at making things, Tom conceived of a solution to the ball retrieval problem, which made him a very popular kid on the block. The ex-farm boy nailed a v-shaped piece of tin to a two-by-four. Carefully extending the v-shaped end of the board into the sewer, the boy was able to grab the spaldeen from the bottom of the foul-smelling sewer.

CHAPTER 16

The Drinking Dads of Elm Park

Sleeping arrangements in the Haley household on Staten Island were different from those in the small Smith farm house. In Bloomington, Tom shared a bedroom with big brother Harry, while Cara slept with big sister Helen in the middle room, which functioned as a dining room during the day. Of course when there were visitors from Jersey City, the kids often wound up sleeping on mattresses in the finished part of the attic. The unfinished part, which lacked floor boards, was used to store old clothes, unused furniture, photos, report cards, and various memorabilia—including Thomas Haley's paintings. In the Haley house, Cara slept in the middle room and Tom had his own room on the sun porch.

However, there were some problems with the many windowed sun porch. It had an outside door to the front porch, but no inside door to the rest of the house. If the boy had to go to the bathroom in the middle of the night, he had to climb through an open window that led to the parlor. Secondly, the sun porch was not heated. So by the end of October—it was quite chilly at night and in the early morning. Once the cold weather of November set in, Tom would have to sleep on a studio couch in the parlor.

1950s-1960s Fable

Nevertheless, the children adapted to these new sleeping arrangements—as children tend to do. Nonetheless, there were unpleasant interruptions to their nocturnal slumbering—loud arguments between their birth parents over Thomas Haley's out-of-control drinking.

Alcoholism was the major impediment to the well-being of the working-class families of Elm Park. Reeking of alcohol fumes and cigarette smoke, the dimly-lit neighborhood bar was a fixture of Staten Island's North Shore. Tom and Cara would sit on the front stoop on Friday nights and observe the shambling walk of the neighborhood dads— stumbling along the sidewalk and slowly mounting the front steps of their respective houses. A hypothetical list of the heavy drinkers of Elm Park would include men of every occupation and every ethnic category. There was the red-faced Mr. Schmidt, Doris's dad, marching home quickly after a Friday night session of elbow-bending at KC's bar—situated on the corner of Morningstar Road and Booker Place. Then, there was Mr. Palermo, Mike's father, a quiet, hard-working mason, whose drinking was less frequent. He would come shuffling home slightly befuddled about once a month—usually on a Saturday night—after drinking at Kaffman's bar, located at the corner of Morningstar Road and Walker Street. There were also the noisy, unruly drunks like Mr. Taglia, Elena's dad, who drank heavily during the holidays. Drinking made Mr. Taglia, who lived upstairs from Tom and Cara combative—causing him to pick a fight with his long-suffering German-born wife, Inga. The kids would hear lots of hollering back and forth—ending with a crashing sound as the heavy-handed Wolstein factory worker knocked poor Inga to the floor.

Tom and Cara discovered that heavy drinking was not restricted to the Irish, Italian, Polish, and German blue-collar workers of Elm Park. Mr. Coombs, native of the West Indies, was a quiet, introverted drinker—sipping his Scotch whiskey while reading Shakespeare's plays and sonnets, after a long, stressful day on Wall Street.

His son, Neil Coombs, a fast runner, clever boxer, and skilled punch-ball player, often talked about his "old man's love of Shakespeare and Scotch whiskey." In addition to Doris Schmidt's alcoholic dad and shut-in mother, she had a cranky grandmother who trekked back and forth from Dooley's liquor store with a shopping bag containing a couple of bottles of cheap wine. It was the influence of this low-priced wine that caused the old woman to harangue the neighborhood kids from her second-floor bedroom window. Of all the neighborhood fathers, only Joey Caprino's dad seemed to have escaped the alcohol plague. A New York City transit bus driver, Mr. Caprino's addiction was gardening. The mild-mannered bus driver spent evenings and weekends tending his back-yard flower garden, where red, yellow, and white roses bloomed, along with petunias and lilies—creating an oasis in the urban desert of Staten Island's North Shore, where neighborhood bars were more frequent than grocery stores.

There were times when Thomas Haley was able to hold off his drinking demons and behave like a typical American father enjoying his children on a family outing. After a hard day's work painting houses in the nearby section of Port Richmond, the kids' birth father arrived home in a good mood, humming "How much is that doggy in the window? The one with the waggly tail."

1950s-1960s Fable

About a half-hour later, the children's birth mother, walking quickly from the bus stop on Morningstar Road, bustled into the house with a bag of groceries from the Staten Island Ferry terminal food market. The kids noticed their parents hugging each other in a friendly greeting and their dad bestowing a rare kiss on their frazzled mom. After a quick supper of franks and beans, in which Thomas Haley tooted loudly to their mom's disgust and the kid's amusement, their dad suggested a drive to South Beach to cool off. The 1950s was an era when the floor fan was the sole means of cooling a house on a hot summer night. At that time, air conditioning could be found only in the homes of the wealthy and in movie theaters.

Mom grabbed a big blanket and a bottle of cold apple juice (Kool Aid was frowned upon by the Haley family). The entire family piled into their beat-up old De Soto and drove on Richmond Terrace along the water front, past the Staten Island Ferry terminal, and then east on Bay Street towards Staten Island's south shore. Entertaining Tom and Cara, their birth parents began singing a romantic song in good two-part harmony:

"Oh, shine on, shine on harvest moon Up in the sky; I ain't had no lovin' Since January, February, June, or July. Snow time ain't no time to stay Outdoors and spoon; So shine on, shine on harvest moon, For me and my gal." Amidst a darkening sky, the glowing red sun hung precipitously above the horizon—already losing its fire-like intensity. Nearly deserted, the sandy beach was marked by rocks, bottles, and pieces of driftwood. A gentle breeze cooled the Haley family as they sat on the blanket, sipping the cold apple juice. Thomas Haley was telling Tom and Cara about his coal-mining days when he worked in the anthracite mines of western Pennsylvania with two of his brothers and his father.

"After a few years in that hell-hole, I made up my mind that coal mining was not for me." Then he began reciting a poem:

"To one whose love was more Than worthless gold, Who loved both rich and poor Within his fold. Whose love was ever strong, With sympathy for each and all the throng— Or such as me.

God grant him graciously
Heavenly bliss
Peace in eternity
And happiness!"

Thomas Haley smiled wistfully, "I dedicated that poem to a priest, Father Kumerant, who was like a second father to me." Tom and Cara were amazed by their dad's poem. "Pop, I didn't know you could write poetry!" exclaimed Tom. Both children referred to their birth father as "Pop." —to their birth mother's dismay.

"Your father has many talents: painting, poetry, interior decorating—once he puts his mind to it." observed their mother.

Thomas Haley smiled bitterly, "They don't pay you for those kinds of things. Make sure you study something useful in school—like business or engineering, Tom. We have too many starving artists in the world. And whatever you kids do—don't drink!"

Their mother agreed whole heartedly: "Do as I say and not as I do."

Grimacing, Thomas Haley replied, "My sanctimonious old man used to say the same thing—the penny-pinching son of a bitch!" On that unhappy note, the Haley family packed up their stuff and headed for their beat up old De Soto.

1950s-1960s Fable

There were other times after a long day of house painting when Thomas Haley was unable to resist his powerful thirst for alcohol. Driving through Staten Island's North Shore, he would pass the ubiquitous neighborhood bars—fixtures on every block of this working class area. The haze of tobacco smoke and the fumes of stale beer wafting from each saloon acted like a magnet—drawing the hard-drinking men inside, where an empty bar stool awaited them. For an incurable alcoholic like Thomas Haley, all it took was one sip of beer, wine, or whiskey to set him off on a drinking binge. Even when abstaining, an alcoholic has a thirst for liquor that haunts him every minute of his waking existence. The artist-turned-house-painter had been enjoying his new role as father to Tom and Cara, along with the company of his long-suffering woman, Claire. But his family ties, though strong, could not keep him out of the saloons of Staten Island very long. So he stopped at KC's bar, put down a twenty dollar bill on the counter and ordered a beer and a "whiskey chaser." In a sporting mood, Thomas Haley bought a beer for the grizzled old man sitting next to him—drinking to his health.

Three hours later, Thomas Haley drove his beat up 1948 De Soto to the familiar white stucco house on Pulaski Avenue. The children had finished supper and were watching "Dragnet" on TV, in which detective Joe Friday gathered information from a reluctant witness: "The facts madam, just the facts." Their mother was putting the food away and finishing the dishes, when their father entered the house in a drunken whirl—bidding his family a too-hearty hello in a boisterous voice.

Claire returned his greeting with a rhetorical question: "Where the hell were you, Tom? Drinking again—you son of a bitch! The mortgage is due Monday and you're pissing away your pay check on beer."

Thomas Haley gave his common-law wife what was left of his salary—a big chunk of which had been squandered at KC's bar. Counting what was left, Claire burst into tears, "You selfish bum! Get out of my house!"

Taking a conciliatory tone, their father lowered his voice—trying to patch things up. He approached the petite woman and clumsily embraced her, but she would have none of it, pushing her drunken husband away.

"So you're giving me the brush-off you cold-hearted bitch." Using his considerable strength, Thomas Haley grabbed his angry wife, who resisted vehemently.

"Get off me, you bum!" At this point, the children ran into the kitchen to intervene. The boy got in between his parents momentarily—only to be slammed against the kitchen wall by his drunken father. The kids' mom screamed as their dad mumbled an apology to his son, while Cara burst into tears. Awkwardly trying to console his children, the alcoholic house painter said something about Jesus suffering the little children. Their mom ran into the middle room, grabbed the phone, and called the police. Returning to the kitchen, Claire corralled her children into her bedroom and slammed the door shut. Thomas Haley sat down in the kitchen, singing a drinking song off key:

"Here's to old King Montazuma
For fun he buggered a puma
The puma one day
Bit both balls away
An example of animal humor."

Resting his head on the table, the artist-turned-house-painter awaited the arrival of the cops.

1950s-1960s Fable

A knock on the front door announced the arrival of two tall policemen, who had mistakenly entered Tom's sun-porch bedroom. Claire ran into the long hall way and gave them a quick description of her drunken husband's behavior. In the 1950s, police routinely settled domestic disputes in which drinking was involved by throwing the husband in jail. Since Thomas Haley was clearly inebriated, the police sergeant said they would keep him there for a week to dry out. Looking at the mother and children, the policeman declared, "You have a nice family, Mr. Haley, and you better stay off the sauce." Whether from fatigue, discretion, or the depressing effects of alcohol, the house painter was subdued and cooperative.

Holding his hands out to be cuffed, bowing to his common-law wife, and winking at the kids, their dad left the house with the two policemen, who towered over him. The children followed the adults through the front door to the porch, where they could see their neighbors on the sidewalk watching their hand-cuffed dad entering the New York City police car. Both kids were deeply ashamed and mortified that everybody in the neighborhood was witness to this spectacle.

In the wake of Thomas Haley's one-week holiday in jail, there were few squabbles within the white stucco house and no repercussions from the neighbors. After all, Elm Park was a working-class area known for its friendly neighborhood bars, including KC's and Kaffman's — situated on successive corners of Morningstar Road. These saloons functioned as sanctuaries on weekend nights for the blue-collar dads of Elm Park after a long week of hard work. Thus, Thomas Haley's drinking habits were quite typical, although the intensity of his binges exceeded the norm for the majority of the area's family men. After a long night of drinking, most of the Elm Park fathers returned quietly to their homes to sleep off the effects of heavy drinking.

Getting thrown into the slammer was unusual for even the most notorious drinkers of this quiet neighborhood. Above all, these men realized they had a family to provide for.

The peace and quiet that reigned in the Haley household was marred by certain budgetary restrictions caused by the father's absence. With only one paycheck coming into the house, money for both necessities and extras was substantially limited. Denied their usual 50 cents per week allowance, Tom and Cara were motivated to think about earning some pocket money on their own.

The two kids began scrounging the neigborhood for five-cent deposit bottles and newspapers. The five-cent bottles were washed, collected, and brought to Karisi's grocery store on Morningstar Road for redemption. Old newspapers were collected and tied in large bundles — to be brought to Perry's junkyard for sale at the rate of two cents per pound. Perry would weigh the newspaper bundles carefully on a big floor scale, which was also used for weighing scrap metal. Mike Palermo, an experienced newspaper bundler, suggested placing some rocks and heavy cardboard in the tied newspaper bundles.

To his credit, Tom ignored his friend's advice, choosing to operate as an honest broker in all his business transactions. Tom also offered his services to the elderly homeowners in the neighborhood — raking leaves in the fall, shoveling snow in the winter, and trimming hedges in the spring. Tom got a lot of practice trimming hedges because the front of their white stucco house was set off by a long, six-feet high hedge. As soon as the children moved in, Tom was assigned the job of trimming the hedge bi-weekly — a job he would have for many years.

1950s-1960s Fable

In any case, having money in your pocket as a result of your own hard work, gave the kids a feeling of independence and a sense of control over the vicissitudes of fate.

Back from his one-week drying-out sentence in jail, Thomas Haley resumed his drinking with a vengeance. His absence from work caused him to lose his house-painting job, so there was plenty of time to indulge his drinking habit at KC's and Kaffman's bars on Morningstar Road.

Taking matters into her own hands, Claire went to these two establishments plus Karisi's grocery store and told them not to sell liquor to her husband. Ironically, the two saloon owners readily agreed to refrain from serving the troublesome Thomas Haley. But Mr. Karisi objected to anybody infringing on his entrepreneurial rights to sell his goods to whomever entered his store. Approaching the bear-like grocer with customers in the store, Claire shouted, "It's bad enough you sell us your rotten pickles and your sour milk, but selling beer to alcoholics is blood money!" When provoked the petite, fast-talking high-energy woman could be formidable adversary. The children's father complained that his wife had "blacklisted" him from the neighborhood establishments forcing him to venture into the adjoining areas of Mariners Harbor and Port Richmond to do his drinking. But in order to indulge his drinking habit, an alcoholic must have the money to pay for his beer, wine, and whiskey. To the children's surprise, he began taking things from the house—pots, dishes, a toaster, an iron, and table lamps to hock at the pawn brokers for beer money. At this point, Claire banished her common-law husband from the house.

Whenever he showed up at the white stucco house, the kids' mom would call the police, which send him scurrying down Pulaski Avenue — only to return the next afternoon while Claire was working in the city.

Tom and Cara were astonished at the profound changes occurring in Thomas Haley when he was drinking heavily. His personality changed to that of a petulant child— demanding money from his wife and even the children themselves for that one drink to get him through the morning. Then, he said he would clean up his act — stop drinking, take a shower, shave himself, and look for a job that very day. Sometimes he would squeeze Tom's hand too hard and laugh at Cara's sketches — acting like a teenaged bully. Even his voice changed when he was drunk — taking on a harsh, strident tone, with a perpetual scowl on his face. Thomas Haley talked about his common-law wife in a peculiar manner — referring to her
as a guy: "Claire is a tough customer. She's a real wise guy — going around to my favorite bars and telling them not to serve me."
Sometimes their father would change his tactics, praising Tom for his good grades and commending Cara for her art work. Then, he would ask the kids for money or try to find out from them where Claire had her money stashed. He even asked them if their mom had any bank books. To all such leading questions, the children maintained truthfully that they had no idea where their mother kept her money.

The children had begun to understand that alcoholics were crafty individuals — always looking for an edge to obtain what they most desire — a drink. There were mornings when Thomas Haley looked well-groomed and sober. He spoke clearly, acted reasonably, and exhibited a surface calm that fooled those around him.

1950s-1960s Fable

But the ex-artist was playing a role. Like all alcoholics, Thomas Haley had something to hide—his gnawing thirst for alcohol. And alcoholics have to be smarter, quicker, and more energetic than regular people. That hidden lie about themselves, which most alcoholics never admit to, is the source of their psychic energy. The kids' mom said that their dad had a disease, called alcoholism, and unless he joined a self-help group like Acoholics Anonymous, it would only get worse. When Tom and Cara lived in South Jersey, Claire had taken her husband to AA meetings, but he said that a bunch of old drunks talking about drinking would never cure them of the habit. "If it is God's will for a person to stop drinking, then he will stop through divine intervention."

Claire replied to her common-law husband that "God helps those who help themselves." Nonetheless, their mom told Tom and Cara that their father's drinking caused him to live in a fantasy world, instead of dealing with the every-day real world. "Remember, you can only live life on a basis of reality. And we all have to work to obtain the necessities
of life: food, clothing, and shelter," she told her children solemnly.

With Thomas Haley banished from the white stucco house, an uneasy calm descended over the Haley household. Hard-working, dependable, and pragmatic, the children's mother got up early each day for work as a bookkeeper, taking the # 3 Castleton Avenue bus to the ferry. She did not return from the city until 6:30 in the evening. Tom and Cara were largely on their own—getting themselves to school on time and doing their homework in the afternoon by themselves. Their after-school snack was always the same—peanut butter and jelly on white bread. Between school lunches and snacks, the Haley family went through a big "Pullman" loaf of bread every week.

Todd M. Daley

It was understood that all homework assignments had to be completed before the kids could go outside to play with their friends. Tom usually wounds up at the P.S. 21 schoolyard to play stick ball or basketball, while Cara remained in the Pulaski Avenue neighborhood — hanging out with Doris Schmidt and Elena Taglia on the front porch.

With their alcoholic father not around to supervise domestic activities, the children were assigned added house-keeping and cooking chores which they fulfilled satisfactorily. Usually their mom made a three-pound meat loaf and a big pot of mashed potatoes, which provided supper for most of the work week. It was Tom's job, with Cara assisting, to heat up the supper each night — meatloaf, mashed potatoes, and canned peas or string beans. He was taught how to turn on the gas burners on top of the stove and how to light the gas oven. The gas oven had to be ignited with a match — after the gas was turned on. Once, the boy couldn't get the wooden match to light right away, with the oven emitting the strong-smelling natural gas for several seconds. When the oven did ignite, there was a mini-explosion which singed the boy's eyelashes.

Then, there was the time Tom tried to repair a leaky toilet with a block of wood driven between the tank and the bathroom wall. The result was a cracked toilet bowl and a small flood in the bathroom. Another time, Cara was doing the dishes and didn't know what to do with some chicken bones. Instead of disposing them in the garbage, she flushed the bones down the toilet. The result in this case was another call to the plumber, who retrieved the offending chicken bones after a half-hour of snaking the toilet with a rotating, sinister-looking metal wire.

At school, both children continued to maintain good grades, while extending their network of friends and

1950s-1960s Fable

acquaintances. Imperceptibly, their accents and manners became more city-like—demonstrating the uncanny ability of children to adapt to the ways of their friends. There was a new girl in Tom's classroom, Bonnie Rosolio, a bright, curly-haired girl, who gave him a run for his money as the top student in his class. The well-mannered girl was matter-of-fact in her approach to the ex-farm boy, rebuking him when he acted up in class. Tom soon found himself paying attention in class and behaving more respectfully.

He resisted the impulse to call out answers to Mrs. Howard's questions before anyone else got a change to respond. In the playground, Bonnie was singularly unimpressed with the boy's athletic prowess, devoting herself to reading stories and poetry while the other kids wore themselves out with the usual playground games. Tom was puzzled by the girl's dedication to academics and she responded that she loved everything in school—except recess.

CHAPTER 17

Poetry Recital

With the arrival of June, Mrs. Howard strived to maintain the flagging interest of her students in their school work. After much deliberation, the veteran teacher issued her class a challenge—they could earn extra credit by memorizing a poem from their poetry anthology book. The students would be given two weeks to memorize their poem, which had to be at least forty lines. The response of the class, worn down by a year of class work, homework, and tests, was not enthusiastic. Tom looked around at the other boys in the class, whose distaste for poetry (which they labeled as "sissy stuff") was the same as their appetite for a plateful of spinach. To his surprise, Mike Palermo, who seldom volunteered for anything in school except to carry out softballs and bats for gym class, offered to memorize a poem—"Casey at the Bat." Looking it up in the poetry book, Mrs. Howard approved this well-known forty-eight-line poem about "mighty Casey," the slugging star of the Mudville nine striking out with two men on base in the bottom of the ninth inning.

Then, Bonnie Rosolio whispered something to Tom about a favorite poem of hers that they could work on together. Raising her hand, his pretty classmate said that Tom and herself would memorize Alfred Noyes' epic poem, "The Highwayman," as a joint project. Surprising Mrs. Howard, Bonnie said that the poem consisted of about one hundred lines.

1950s-1960s Fable

She would recite the first fifty lines and Tom would recite the second fifty lines.

After a quick perusal of the Noyes poem about the deaths of a medieval bandit and his heroic sweetheart, Mrs. Howard gave her approval of the joint project to the amazement of the class.

For the next two weeks, Tom and Bonnie spent their recess time plus Saturday afternoons huddled over the poetry anthology book—reciting the stirring lines of Alfred Noyes' romantic poem about love, sacrifice, and death. This enchanting poem is filled with picturesque metaphors in which the wind is likened to a "torrent of darkness," the moon to a "ghostly galleon," and the road ridden by the highwayman to a "ribbon of moonlight." Both youngsters were moved by the bravery of the "landlord's black-eyed daughter" who "shattered her breast in the moonlight" with a gunshot to warn her lover, the highwayman, of the presence of the king's soldiers.

The pure romanticism of this epic poem moved the idealistic youngsters. Indeed, the noble idea that love not only trumps the everyday concerns of the world, but that love transcends death—was most appealing to the two kids who came from such divergent backgrounds. One day, Mike Palermo joined them—forming a poetry-memorizing threesome in which they functioned like the three musketeers: "All for one and one for all." Occasionally, Mike's gum-cracking girlfriend, Elena Taglia, joined them to help the stick ball champ master his poem: "I like the part where it says that hope springs eternal in the human breast." Mike nodded in agreement, glancing at Elena's budding breasts.

Todd M. Daley

At last, the day of poetry recitals arrived, in which the participants from all the classes would recite their poems in the P.S. 21 auditorium—before the entire school, including parents. In Mrs. Howard's class, Mike Palermo bravely leads off reciting Ernest Thayer's "Casey at the Bat" flawlessly, with a few gyp notes cleverly written on the back of his hands.

"The outlook wasn't brilliant for the Mudville Nine that day; The score stood 4 to 2, with but one inning more to play, And Casey stood a-watching it in hauteur grandeur there.
. . . .
And somewhere men are laughing and somewhere children shout, But there is no joy in Mudville—mighty Casey has struck out."

There was a well-deserved, resounding applause for Mike from the audience, who acknowledged their accolade with a sweeping bow.

Then, it was time for Bonnie and Tom to recite their poem—Alfred Noyes' "The Highwayman." As they mounted the stage, Tom became more nervous while Bonnie exuded the composure that was a product of her secure family background. Looking out at the audience, Tom was astounded upon observing his father in the audience. Drinking relentlessly for the past few weeks, Thomas Haley no longer resided at the white stucco house on Pulaski Avenue. Bonnie dramatically recited her portion of the Noyes' poem without missing a line.

"The highwayman came riding up to the old inn door.
He whistled a tune to the window, and who should be waiting there, But the landlord's blackeyed daughter, Bess the landlord's daughter, Plaiting a dark red love-knot into her long black hair.
. . . .
One kiss my bonny sweetheart, I'm after a prize tonight, But I shall be back with the yellow gold before the morning light;

I'll come to thee by moonlight, though hell should bar the way."

Then, as Bonnie acknowledged the audience's polite applause, Tom stepped forward — eying his father nervously.

Taking a deep breath with a moment's hesitation, the boy started to recite:

"They tied her up to attention, with a sniggering jest; They had bound a musket besides her, with a barrel beneath her breast."

He continued to recite in a halting fashion, cued by Bonnie who had discerned the source of his discomfort. As Tom recited his lines, he never took his eyes off his father — wishing that the alcoholic house painter would magically disappear from the auditorium.

"Up she stood at attention, with the barrel beneath her breast, She would not risk their hearing; she would not strive again;"

Again, the boy lost his place in Noyes' lengthy epic poem. At this point, Thomas Haley got up from his seat and shouted, "Calm dawn, Tom. You know the poem — just speak clearly and slowly. Then, the principal, Mrs. Stimp walked over to Tom's father and told him to quiet down. Annoyed, the inebriated house painter told her to "F_off" in a booming voice. Tom had just finished the line:

"Her musket shattered the moonlight, Shattered her breast in the moonlight and warned him with her death."

As if in concert with his son, Thomas Haley continued the recital: "He turned; he spurred to the West; he did not know who stood there bowed with her head o'er the musket, drenched with her own red blood."

This time, Mrs. Howard said something to the boisterous house painter, who laughed loudly. Totally distracted by the ongoing commotion between his alcoholic father and the school's staff, the rest of the poem was lost to the boy. Despite Bonnie's spiritual support, Tom wanted out of his embarrassing situation. His eyes filling with tears, the boy stormed off the stage in a fit of frustration.

August 5, 1957

Dick Clark's "American Bandstand" show premiered live on the ABC network from Philadelphia. Once called "the world's oldest teenager," Clark presented rock and roll music in a respectful manner, interviewing teenagers about their opinion of new songs played on the show in his "rate-a-record" segment. The most common accolade for a potential pop music hit was that "it had a good beat and you can dance to it." Clark's congenial manner gave him a good rapport with teenagers as well as the rock and roll stars appearing on the show. Over the years, rock and roll performers featured on "American Bandstand" included Chuck Berry, Buddy Holly, Little Richard, Stevie Wonder, Paul Anka, Frankie Avalon, Fabian, Bobby Rydell, Sam Cooke, the Platters, the Jackson Five, Jan and Dean, and the Beach Boys. The show ran daily on week-day afternoons – capturing a big portion of American teenagers. "American Bandstand" influenced music, dance, and fashion for an entire generation of young people – creating the uniquely American phenomenon of a "youth culture."

Dick Clark's clean-cut, boy-next-door image facilitated the acceptance of teenage music by parents throughout the country. To overcome the anti-rock-and-roll mentality of American adults, the youthful Clark projected a conservative middle-class facade. Consequently, Dick Clark bridged the musical gap between teenagers and their parents. There was a dress code for the teenaged dancers on the show: the boys wore jackets and ties, while the girls wore modest skirts and blouses, with coifed hair. There were a few black couples appearing on "American Bandstand," but everybody had to look nice and wholesome — as if they were going to their high school prom. Despite his shrewd businessman's approach to his TV and radio programs over the years, Clark defended the artistic freedom of his rock-and-roll performers and condemned all forms of censorship in the broadcast forum. "American Bandstand" laid the groundwork for the baby boom generation — defining what teenagers listened to, how they danced, and what they wore, ate, and drank.

Dick Clark insisted that his "American Bandstand" was a pioneer in breaking down racial barriers in the 1950s and 1960s. Black teenagers did participate as dancers on the show in small numbers, but Bandstand producers screened out minorities by scrutinizing the names and addresses of advance ticket subscribers. During the 1950s, the new musical genre of rock and roll was associated by many white people as an engine for racial mixing. Furthermore, the teenagers participating in "American Bandstand" in the early years were overwhelmingly white and not reflective of the ethnic diversity of American youth. However, Dick Clark was a pioneer with regard to TV appearances of black rock and roll artists. The list of black singers appearing on the show is extensive: Chuck Berry, Little Richard, Stevie Wonder, Mary Wells, James Brown, Smokey Robinson, Marvin Gaye, Prince, plus many R and B singing groups. Dick Clark brought African-American performers to "American Bandstand" in an era when such national TV exposure was almost non-existent. Though Clark's claims that his show was integrated in the 1950s and early 1960s is an exaggeration, there were significant racial breakthroughs on "American Bandstand." As the years progressed into the 1970s and the 1980s, the show increased its ethnic diversity — moving from a weekday format to a Saturday afternoon show originating from southern California. In his retelling of the "American Bandstand" saga, Dick Clark may have embraced a more comforting narrative of the show's history: "I don't think of myself as a civil rights activist for integrating the show; it was simply the right thing to do."

The best description of Bandstand came from Dick Clark himself: "I played the records, the kids danced, and America watched."

After the poetry recital fiasco, Tom spent recess time playing hand ball and catch with his classmates — using a spaldeen he brought to school each day, along with his school books, loose leaf, and brown-bag lunch. For reasons unknown, he kept his distance from Bonnie Rosolio, his recital partner. And he learned how to maintain a poker face when confronted with wisecracks about his girlfriend shooting herself in the chest to save

Tom from the king's soldiers. Then, there were the cutting barbs about his father's drinking habits: "Your dad sure likes his poetry. Almost as much as he likes his booze." The fact of the matter was his dad's reputation as a hard drinker was well-known in that working-class neighborhood. Elm Park had its fair share of neighborhood bars and saloons, where the consumption of alcoholic beverages by the men of the neighborhood was the accepted norm. But Thomas Haley went beyond the norm of the typical barfly — his drinking binges dragged on for weeks on end. The unemployed house painter had fallen into an alcoholic never-land, in which the needs of his family and the demands of the work-a-day world no longer mattered.

Trying to maintain a tough street-kid image, Tom deliberately avoided contact with Bonnie Rosolio during recess. The pretty book worm sat in a quiet tree-shaded corner of the playground — reading poems and short stories from Mrs. Howard's anthology book. Occasionally, Cara would join Bonnie in her quiet corner — sketching a shrub-and-tree filled cemetery situated across the street from P.S. 21. Cara's renewed interest in sketching the world around her indicated that despite her father's alcoholic shenanigans — she had adapted to Staten Island. Eventually, her brother's notoriety as the "Highwayman Poet" diminished over time, and both children learned that people are mostly concerned with their own problems and not with anybody else's affairs.

Mike Palermo, an athletic star of recess, was more popular than ever after his stirring rendition of "Casey at the Bat." Tom hung out with his neighborhood friends during recess—Mike Palermo, Joey Caprino, Neil Coombs, and other kids from Pulaski Avenue—who were accustomed to the ups and downs that went with hard-drinking dads.

Sometimes, Tom longed for the halcyon days in South Jersey with the Smith family in which everyone did their part—working in the local canning factory and running their twelve-acre farm, with its corn fields and vegetable gardens and its chickens, turkeys, and mud-rolling pigs.

What puzzled the boy was his father's uncanny awareness of his children's activities at the school—honor roll, poetry recitals, spelling bee, art shows, and other events at P.S. 21. His mother remarked that the unemployed Thomas Haley spent most of his time elbow bending in the Elm Park saloons, where he gleaned from the neighborhood dads the kids' latest doings at P.S. 21. Running back and forth to work, maintaining the white stucco two-family house, food shopping, and preparing meals, the children's mom had little time to attend the school's functions.

Nevertheless, Claire Haley examined Tom and Cara's report cards under a microscope, and any scholastic declines resulted in a firestorm of motherly consequences which the kids strove to avoid.

When their mother tossed her common-law husband out of the house, his beat-up 1948 DeSoto went with him. Consequently, commuting to work, shopping, and family trips were accomplished via the New York City transit buses.

Fortunately, during the 1950s public buses and trains ran on reliable 15 to 20 minute schedule, 24 hours a day, seven days a week. When the kids grumbled about having to take a bus to go food shopping at the A & P supermarket in Port Richmond, their mom would always reply in her sing-song voice: "A car is a luxury!"

CHAPTER 18

Church Issues

When Tom and Cara first moved to Staten Island, the thorny issue of which church to attend inevitably arose. The children were raised Catholic by their foster parents—receiving the sacraments of communion and confirmation in South Jersey. They were heavily influenced by big-sister Helen's idealistic lectures about Jesus's Sermon on the Mount in which Jesus blessed the meek, the poor, the downtrodden and persecuted people of the world. Thomas Haley asserted that the children should continue in the Catholic faith: "After all, they were raised Catholic by the Smiths—to force them to change their faith would be unfair to the kids." Claire Haley, had a Marxist disdain for organized religion, which she called "the opiate of the people." Their father winced at this expression, "I hit the jack pot with your mother—a Red and a Jew, no less!" The children's memories of the Catholic Church weren't very positive—especially Father Sullivan's hell and brim fire sermons, as well as his awful treatment of Tom's black friend, Earl Jones. However, their father won the argument with his common-law wife, and the kids reluctantly began attending St. Francis's R.C. Church in Port Richmond.

Before receiving communion one Sunday, Tom and Cara had to go to confession the Saturday before. When the children admitted to the priest that they had not attended church all summer, they received a severe tongue lashing from the ill-tempered priest, who said they were in great danger of burning in Hell.

The angry priest ordered them to say a dozen "Our Fathers" and "Hail Marys" and demanded to speak with their parents. But after a brief interview with Thomas Haley, who reeked of alcohol from an afternoon of beer drinking, the priest stormed out of the sanctuary, shaking his head and muttering to himself. The kids attended St. Francis's for a few Sundays—finding its unfriendly atmosphere neither spiritually enlightening nor uplifting to their souls. Complaining about the priest's hostile attitude each time they went to confession, their mother stepped in. She opted for the Protestant faith, which she believed to be less dogmatic than Catholicism.

After some research, Claire Haley settled on a small Methodist church on Richmond Avenue in Port Richmond. The white steepled church had no stained-glass windows and a simple interior. The minister, Reverend John Hays, a smiling chubby man, was friendly and welcoming—along with the congregants, who numbered around forty. The service was less ritualistic than the Catholic mass, but it had an upbeat note—stressing a kind and gentle Jesus who welcomed all people to his flock. The children's Sunday school went over biblical passages that taught a moral lesson, like the parable of the good Samaritan. Tom and Cara liked the church because nobody threatened them with the fires of hell, nor did anyone ask them embarrassing questions. Of course, there were repercussions from the Elm Park kids on the block: some of the Catholic kids exclaimed that they had stabbed Jesus in the back by switching churches. Mike Palermo, who seldom attended St. Francis's R.C. Church on Sunday mornings, told them to shut up: "As long as it doesn't affect his stick ball game, who gives a shit!"

With the arrival of June, the pupils of P.S. 21 had begun chanting the traditional year end school's out song:

1950s-1960s Fable

"No more pencils, No more books, No more teacher's dirty looks!"

Near the end of the semester, the students in the upper classes took an exhaustive battery of achievement tests, called the Iowa tests. These tests purportedly measure general aptitude plus academic achievement—covering reading, writing, history, geography, science, and arithmetic. As a result of his unusual background—going back to his early days in South Jersey reading the novels and nonfiction books in the Smith's cellar bookcase—Tom did unexpectedly well. His mother was notified that in the fall, the boy would be attending P.S. 20 in Port Richmond—enrolling in a special IGC class for gifted children. The boy was not happy to be leaving his friends at the Elm Park school, but in the 1950s children obeyed their parents in all matters related to school.

With summer looming, Tom and his friends looked forward to endless games of stick ball, punch ball, soft ball, and hard ball, while Cara and her friends anticipated the sidewalk games of jump rope, hopscotch, jacks, and plenty of girl's gossip. Tom noticed that Cara already had an interest in clothes, pop music, dancing, and boys. She had begun watching "American Bandstand" on television, in which a youthful, well-spoken host, named Dick Clark, played rock and roll music, while neatly-dressed teenagers from Philadelphia danced. Dick Clark introduced rock and roll music to the American people and bridged the generation gap between teenagers and their parents. Although rock and roll was the music phenomenon of the 1950s, Tom and his Elm Park pals were not interested in that "girly stuff" which they equated with jump rope and hopscotch.

The boys of Elm Park were concerned with more serious matters: who was the best of New York's three centerfielders? In 1956, the Yankees' Mickey Mantle hit 52 homeruns and batted .353, winning the American

League's Most Valuable Player award. That same year, the Dodgers' Duke Snider hit 43 homeruns and drove in 101 runs, while the Giants' Willie Mays hit 36 homeruns and stole 40 bases. Tom favored Willie Mays because of his fielding and base running, and his famous "basket catch" method of snagging a fly ball. Joey Caprino liked Duke Snider because he was a Dodger fan, while Mike Palermo leaned towards Mickey Mantle because of his tape-measure homeruns. It intrigued the ex-farm boy that Willie Mays reportedly played stick ball on the streets of New York with average kids like himself. When Tom brought up his childhood hero, Robin Roberts, both Joey and Mike labeled the Phillies workhorse pitcher as a "has-been." Tom had to agree that Roberts had already experienced his best pitching years—failing to win twenty games in 1956 for the first time since 1950. Joey asserted that twenty-seven game winner Don Newcombe was the best pitcher in baseball at that point in time. Baseball batting champs Ted Williams and Stan Musial earned more than $100,000 in 1956—reportedly surpassing President Eisenhower's salary that year. "Why not?" said Mike, "They each had a better year than Ike, who only plays that old-man's game of golf!"

In that second summer on Staten Island, Tom and Cara anticipated a fun-filled time of street games like stick ball, punch ball, and hide-and-seek, jump rope, and hopscotch. For the kids, summer was a hard-earned break from school lessons and homework, and from the hardships inflicted by their father's out-of-control drinking. There were some new participants in the Elm Park street games, one of whom was a fast-running skinny kid named Gene Munski, whose father was an alcoholic carpenter who carried a shopping bag full of beer bottles home each afternoon. Gene was an adept street ball player with an unusual interest in his friends' religious backgrounds.

1950s-1960s Fable

Through the neighborhood grapevine, Gene learned that Tom and Cara had forsaken Catholicism for a Protestant church. Gene was a walking contradiction—an alter boy who cursed frequently, and a fan of black National League batting champion Hank Aaron with an open disdain for black people. Gene liked to use the "n-word" to indicate his worldliness, but was smart enough to refrain from using that epithet in front of the West Indian.

Neil Coombs, who would have bloodied his nose without hesitation. Gene was one of the Pulaski Avenue kids who labeled Tom and Cara's leaving the Catholic Church for a Protestant church as "stabbing Jesus in the back." He also possessed a preternatural curiosity about Tom's ethnic background—asking him point blank: "What are you?" After hesitating, Tom said he was "American like everyone else. A person's religion or color shouldn't matter. How he treats others is what counts."

Gene replied that this was "bullshit. You sound like a Communist to me." Tom couldn't understand the importance some New Yorkers placed on ethnic background—he intuitively felt that environment trumped nationality.

Then, Mike Palermo, who had no interest in such matters, brought the religious discussion to a halt by telling Gene to "Shut up, play ball, or get the f_____ out of here!"

There was a new player of the street games of Pulaski Avenue, who rivaled the kids in his passion for stick ball. He was a handyman and neighborhood father of toddler twins, whom the kids called "Harry the Horse." And unlike the other neighborhood dads, Harry always had the time and the energy for street games.

Most evenings, he would come strolling down Pulaski Avenue with his three-year old twins in toll, which he handed off to Cara, Doris, and Elena while he took to the street—choosing up sides, formulating ground rules, and organizing a big game of bouncing-pitch stick ball involving all available kids on the block.

Occasionally, Harry would opt for the fast-pitch stick ball, played against a concrete wall. He would mow everybody down with his blazing fast ball until the eighth or ninth inning, when his arm gave way and he would lob the ball so that even Tom could whack it with the skinny broomstick bat. Harry loved street games, played by the rules, and was not unduly concerned with winning. All the Elm Park kids loved Harry the Horse because he was a big kid himself.

One day Harry the Horse and the neighborhood boys were playing a marathon bouncing pitch stick ball game on Pulaski Avenue—in front of Joy Eggert's house, which was directly across Tom and Cara's white stucco house. One of the few neighbors who wasn't tolerant of the street games was Mrs. Eggert—Joy's mom. Harry bounced a tantalizing, slow bounce pitch to Tom, who lined it hard directly towards a window in the Eggert house. The fast-moving spaldeen broke the first-floor window with a sharp tinkle. Within seconds, Mrs. Eggert stuck her head out of the window and began screaming at the kids—singling out Tom. Ever since the Haleys had moved into the neighborhood, especially with Thomas Haley's drinking and the police car visits to the white stucco house, Mrs. Eggert had a vendetta against Tom and Cara, whom she labeled as "trouble-makers." Screeching in a high-pitched voice, the middle-aged blonde woman yelled, "You see what you did? Go play in the school yard! You hoodlums!"

Harry, looking at her like she was a giraffe in the zoo, yelled back up to the woman: "What's the matter lady?

1950s-1960s Fable

You need a drink like Granny Schmidt on the other side?"

This remark made everybody laugh because one of the stick ball game's rancorous spectators was Granny Schmidt, the alcoholic grandmother, who regularly harangued the kids playing in the street.

Then, Mr. Eggert, a stern-looking manager at the Wolstein factory stuck his head out the window and threatened to call the cops. Discretion being the better part of valor, Harry and the kids decided to suspend the stick ball game for the night, and it was agreed that everybody would chip in to pay for the broken window. The epithet "hoodlums" seemed to sting the good-natured Harry and his merry gang of stick ball players.

CHAPTER 19

Return to the Farm

Towards the end of that second summer, the Haley family received a letter from the Smiths inviting the children totheir son's wedding. Though only 18 years old, Harry was about to marry a girl, named Amy of the same age, who lived on the Geratty farm—Harry's first employer. Harry had transitioned from working at the Geratty poultry farm to a full-time job at the Bloomington canning factory, where his mom and dad had worked for years. Well-liked at the factory, the hard-working Harry had quickly attained a promotion to foreman. Big sister Helen was already married with a baby and living in an apartment in downtown Bloomington. During the 1950s, particularly in rural areas, it was typical for young people to marry within a year or two of high school graduation. The profound changes in people's living status wrought by the passage of time perplexed Tom, who realized that life is ever changing.

With Thomas Haley's beat-up 1948 De Soto no longer available, Tom, Cara, and their mom made the 100-mile turnpike trip to South Jersey on a ponderous Greyhound bus. They passed big natural gas storage tanks, flame-spouting oil refineries, and smoke-spewing factories of North Jersey, giving way to quaint farm houses and barns, rolling corn and wheat fields, and the woods of South Jersey. The idea that big brother Harry, hardly more than a carefree teenager, was about to shoulder the responsibilities of grownups—running a household,

paying bills, and raisin children—was unnerving to Tom. His perception of the adult world, from the unending toil of the Smiths working in the factory and running the farm, to his mother's struggles to put food on the table amidst their father's drinking binges, was tantamount to a lifetime sentence of involuntary servitude. Tom, for sure, was in no hurry to grow up and enter that scary realm of mind-numbing responsibilities.

Upon their arrival on Eden Avenue, Tom and Cara were surprised by the changes in the Smith twelve-acre farm and in the Smiths themselves. Mom was energetic as ever, but her smiles, her quaint expressions, and even her hugs were more restrained than in the past—as if she burdened by some nagging cares and concerns. Dad's joy at seeing the children was also tempered. He appeared older and frailer than when Tom and Cara had last seen him last summer at their secret meeting on Staten Island. With their own children no longer around to help, the Smiths had stopped raising turkeys—their cash crop for the year-end holidays. The troublesome pigs, who often escaped their smelly pig-pen, were gone except for one lonely sow. This friendly 300-pound behemoth was treated with choice table scraps, like a pet dog. There were still several egg-laying hens and a noisy bantam rooster in the chicken coop, plus a few ducks and geese who wandered about the farm and its surroundings.

As always, Mom had her flourishing one-acre truck garden of carrots, tomatoes, lettuce, cucumbers, green beans, melons, and strawberries, which she took care of religiously. The rest of their land was rented out to a neighboring farmer, who planted the fertile fields with corn, wheat, and soybeans. Across Eden Avenue, was the sweet-sour smelling apple orchard, laden with ripening red apples. Initially, Tom and Cara looked for the friendly Puerto Rican man who played catch with them and had helped them find a turtle in Hunt's Creek.

But their searches were in vain—his absence from the big farm across the street was one more change wrought by the passage of time. The irretrievable nature of the past was continually hammering away at the kids, who sensed the destructiveness of time itself. The relentless passage of time forces everyone to depend on the vague memories of childhood which are not always reliable.

It was strange for the kids to visit the empty fenced-in turkey cage—now devoid of the noisy, restless turkeys but marked with the stray feathers of turkeys who wound up on the Thanksgiving menus of so many Bloomington residents. The abandoned cage emitted an odor of turkeys and turkey droppings. The Smiths had mentioned that work men would be coming to the farm to dismantle the turkey cage—leaving an area of fertile soil for crops. Tom thought that the area ought to be left fallow and turned into a wilderness area as a memorial for all the turkeys dispatched by Mrs. Smith's sharp knife. He imagined that this segment of the Smith farm would forever be haunted by the spirits of the dearly departed turkeys. Out of a sense of melancholy remembrance, rather than true need, Mr. Smith and Tom ventured to the pigpen with a hammer, a saw, wire cutters, nails, chicken wire, and a fencing post to repair a torn portion of the pigpen fencing. Working quietly together as they had done so many times in the past, father and foster son repaired the pigpen fence, as the docile 300-pound sow watched them intermittently—nosing around and munching the soggy vegetables, corn ears, and slop which provided her lunch.

Then Cara joined them for a leisurely tour of the chicken coop, where the remains of Tom's science experiments, along with the stacked wood from his disassembled wooden shack, were left in one chamber of the coop.

1950s-1960s Fable

After their foster father left the children to take an afternoon nap, Larry Hunt and Richie Neeman joined Tom in a fast-pitch stick ball game, in which a strike zone was chalked on a chicken coop wall.

Larry and Richie had little trouble mastering the rules and even hitting the fast moving spaldeen with a broomstick bat, but they would have preferred playing with a hard ball had one been available. A few days before the wedding of Harry and Amy, Father Scanlon, the young priest at St. Teresa's church in Bloomington visited the Smith family and spoke with Tom and Cara. The youngsters had mentioned to their foster parents that they were attending a Protestant church on Staten Island, after some problems with the local Catholic church. Naturally, the children were nervous about the interview with the youthful cleric—bracing themselves for a stern admonishment by the priest. But Father Scanlon's kind demeanor and patient attentiveness to their story, including their dad's alcoholism, was a pleasant surprise to the kids. Though he believed in the spiritual supremacy of the Catholic Church, Father Scanlon indicated that there was more than one path to God. He referred to Protestants and Jews as "our friends searching for the Light," a term he used interchangeably with God.

Father Scanlon was happy to learn about big sister Helen's lectures on good vs. evil in relation to Jesus's Sermon on the Mount—in which Jesus blessed the poor, the meek, the sick, and the pure in heart. He declared that Jesus's message to the world could be summarized by the Golden Rule: "Do onto others what you would have them do onto you." Father Scanlon indicated that St. Teresa's has moved forward with the times— "opening its doors to believers from all walks of life."

At this point Cara interjected, "You mean you don't throw colored people out of the church anymore?"

The young priest smiled benevolently, "Some of my brethren, being human and subject to the practices of the past, have made mistakes." The youthful cleric invited the children to St. Teresa's on Friday, where he would

hear their sins and purify their souls—so they could receive communion on Sunday. This sounded good to the kids, who readily consented to the congenial priest's proposal. Theidea of receiving communion on Sunday in their childhoodchurch brought back fond memories of the past and made their foster parents very happy. What their birth mother didn't know—beset with making ends meet without her common-law husband's help—wouldn't hurt her. Yet, both kids felt they were betraying their mom, who was a "fellow sufferer" deserving all of God's compassion.

The wedding of Harry Smith and Amy Geratty took place on a sunny Saturday afternoon at St. Teresa's under the spiritual guidance of Father Scanlon. He quoted from St. Paul in Corinthians: "Love is patient and kind; love is not jealous or boastful . . . . Love bears all things, believes all things, hope all things." Harry, in his new blue suit, and Amy, in her dazzling white gown, looked more like movie stars than ordinary country people. The blue sky with nary a cloud and the bright sunlight reflected the cheery optimism that always accompanies the matrimonial ceremony. After all, this was the fabulous fifties—an American era marked by a universal sense of optimism in nearly all events familial and national. Everyone was dressed up in the Sunday clothes, including Tom and Cara, who wore nice outfits borrowed from the Smith's Jersey City relatives attending the wedding.

Looking around in the crowded church, Tom noticed his childhood sweetheart, Connie Mullin, among the audience.

1950s-1960s Fable

Tom remembered that Connie had an older brother, William, who was one of Harry's friends at Bloomington High School. After the ceremony, when everybody was tossing rice on the newly weds, Tom got the chance to talk to Connie. She was surprised at how much he had grown in one year and the way he spoke so quickly.

Tom asserted that if a person did not talk, walk, or act quickly in New York City, he would be run over by a car, knocked down by pedestrians, and robbed of his money by pickpockets. The native New Yorker told Connie about the street games they played in New York—stick ball, punch ball, handball, hide-and-seek, and ring-o leerio. He talked about his father's drinking habits—stressing that the phenomenon of drinking dads was commonplace on Staten Island, where saloons could be found in every neighborhood. Though impressed by Tom's bravado in describing these social maladies, Connie indicated her preference for the country ways of South Jersey. Tom had to agree with his former sweetheart: "Sure, I miss living on the farm but there's a lot to be said for the big city—lots of friends, plenty of places to see, and all kinds of things to do." Listening to himself talk Tom understood he wasn't as convinced as he sounded.

The congregation was breaking up—heading for the wedding reception to be held at the Smith's house. Mom and Helen had been cooking for days, preparing a sumptuous wedding feast of roast beef, turkey, chicken, potato and cucumber salads, plus pots of vegetables from Mom's truck garden. Tom and Connie said their sad goodbyes, both kids realizing that this time it was for good. Somewhere in his reading Tom had come across the expression "vale of tears." And he now understood the meaning of this description of life.

Todd M. Daley

CHAPTER 20

The Space Race

Back on Staten Island, the children started a new school year with Cara remaining at P.S. 21 in Elm Park and Tom transferring to P.S. 20 in Port Richmond, which was a large elementary school with special programs for severely handicapped children, as well as academically exceptionally children. Typical for his age, Tom was often more interested in playing stick ball, baseball, and basketball than in the acquisition of knowledge. But his mom scrutinized his report cards and insisted that he spend a minimum of 1 ½ hours on homework each day, plus do outside reading. This was the era of sputnik, when the Russians surprised the world by putting a sizeable satellite in orbit around the earth.

Suddenly Tom and his classmates began reading about jet planes, booster rockets, and space exploration. Fortunately, P.S. 20 was situated only one block from a public library via a short walk through a tree-lined public park. A new friend from P.S. 20, Gary Lukovski, shared his interest in science in general and rockets in particular. They understood that both rockets and jet engines apply Newton's third law of motion, which states that for every action, there is an equal and opposite reaction. Working in Tom's cellar, the two boys built a workable rocket from a tin can with a fire cracker protruding from one end. When the fire cracker went off, the can catapulted thirty feet into the air. Next, they got the idea of using cutoff match heads as the fuel because

1950s-1960s Fable

clumped match heads burn rapidly.

The boys would push approximately forty match heads into a small tin can with a narrow opening at one end. A twisted piece of paper pushed into the opening worked well as a fuse.

The first match head rocket was set off in the cellar by Tom and Gary just to see if it would work. As it turned out, the match head tin can rocket worked quite well — rocketing across the cellar from one end to the other and spewing out a hot flame of burning sulfur. After a couple of tin can rocket launches, the cellar was filled with a sulfuric smoky haze. Since smoke rises, Cara inquired about the scientific experiments going on in the cellar. Then, Mr. Taglia, the hot-tempered Wolstein factory worker, who had little interest in science or rocketry, stormed downstairs and demanded that the boys "cut the shit!" Observing the various materials in the cellar — assorted tin cans, boxes of wooden matches, and gun powder scrapings from fire crackers — the hard-edged blue-collar worker mumbled something about "mad scientists blowing up the world" and left in a huff. Tom indicated that they would conduct their rocket experiments in the backyard, where the sulfur fumes would dissipate into the atmosphere.

Later, Gary inquired about the identity of the irascible Mr. Taglia, to which Tom replied that he was "the loud-mouth SOB who knocks his wife around when he's bored." In any case, the rocket experiments continued outdoors where one of the match head tin can rockets hurtled above the trees — roughly sixty feet above the ground — as the two amateur scientists jumped up and down in celebration. America's youth had joined the space race!

Todd M. Daley

December 29, 1958

Fidel Castro rode into Havana in an army tank after his Fidelista Army defeated Fulgencio Batista's Cuban army at Santa Clara. The dictator Batista lead a corrupt, repressive regime in which American gangsters ran gambling casinos in Havana. Cuba, known as the "Pearl of the Antilles," is a Caribbean island of rich soil, sugar and tobacco crops, and rich mineral deposits like nickel. Despite these assets, Cuba was an impoverished country with widespread political corruption and economic woes. The sugar plantations were owned by wealthy land owners who exploited the peasants working the land.

Fidel Castro was the illegitimate son of a wealthy sugar cane farmer from Oriente province, who attended a Jesuit prep school and the University of Havana Law School. An excellent baseball player, Castro carried a revolver and joined a terrorist group dedicated to the overthrow of the Cuban government. In the 1950s, Castro set up a private law practice that floundered because his clients were poor and he was heavily involved in political intrigues. Despite Cuba's extreme poverty and widespread corruption, the Eisenhower administration supported the dictator Fulgencio Batista. But by the mid1950s, Fidel Castro, his brother Raoul, and Ernesto "Che" Guevara had organized a small force which attacked the Cuban army utilizing guerilla (hit-and-run) tactics from the safety of the Sierra Maestra Mountains. The local peasants supported Castro's guerilla band against the Cuban government and rich landowners. In March 1957, Castro attacked the El Uvero army barracks and captured a large stock of arms. In 1958, Batista launched an all-out offensive against Castro's guerillas in the mountains, but was defeated. The will of the Cuban army was shattered and Batista's forces were routed at Santa Clara.

The unpopular dictator Fulgencio Batista fled Havana before Fidel Castro arrived triumphantly in Cuba's capital city on an army tank amidst cheers of the Cuban people. Castro promised free elections and economic reforms, but soon began purging democratic officials – replacing them with revolutionaries. He had six hundred

1950s-1960s Fable

alleged war criminals executed and declared himself a Marxist-Leninist, allied with the Soviet Union.

Like all dictators, Castro believes that only he knows what is best for the Cuban people. Fidel Castro immediately broke up the large sugar and tobacco plantations into small peasant communes – driving middle-class farmers off the land. Much of the Cuban middle class fled Cuba.

The Cuban economy faltered as the sugar and tobacco harvest declined and shortages of consumer goods, rice, beans, eggs, meat, fish, chicken, and potatoes resulted in rationing. On the plus side, the Castro government eliminated prostitution, gambling, drugs, and political corruption. There is free education, nearly 100% literacy, and universal free medical care in Cuba. Castro has failed to export his revolution to the rest of Latin America, but Cuba does send its doctors and nurses to help third-world countries with their medical programs. The Catholic Church exists under the watchful eye of the Castro regime and the Pope has visited this island country. In 1961, the U.S. helped organize the Bay of Pigs invasion involving 1,400 Cuban exiles, but Castro's forces captured the rebel army. Eventually, ninety of these Cuban refugees were returned to the U.S. in exchange for $25 million in food and medicine. In recent years, the U.S. has reconciled itself to co-existing with Communist Cuba, and some travel and trade has been permitted between the two countries.

To the relief of Tom and Cara, several weeks had gone by without any sign of their alcoholic father. Their mother had mentioned to the kids that she had seen their hard-drinking dad in New York City. He told her that he was now living in the Bowery — the bottom-of-the-barrel neighborhood for drunks and derelicts. After hitting her up for beer money, Thomas Haley said he was sharing a room with his nephew Rusty, who like most of the men in his family, had drinking issues.

Their mom had to laugh when her common-law husband said he was helping Rusty with his drinking problem.

"After hanging out with your father, Rusty will progress from a pint of whiskey a day to a quart of whiskey a day." The kids were hardly reassured by their mother's joke—the only thing worse than having one alcoholic in the family is having two alcoholics to deal with. In any case, the Haley family went about their daily business of work, school, and play occupying themselves while waiting for the proverbial shoe to drop.

1950s-1960s Fable

CHAPTER 21

Basketball Tournament

During the winter of that final elementary school year, Tom participated in the P.S. 20 intramural basketball league. His IGC class competed against the other eighth-grade classes. The contests took place on the third-floor gymnasium of the school's older building.

P.S. 20 consisted of two distinct buildings connected by an enclosed glass-and-brick walkway. One building was a twentieth century red brick school building and the other was a nineteenth century brownstone building, which resembled a monastery complete with an imposing bell tower. The third floor gymnasium was rather small, with narrow stands on either side, and baskets mounted on wooden back-boards on opposite ends of the gym. Consequently, the basketball court was approximately ten feet shorter than the standard high school basketball court. Refereeing the games was the school's superb science teacher, Mr. D, who devoted much of his science class to lectures about jet planes, space rockets, gravity, and Newton's laws of motion. As a referee, Mr. D kept tight control of the game by blowing his whistle every few minutes upon the slightest infraction of the rules.

Since the IGC class consisted of only eight boys, there were only three substitutes available—forcing the starters to play most of the forty-minute game. With the exception of Tom, the IGC boys were short in stature, though they were a scrappy bunch.

The other eighth-grade classes were not only taller and more athletic, but more aggressive around the backboard than the IGC kids. Thus, the IGC team was limited to one shot before their opponents grabbed the rebound and rushed down the court for a fast break. The IGC team had lost their first two games to the 8-2 and 8-3 teams by fairly wide margins. Desperately trying to avoid a clean sweep and last place in the league, they played their final game against the 8-1 class which was close to IGC in academic talent and physical stature.

The 8-1 team was led by a fast-talking, fast-moving point guard named Tommy Spider. Spider, from the black Avenue B section of Port Richmond, was an adept ball-handler and deadly jump shooter. However, Spider was somewhat off his game, as he tried to carry his team on his sturdy shoulders. Hence, the score remained close as Gary Lukovsky and Donald Uberow scored on two-handed set shots from twenty feet away. Tom made a few bank shots, which had become his offensive specialty, and even blocked several shots of his opponents who preferred to post themselves close to the basket. With the score tied, Tommy Spider threaded his way through the IGC defenders for a spinning lay-up. With just twenty seconds remaining, Donald Uberow brought the ball up for the IGC-ers and bounced a pass to Tom, who happened to be standing alone under the basket. Tom almost fumbled the ball but managed to bank a lay-up for a basket — while being fouled by an 8-1 grader.

With the game on the line, Tom sank the foul shot to win the game for the ICG-ers. The gymnasium resounded with the cheers of his teammates and IGC cheerleaders, led by the leggy Leah Stith. Leah was a tall brunette, who aided the IGC cause by repeatedly distracting the streetwise 8-1 basketball players throughout the game. All's fair in love and sports!

1950s-1960s Fable

CHAPTER 22

The Return of Thomas Haley

Just as Tom and Cara were beginning to wonder if their father would ever show up at the white stucco house on Pulaski Avenue, Thomas Haley arrived looking clean-shaven and sober. Hesitating for a moment, their mother let him in the house and offered him a cup of coffee. Her errant common-law husband sat down at the kitchen table comfortably—as if he had just gone for a walk around the block. The lifelong alcoholic declared that he had been "off the sauce for six weeks" and was attending AA meetings faithfully. His motivation in giving up drinking was to prove to his nephew Rusty that through self-discipline and the support of like-minded people, one could kick the drinking habit. "Yes sir, I have tossed the booze monkey off my back. And I got a job through a rehabilitation agency." He indicated that he was working on Wall Street delivering securities to other firms in lower Manhattan. He asked the children's mom if he could once more stay at the house.

The vulnerable woman sighed and shook her head, then pausing for a few seconds while looking out the kitchen window at her neighbor Mr. Caprino, working in his garden. The kids looked from one parent to the other—trying to understand adults. "OK, but the minute I smell a whiff of booze on your breath—you're out!" For the next few months, the Haley household ran smoothly as both parents left together in the morning for work. Somewhere along the line, Thomas Haley had lost his battered 1948 De Soto. It wasn't clear whether he had smashed up the De Soto or the old sedan had finally stopped running. So the kids' parents, as odd a couple as ever walked the streets of Elm Park, took the # 3 Castleton Avenue bus to the Staten Island Ferry, where they rode across New York Bay to Manhattan. Claire wore her usual neat skirt and white blouse, while Thomas was attired in a thread-bare gray business suit. While both parents were at work, the kids got themselves to school—Clara walking up the Walker Street hill to P.S. 21 and Tom taking the bus to P.S. 20 in Port Richmond. It was Tom's responsibility to heat up the meat loaf dinner each night and Clara's job to wash the dishes and keep the house neat.

Sometimes the children were amazed at how mismatched their parents were—not only in their backgrounds, attitudes, and habits—but in their political views. One evening, there happened to be a political discussion at the supper table about Cuba's new leader, Fidel Castro. After a hard-fought revolution, Castro had driven the Cuban dictator Batista from the Caribbean island country. Thomas declared that Castro was "a tin-pot dictator and a Communist to boot. He's no better than the crook he threw out."

Claire objected vociferously, asserting that Fidel Castro was "a man of the people" who would help the poor people of Cuba. "Before the revolution there was corruption, gambling, and hunger in Cuba. The people would take food from rich people's garbage cans in order to eat and the peasants worked the sugar plantations for slave wages."

She said that under Castro there was food for the poor and free education and medical care for everyone—rich or poor. "If that's Communism—I'll take it!"

Turning to the kids with a wry smile, which was more like a grimace, Thomas intoned: "Do you see what I hitched my wagon to? A fast-talking, fast-walking Red who parrots the Soviet line and reads too many books!"

Claire smirked: "Don't be a nudnik. Now that you work on Wall Street, you talk like a rich capitalist—with hardly a pot to piss in!" Everybody laughed, including the children, who were happy to witness an argument that was not about drinking.

A few weeks later, the Haley family was having their usual meat-loaf supper when the doorbell rang and the kids ran to the front door. It was Thomas Haley's hard-luck nephew Rusty, looking nervous and asking to see his uncle. Thomas Haley went out on the porch, closed the door, and conferred with his nephew, who gave him a canvass bag. At this point, Claire barged onto the front porch, grabbed the bag from her common-law husband. Upon unzipping the bag, she discovered that it was full of dollar bills—ones, fives, tens, and twenties. Slamming the front door on Thomas Haley and his nephew Rusty, she rushed to the phone and called the police. Within minutes, a squad car pulled up to the white stucco house and Rusty was arrested for the robbery of a liquor store in Mariners Harbor.

Thomas Haley was furious at Claire for calling the cops— calling her a snitch. After the police left with Rusty in handcuffs, the children's father stormed out of the house. Tom and Cara understood that the recent honeymoon between their parents was over.

And what's worse, the local Staten Island newspaper, "The Advocate" had a banner headline story about a liquor store robber coming to an Elm Park house with the intent of hiding his booty.

The kids' mom was furious at "The Advocate" which she called "a rag—always sweeping the gutter for sensational news stories." For the next few weeks, Tom and Clara had to endure comments from classmates and neighbors about their "jailbird cousin."

1950s-1960s Fable

CHAPTER 23

Newspaper Route

Trying to earn some pocket money, Tom got a paper route for the New York Herald Tribune after fruitlessly trying to get a Staten Island Advocate paper route. The Advocate was a popular Staten Island tabloid covering civic events, local crime, high school teams, and little league scores on the Island. The inside story was that you had to "know somebody" in order to get an Advocate route. The perpetual outsider, Tom had no Staten Island relatives who could pull strings for him. The disadvantages of a Tribune route were many: Unlike the afternoon Advocate, it was a morning paper which had to be delivered before school. Secondly the Tribune was a seven-day newspaper, which included the burden of a heavy Sunday paper. Thirdly, unlike the compact three or four-block Advocate paper route, Tom's Herald Tribune route extended from Port Richmond to Elm Park to Mariners Harbor—an area of 2 ½ square miles. The Tribune customers were widely scattered with little loyalty to the paper. Many of his customers would quit after two or three weeks—claiming the paper had stale news and wasn't worth its cost of 65 cents per week.

In trying to increase the newspaper's circulation, the Herald Tribune people would solicit customers over the phone. From his customers' remarks, Tom learned that they would resort to sob stories in their sales pitches—asserting that the newspaper boy was an indigent person saving up for college.

This in itself was annoying to Tom, who didn't want the sympathy of strangers. Sometimes, the circulation of people would get him customers who were unable to pay for the paper. They would run up a tab for several weeks and then declare that they had no money to pay for the newspaper. Some of the Tribune customers were black people living in run-down areas of Port Richmond and the high-rise housing projects of Mariners Harbor. They would order the newspaper for a few weeks, paying their bill dutifully, and then suddenly cancel the Tribune because they could no longer pay for it. One Tribune customer was a scary-looking old man with a long red beard, who lived in a shack in a wooded area of Elm Park. When Tom knocked on his door to collect the bill, he was so frightened by the hermit's strange appearance that he turned and ran away.

Another problem for Tom was that the Herald Tribune people would regularly send him too many newspapers. Often, he would be sent 35 newspapers when he had only 25 customers. And he would be charged for the extra newspapers. Whenever Tom mentioned this discrepancy to the circulation manager who came to the white stucco house to collect his money, the gruff-mannered man would get angry. Because of this short-fall, Tom wasn't earning any money for several months. In fact, he was falling in debt to the Herald Tribune company. Tired of getting up early each day and not getting paid for his efforts, Tom tearfully pleaded to his mom that he wanted to quit. When she understood the reason for his lack of spending money, the feisty petite woman met the Tribune circulation manager at the front door — blasting him vociferously. Using choice vocabulary, Claire Haley told the unsmiling man he ought to be ashamed of himself for taking advantage of a twelve-year old boy: "You repeatedly sent him more newspapers than he had customers. And billed him for the extra papers. You crook!"

1950s-1960s Fable

After that discrepancy was removed, Tom began to earn some decent pocket money from his far-flung newspaper route.

On holidays like Christmas and Easter, the Tribune customers were especially generous and he would earn from $25 to $30 in tips alone — a small fortune for a kid in that era. Riding his bike, toting his heavy bundle of newspapers (particularly on Sundays) in all kinds of weather — rain, sleet, snow, wind, and bitter cold — took true grit for the twelve-year old boy. But for the five years he had his Herald Tribune paper route, Tom never caught a cold, the flu, or even had a cough. In addition, the rigorous exercise biking three miles seven days a week gave him strength and endurance which improved his athletic ability.

There was a new boy in the neighborhood a sullen bully named Wayne O'Toole, who for no particular reason, would pick on Tom — shoving him to the ground and calling him "Tom Thumb." Originally, Tom thought he was angry because of family problems like alcoholism or poverty. In fact, Wayne lived in a nice house on the Walker Street hill near P.S. 21. One day, Wayne went so far as to pick up Tom's bicycle and slam it to the ground — causing the front wheel to be bent. From that point on, the red bike wobbled whenever the boy pedaled it on his morning paper route. After a while, the other neighborhood boys, Mike Palermo, Joey Caprino, and Gene Munski, steered clear of the neighborhood bully. As luck would have it, Wayne's family became one of Tom's Herald Tribune customers. Reluctantly, the boy delivered the newspaper to his house for a week, and then went to his front door to collect the bill. Wayne opened the door with a big sneer on his face: "What the f do want Tom Thumb?"

His mom, who happened to be standing in the front room, overheard her son. "Is that any way to talk to this nice paper boy, Wayne?" Embarrassed, the unhappy bully smiled sardonically and retreated. The boy's mom stepped outside to pay the bill, giving him a nice 25-cent tip. Then, she noticed the bent front wheel on his bicycle.

"Good heavens! What happened to your bike?" With a little hesitation, Tom said that he had ridden off a curb while carrying a heavy sack of Sunday papers — bending the front wheel. After that for reasons known only to Wayne, the miserable bully left the newspaper boy alone. Eventually, Tom found a front bicycle wheel at Perry's junk yard and put it on his old red bicycle — grateful that it wasn't the wheel rear which would have cost more.

Delivering the New York Herald Tribune early each morning gave Tom a new perspective on the world. The streets were quiet and the air had a fresh scent — free of the dust and exhaust caused by rush-hour traffic. The pinkish gray sky formed by the rising sun bursting through the dark clouds and the twittering chirps of early morning birds provided a pleasant background for the biking newspaper boy. The other early risers — the milkman, the bread man, the mailman, the bus drivers and truck drivers — were quietly going about their business. The pre-dawn quiet was scarcely marred by the occasional barking dog, the wandering alley cat, the slinking raccoon, and the solitary pedestrian walking to the bus stop. Tom noticed a certain courtesy among early morning people — cars would stop to let him cross the street and people waved to the bicycling newspaper boy as he passed them — usually at the same time each morning. Once when his bike had a flat tire, a bus driver stopped to give him a ride along the half-mile trek of Forest Avenue.

1950s-1960s Fable

Tom was amazed by the variety of Tribune customers that existed on his wide-ranging newspaper route — from the affluent living in big Victorian houses to the very poor living in shabby apartments, who could hardly afford the 65 cents-a-week newspaper. It moved him that even his poorest customers invariably tipped him from 10 to 25 cents. In fact, Tom observed that poor people were generally better tippers than wealthy people. Once on a windy March day, a customer was paying him, while he held the outside storm door. A sudden gust of wind slammed the door shut — breaking the glass. The boy was so upset that he burst into tears — apologizing profusely. The woman reassured Tom that it was not his fault and paid the bill with a 25-cent tip. The kindness and generosity of people in general made a great impression on the boy.

The New York Herald Tribune was an excellent newspaper — on par with the world renowned New York Times in terms of its breadth and depth of news events coverage. The boy developed the habit of reading the Herald Tribune everyday, becoming well informed of national and international events. He became aware of the national effort by black people to expand their fundamental human rights, as well as the increasing tensions of the Cold War between America and the Soviet Union. Under his mother's influence, Tom became a supporter of the Democratic Party because he perceived them to more sympathetic to working people and to the civil rights movement. Despite the uncertainties of the weather, the hardship of getting up at six AM seven days a week, and the burden of the heavy canvass newspaper bag on his shoulder — Tom kept his paper route for five years. Enduring flat tires, bent wheels, ripped canvass bags, rain-soaked newspapers, riding his bike, or walking the three-mile route, Tom rarely complained to his mother.

He was well aware of Claire Haley's sing-song response to any notion of his quitting his paper route: "Nobody ever died from hard work!"

Despite his drinking episodes, Thomas Haley continued to work in Manhattan, commuting with Claire by public transit during the work week. His weekends, especially Friday and Saturday nights, were spent within the friendly confines of KC's or Kaffman's bar—"bending elbows with the folks." The children's mother had thrown in the towel and accepted his weekend drinking habit as long as her husband got up for work on Monday morning and "Shlepped into the city." However, when it came to bringing liquor into the white stucco house, the feisty woman put her foot down. She also collected all of Thomas Haley's weekly pay check—except for twenty dollars of weekend spending money. This amount "he could spend on bupkes" for all she cared. The kids noticed that their mother's vocabulary included Yiddish words when she was venting her frustration with the ups and downs of everyday life. Remembering the days when their mother would storm into local bars to harangue the proprietor for serving her husband, the kids were surprised at this compromise—wondering about its cause and its duration.

Occasionally his dad would help Tom with his outdoor chores—cutting the front hedge and mowing the backyard crab grass. When Thomas Haley pushed the rusty old hand mower around the small backyard, the boy noticed him huffing and puffing after cutting the grass for a few minutes. The former house painter said it was just shortness of breath from years of smoking and drinking. He made the boy promise to refrain from these bad habits, to which his son readily agreed. Tom recalled that his idol, Phillies pitcher Robin Roberts, was a nonsmoker and teetotaler.

Pausing to look at the big mulberry tree which dominated the backyard, his father said he was feeling "the burden of my bad habits weighing upon me. Remember whatever happens to me, I want you to take care of your mother and your sister."

One Saturday night, Tom was playing stick ball in the street with Mike Palermo, Joey Caprino, Neil Coombs, and Gene Munski, when he noticed his father stumbling and staggering along Pulaski Avenue. Abruptly collapsing by a telephone pole, he sat leaning against the pole—rubbing his face and gasping for breath. Everybody stared at the panting man. When Gene started to laugh, Tom threw his baseball glove at him, telling him to "shut the f_up!" Then he ran over to his

dad, helped him up, and supporting his weight—guided the ex-house painter home. Shuffling into the house and collapsing in bed, he asked his frightened wife for a glass of water. Claire noticed he was sweating profusely and gave him some aspirin. Thomas Haley remained in bed for the rest of the weekend, but was able to get up and go to work in Manhattan on Monday morning. The sudden decline in their father's health had one good consequence—he ceased drinking on weekend nights.

Thomas Haley continued on the straight and narrow path of sobriety for several weeks until his nephew Rusty showed up on a Saturday afternoon. Claire refused to allow the troubled Haley family member (whom she referred to as "the schmuck") into the house, so the two men left with the intent of "going for a stroll along Morningstar Road" according to their dad. As the afternoon turned into evening, Claire remarked that it wasn't just a stroll through the neighborhood. It was more like a "trip to hell and back." She correctly assumed that the two Haley men were "ensconced in a saloon drinking the night away."

Sadly, his nephew's visit triggered another Thomas Haley drinking binge that would go on indefinitely and result in the loss of his Wall Street messenger's job. After enduring so much grief from her alcoholic husband, the kids' mom was beyond the point of tolerance and compromise. She
packed Thomas Haley's belongings into a large suitcase and some cardboard boxes, and put them on the front porch. "Your father has burnt his bridges behind him. It's over!" she announced to Tom and Cara. From that point on, the children would only catch glimpses of their father entering or leaving neighborhood bars.

Cara said she saw Thomas Haley and his nephew sitting on a bench in Port Richmond when she was shopping at Woolworth's for some art supplies. He told her to pursue her drawing and that his biggest regret in life was not continuing with his painting. In a rare outburst of temper, Cara yelled at her father, "Well Pop, if you didn't drink so much, maybe you'd have time to paint again." Early one morning while delivering the Herald Tribune, Tom noticed Thomas Haley sleeping against a warehouse wall in Mariners Harbor. The boy went up to his father, asking him if he was OK. The down-on-his-luck alcoholic said he needed some money to get breakfast. Tom got off his bike, gave him all his pocket change, and then went on his way. All day at school he thought about his father—how could he wind up in such a terrible state?

Finishing his morning paper route, Tom noticed an article in the Herald Tribune about the articulate young senator from Massachusetts, John Kennedy, who was running for President on the Democratic ticket. Kennedy was a voracious reader of novels, history, and poetry. The World War II hero talked about the different forms of courage—in particular the courage of poets who "illuminate the nature of man and the world in which he lives."

1950s-1960s Fable

Kennedy was opposed by Republican Richard Nixon, who had been Vice President under Dwight Eisenhower, the popular 1950s American President. Nixon had made a name for himself by holding his own against Russian Premier Nikita Khrushschev in the famous "kitchen debate" in Moscow. In this debate Nixon had argued that the typical American factory worker could afford a nice suburban house costing $15,000 — paid for with a 25-year mortgage. Khrushchev replied that American capitalists build homes that do not last 25 years, while Russians build homes and apartments that last for generations.

Tom's mother despised Nixon for his history of "red baiting" — accusing political opponents of being Communist sympathizers. In 1948, Nixon was instrumental in getting Alger Hiss, a U.S. State Department official indicted for perjury for denying that he was a member of the Communist Party during the

1930s. The feisty left-leaning woman declared "only a fool would believe Nixon's spiel about American prosperity with millions unemployed and struggling to pay their bills." At this point, both Tom and Cara reminded their mother about their father's plight — wandering around homeless in Mariners Harbor. Turning red with anger and frustration, Claire Haley shook her head: "I'm done with his drunken antics — he'll drag us into the gutter!"

September 26, 1960

Nearly 70 million viewers watched the first televised debate between John Kennedy and Richard Nixon — opposing candidates for President. Kennedy appeared tanned, relaxed, and confident, while Nixon looked tense and pale, with a five o'clock shadow.

Todd M. Daley

Kennedy combined a sense of humor with rhetorical aggressiveness by asserting that America was troubled by poverty, unemployment, a missile gap, and discrimination of black people. The consensus was that Kennedy won the debate, holding his own against the more experienced Vice President. Early in the campaign, Kennedy had made a phone call to Martin Luther King, who had been arrested and put in jail in Georgia. An important issue in the campaign was John Kennedy's Catholicism – particularly in the Protestant South. Kennedy responded to the controversy by stating unequivocally that he did not "speak for my church on public matters and the church does not speak for me."

Though John F. Kennedy was from a wealthy family, he had known hardship in his life. A brother and a sister were killed in the Second World War, and Kennedy hurt his back rescuing a crew member when his torpedo patrol boat was rammed by a Japanese destroyer. For his heroism in the South Pacific, Kennedy received the Purple Heart. Kennedy had graduated from Harvard College in 1940 with honors. Operating under the family slogan – "Of those to whom much has been given, much will be required" – the entire Kennedy family was active in public service. After World War II, John Kennedy was elected to Congress in 1946 and to the Senate in 1952. In 1956 while recovering from back surgery, he wrote Profiles in Courage about eight senators who made courageous decisions that hurt their political careers. In John Kennedy's inaugural address, he urged Americans to serve their country in various capacities: "Ask not what your country can do for you, ask what you can do for your country." The new President asked the nations of the world to join together to fight the "common enemies of man: tyranny, poverty, disease, and war itself." The Kennedy Administration was called "the New Frontier" for its emphasis on education, civil rights, medicare for the elderly, economic aid to rural areas, and tax reform. President Kennedy's biggest setback was the Bay of Pigs Invasion of Cuba, in which Castro's army defeated and captured American-trained Cuban exiles. The 1962 Cuban missile crisis, in which Kennedy forced the Russians to remove nuclear-tipped missiles from Cuba in exchange for guarantees of Cuban sovereignty, was the closest approach to nuclear war between the two super-powers.

1950s-1960s Fable

The biggest triumphs of the Kennedy Administration was the 1963 signing of the nuclear test-ban treaty, in which the U.S., Russia, and Great Britain agreed to stop atmospheric testing of nuclear weapons. Another innovation of the New Frontier was the Peace Corps which sent thousands of young Americans overseas to help third-world countries in such areas as education, health care, farming, and construction. In southeast Asia, a conflict was brewing between North Vietnam, led by Communist Ho Chi Minh, and South Vietnam, led by right-wing generals. President Kennedy sent military equipment and American advisors to train the South Vietnamese army, but he stated that "In the final analysis it is their (South Vietnam's) war. They are the ones who have to win it or lose it." In June 1963, Kennedy spoke about world peace – "the necessary rational end of rational men" in which people live together in mutual respect and tolerance.

On the domestic front, the civil rights movement gained momentum as freedom riders attempted to integrate public buses and private restaurants in the South. There were also efforts by black people to integrate the public schools and colleges of the South.

After Mississippi governor Ross Barnett attempted to block the entrance of James Meredith into the University of Mississippi, President Kennedy sent federal marshals and troops to protect Mr. Meredith from rioting white southerners. As a result of the racial conflicts in the South, Kennedy proposed a new civil rights bill guaranteeing the right of all citizens to enter the schools and colleges of their choice. The bill would also guarantee the right to equal service in restaurants, hotels, stores, buses, and trains Kennedy also proposed a bill to guarantee the right to vote anywhere in the U.S. without interference, reprisal, or poll taxes. John Kennedy expressed deep outrage over the violence and killings perpetrated against civil rights activists in the South. "This issue could cost me the election, but we're not turning back." Although John Kennedy's work as the 35th President was cut short by his assassination on November 22nd, 1963, the New Frontier was revered as the era of Camelot representing the youth, the hope, and the idealism of America during the 1960s.

CHAPTER 24

Marxism vs. Capitalism

Claire Haley would often lecture her children about the evils of capitalism—describing American materialism, exploitation, and greed. She said that in an ideal Marxist society there would be no rich and no poor—everyone would be equal. "And the proletariat would own the means of production, the factories. Unlike America," she declared confidently "there's no unemployment in Communist countries like Russia—everybody works." She said they have free education, free medical care, and low-cost housing for all the people. Their mom reiterated the Marxist slogan which the children had heard many times before: "From each according to their ability, to each according to their needs."

Continuing her lecture, Claire asserted that every commodity has "surplus value" representing the labor that produced it. "And surplus value is the source of the capitalist's profit."

Tom wondered what happened to people who couldn't work because of poor education, bad health, or alcoholism. To which Claire replied, "The government gives them rehabilitation and training—there are no slackers in Russia." Tom said he had read in the Herald Tribune that they put political opponents in prison camps in Russia. Claire, growing angry, replied that

1950s-1960s Fable

such stories were "capitalist lies." Cara wondered if artists in Russia were paid the same as garbage men.

Her mother asserted that capitalist pit blue collar workers against white collar workers in order to exploit all working people.

Tom asked why there was no freedom of speech, press, and religion in the "workers' paradise of Russia." He said that the Russian newspaper Pravda "only prints stories that support the Communist line and the government suppresses political dissent."

Raising her voice and getting angrier by the minute, Claire told her children not to believe everything they read in the newspaper or see on television. With regard to religious freedom, she said that Karl Marx called religion "the opiate of the people because it prevents the proletariat from revolting against capitalism. Religion is just pie in the sky." The kids disagreed, citing Jesus's Sermon on the Mount when he blessed the poor, the meek, the merciful, and the pure in heart.

"That's all well and good, but let me tell you about the Great Depression in the 1930s when doctors and lawyers were selling apples on street corners." Their mom talked about banks closing because they had no money and factories shutting down because nobody could afford to buy anything. Thanks to President Franklin Roosevelt, she was able to get a job with WPA but the depression continued until the start of World War II.

Tom declared that now with government regulation of banks and the stock market, and because of social security and unemployment insurance—"there will never be another depression in America."

Claire snickered bitterly, "I wouldn't be so sure of that mister. Capitalism contains the seeds of its own destruction!" The kids used the discussion of Marxist ideals to bring up Thomas Haley's desperate condition — wandering around like a vagrant on Staten Island's North Shore. Tom said he saw his father trying to keep warm in an abandoned warehouse near the Richmond Terrace waterfront. Cara asserted that when she saw him in the Port Richmond shopping area, he was sober. "Jesus tells us to help the poor—love, faith, hope, and charity," intoned Cara. "There you go again with that man Jesus! Besides, I don't believe in charity. The government should help the poor with direct subsidies—taken from the rich," said their mother doggedly. Tom observed that Marxists ought to admire Jesus because he threw the money-changers out of the temple in Jerusalem. "Jesus also said that it's easier for a camel to pass through the eye of a needle than for a rich man to enter heaven."

Claire had to laugh at her children's spiritualism: "I didn't know you were mavins on the Bible. Fine! From me according to my ability, to your father according to his needs." Their mother's joke told Tom and Cara that they had appealed to her conscience and had won their case. But Claire Haley stipulated three conditions for her alcoholic husband's return to the white stucco house on Pulaski Avenue: He must stop drinking, attend AA meetings, and get a job.

When Thomas Haley returned to the white stucco house on Pulaski Avenue, it was a somber, subdued, and weakened version of the children's hard-drinking father. No longer the boisterous, burly house painter who could lift up his kids in either hand, their dad had trouble carrying the A&P grocery bags from the taxicab to the front door. His appearance had changed substantially in the past few years. Thomas Haley's striking blue eyes had lost their luster, his reddish complexion had a

1950s-1960s Fable

grayish tinge, and the lines in his face had deepened. His once robust constitution had a fragile, hollowed out aspect—from years of carousing with no regard to the effects on his health. These changes in his appearance alarmed his children, but reassured his long-suffering wife that at last his drinking days were over. Any kind of physical exertion such as mowing the grass, cutting the hedge, raking the leaves, sweeping the front porch and steps, tossing a football with Tom and Mike Palermo, or turning a jump rope for Cara and Elena Taglia—appeared to exhaust Thomas Haley profoundly. After he complained of stomach cramps and chest pains, Claire took him to the doctor who prescribed vitamins and bed rest for two weeks. When their dad began coughing each morning, Claire suggested that he give up smoking. "I don't drink anymore and now you want me to stop smoking too? Why don't you just shoot me and be done with it," the ex-house painter replied irascibly.

For a while Thomas Haley made the trip to Manhattan with his wife—seeking employment as a Wall Street messenger. But his ashen appearance and impaired health prevented him from securing his former line of work in New York City. Nevertheless, Claire insisted that he make weekly trips to the state unemployment bureau in the city, so he could qualify for unemployment compensation. But the effects of continual rejection by prospective employers on the kids' father impaired both his health and his mood. "Like the horse and buggy, I have been railroaded to the dust-bin by Wall Street. Maybe I'll become a Red like your Mom" he remarked sadly to his kids.

There was one small consolation for the kids. With no work available and little to do at home, Thomas Haley borrowed Cara's sketch pad and began drawing. He sketched tree-and flower filled lakeside landscapes and rustic farmhouses much like the Smith farm—complete with cornfields, a chicken coop, and a pigpen. He also sketched the Staten Island Mariners Harbor waterfront with its rotting warehouses, corroded ships, and decayed docks. There was also a nice view of the Manhattan skyline with its skyscrapers, bridges, and neon signs. Then he sketched compelling portraits of Tom and Cara, plus a dramatic profile of Claire—from her "good side." The children wanted their father to color these hastily drawn pencil sketches, but the former artist shook his head: "My mind is willing but my body is not. You gotta know when to toss in the towel." It was a gloomy day in late November when it seems to get dark by mid-afternoon. Suddenly, their father grew vexed with himself and his kids. "I'm going for a walk by myself." The children objected—they wanted to accompany their moody father. But he was adamant—he insisted on his privacy: "I said by myself!"

Tom and Cara decided to follow their melancholy father, at a safe distance, on his walk down Pulaski Avenue, up Walker Street, and then turning on Morningstar Road—entering Kaffman's Bar as they expected. Talking among themselves, they decided to do the unexpected—they entered the dimly lit, smoke-filled, alcohol reeking saloon. The bartender, a bald-headed stocky man, told them to leave but the kids ignored him—searching the bar for their father, who sat at the end of the bar with a half-empty glass of beer before him. Thomas Haley told them he was having just one beer and then he would return home. "Be good kids and go home before your mother gets worried about your whereabouts."

Cara ran over to her father's place, grabbed the glass of beer and spilled its contents on the floor. At this point, the bartender got mad and told Thomas Haley to leave with his kids or he'd call the cops. Incensed at Tom and Cara, the former house painter left the bar with his children following. On the sidewalk growing red-faced with anger, he turned to Tom and Cara, "I've never laid

1950s-1960s Fable

a hand on you, but if you follow me any further — you'll both get a whupping. Get the hell out of here!"

The children reluctantly left their angry father and headed home — fearing the worst When Tom and Cara returned home, they told their mother, who had gone food shopping at the A&P on Richmond Avenue, about their father's exit from the house. They wondered where Thomas Haley had obtained the money to buy his drinks at Kaffman's Bar. The explanation was simple: He had grabbed his unemployment check from the mailbox before his unlucky wife could have him sign it and cash it at her bank in Port Richmond. "Now your father has enough money to carry own for two weeks. He'll drink himself to death," she declared grimly. The kids felt they had been tricked by the wily alcoholic, who knew how to con people in order to satisfy his gnawing thirst for liquor.

The children suggested that their mom remind the local bar owners of their pledge not to serve their dad. Shaking her head wearily, Claire Haley replied, "He'll just go somewhere else to drink. There's a bar on every corner. Saloons are the big business of Staten Island."

Todd M. Daley

CHAPTER 25

Thomas Haley in Trouble

As a result, everybody in the Haley family went about their daily business—Claire working in Manhattan, food shopping and cooking the meals, Tom delivering his papers each morning and attending P.S. 20 in Port Richmond, and Cara attending P.S. 21 in Elm Park. Thomas Haley must have done his drinking outside of the Elm Park neighborhood, because there was no word of his activities or his whereabouts for a few weeks. Tom wondered what drove a person to drink himself to stupor day-in and day-out—especially when that person wasn't feeling very well.

To ignore the beauty of the living world—the golden sunrise in the morning, the feathery clouds floating across the bright blue sky, the twinkling stars and glowing moon at night, the sweet honey-suckle fragrance of Staten Island's fields and woods, the hustle and bustle of the cars moving along the streets, and busy people going about their daily business— for the mind-numbing effects of alcohol was inexplicable. To forsake the company of your family for a smoke-filled saloon was both mysterious and frightening to the boy. Such a powerful compulsion to drink oneself unconscious was nothing less than a death wish.

Maybe it had something to do with Thomas Haley's childhood. He didn't speak often or fondly of his large

1950s-1960s Fable

family. There were too many mouths to feed, and he hated working in the coal mines of Western Pennsylvania as a young man. He had God-given talent as an artist but couldn't stick to it. Maybe it was about work ethic? In South Jersey, the Smiths taught the value of hard work by example — taking care of their twelve-acre farm in addition to working in the local canning factory. His birth mom trudged off to work as a bookkeeper every day in Manhattan. When the kids lived in South Jersey, she had addressed envelopes at five cents each after work to pay the $32 monthly board for her two children.

The boy himself gained the respect of his friends and neighbors through his early morning work — delivering the Herald Tribune seven days a week — summer, fall, winter, and spring. He amazed the candy-store owner by buying the New York Post, a politically liberal tabloid, on Saturdays. "Why do you want to read the Post? You deliver the Herald Tribune every day." Tom replied that he enjoyed reading other newspapers to get a different point of view on current events.

A new neighbor moved into the house next to the Haley's white stucco house on Pulaski Avenue — a sturdy elderly Italian immigrant, named Antonio. He spoke little English and worked as a mason on Staten Island's South Shore, where a lot of construction was occurring. Antonio would arrive home late afternoons by the #3 transit bus with his overalls covered in gritty white dust. Antonio liked to do fix-up projects on his house — early on weekend mornings. Starting his paper route at six AM, Tom would observe the hard-working mason mixing cement in a big iron tub and hammering the wood frames into which he'd pour the cement.

Some of the Pulaski Avenue neighbors did not appreciate Antonio's early morning industriousness, while they were trying to catch up on their sleep. Mr.

Caprino (Joey's dad) and Mr. Palermo (Mike's dad) were among the indignant loud voices — telling the Italian mason to "knock it off you dumb Guinea!" Pretty soon the kids on the block, Tom included, used the epithet "dumb Guinea" when referring to the hard working but naïve immigrant. For his part, Antonio though unaware of this pejorative term, understood from the tone of his neighbors' language that he was being maligned.

One day, Tom, Mike Palermo, Joey Caprino, Gene Munski, and Neil Coombs were playing one-bounce, running bases stick ball on the street — directly in front of Antonio's house. The latter was busy mixing cement in his big iron tub for a patch-up job on his cracked sidewalk. Tom hit a popup which, as luck would have it, landed with a plop in the cement-filled tub. Mike yelled, "Only you could hit that one-in-a-million shot, Tom."

The boys laughed at Antonio's vexation, as he gingerly picked up the cement-coated spaldeen and handed it to Tom. "You did that on a-purpose. I come from Sicily, nobody makes a fool out of me!"

The boys found his remark even more hilarious — repeating Antonio's words: "I'm a-come from Sicily, nobody make a fool out of me." Becoming incensed at the rude laughter of the boys, the elderly mason waved his shovel at the group, "You keep it up and I'm gonna do something nice!"

This strange remark caused more raucous laughter and comic derision from the boys, who could barely focus on the stick ball game because of their mirth. Mike, the boldest of the Pulaski Avenue boys, kept saying, "watch out 'cause I'm gonna do something nice."

In particular, Mike addressed his remarks to Cara, Elena Taglia, and Doris Schmidt who were jumping rope on the sidewalk. Elena and Doris did their best to ignore

1950s-1960s Fable

Mike, who was staring at them in a suggestive manner: "I'm gonna do something nice." But Cara stopped turning the rope and turned to the boys: "You guys are ignorant! Show some respect for the man." She went into the white stucco house and returned with a cupcake she had recently baked, and gave it to Antonio. "I apologize for these rude boys, Mr. Antonio."

The hard-working mason accepted the cup cake and bowed to the girl. "Thank you for this nice-a-cookie."

The boys howled but an angry look from Cara told them they'd better quit while they're ahead and resume their stick ball game. In spite of his annoyance at Cara's intervention, Tom realized she was right to reprimand his friends. No longer the dreamy-eyed farm girl, Cara was an outspoken city girl with a strong sense of right and wrong. And after some reflection, Tom admitted to himself that it wasn't one of his better moments. Nevertheless, he kept the hardened cement-coated spaldeen as a souvenir of the Pulaski Avenue boys' funny encounter with the Italian mason.

Early one October morning, Tom was delivering the Herald Tribune to a customer on the northern end of Pulaski Avenue, which terminates in a grassy slope running down to some abandoned railroad tracks. Part of the history of Staten Island's North Shore was the demise of the northern branch of the Staten Island Railroad (in the late 1940s), which took commuters from Mariners Harbor, Elm Park, and Port Richmond to the Saint George terminal of the Staten Island Ferry. Tossing a folded newspaper on to the porch of a neat white cottage, Tom noticed a dim light in the small ramshackle house at the very end of the street. Previously, that tumbledown house with the peeling paint had been unoccupied. Out of curiosity, he rode his bike to the front steps of the house and peered through a broken window.

The boy did a double take—none other than a scruffy-looking Thomas Haley was sitting at a table talking to a shabbily-dressed elderly man—evidently a derelict.

Suddenly aware that he was being observed, the ex-house painter turned towards the window and called out to his son: "Well, stop gawking at me, Tom, and come on in—for Christ-sakes!" The loud, too-hearty welcome told the boy that his alcoholic father was drunk.

Hesitating for a moment, Tom got off his bike and walked into the dusty house—entering the kitchen, which had a rickety table and some rusty folding chairs to sit on. There were a couple of mattresses in the parlor, and some cardboard boxes and stacks of newspapers in a side room. His father introduced Tom to his grizzled companion, who did his best to hide his own state of intoxication. "My son is a hardworking newsboy, a gifted student at P.S 20, and a top-notch stick ball player," he told his drunken companion, who nodded slowly while keeping his eye on a half-empty bottle of cheap wine. Then, the former artist asked his son for some spare change so the two men could get some breakfast. Emptying his pockets, the newspaper boy gave his alcoholic father a few dollars in change. Pocketing the money, Thomas Haley unceremoniously told the boy to be on his way, indicating he would be cleaning up his act and returning to the white stucco house shortly—"as sober as a judge." Nodding to the two alcoholics and forcing himself to smile, Tom quickly left the dilapidated house and resumed his early-morning newspaper deliveries.

1950s-1960s Fable

CHAPTER 26

Thomas Haley at Rest

Telling neither Cara nor his mother about the pre-dawn meeting with Thomas Haley, Tom doubted he would ever see his father in a state of sobriety again. Weighed down by a sense of gloom with regard to his father, Tom had difficulty concentrating at school and sleeping at night. He had a recurrent dream in which his drunken father kept on banging on the front door of their house, but was refused admittance by his adamant mother. A few weeks later in early November, Tom was walking home from P.S. 20 — opting to walk from Port Richmond in order to save on bus fare. He ran into some former classmates of his from P.S. 21, who greeted him in a friendly way — asking the boy about his doings at the new school. Even the notorious Wayne O'Toole refrained from his usual nasty barbs as he said hello to the newspaper boy. Arriving at the white stucco house, Tom noticed his upstairs neighbor, Mr. Taglia standing on the front porch — looking sedate and somber. The hot-tempered Wolstein factory worker asked Tom if he could talk to him inside the house. Wondering what he had done wrong, Tom agreed fearing the worst. After a lengthy pause, Mr. Taglia told the boy that his father had suffered a heart attack and died while walking along Pulaski Avenue. "They took him in an ambulance to St. Vincent's hospital, but he was already dead."

Tom became light-headed as the blood drained from his face and there was a hollow feeling in his stomach. Mr. Taglia grabbed the boy by his arm and sat him down on a kitchen chair.

There were no tears—just a sense of melancholy from the irretrievable loss of his troubled father. He would never see his father's striking blue eyes with that empty look, or his sardonic smile—more like a grimace when he cracked a joke about his wife's Marxist views and Jewish background. Walking to the sink, Mr. Taglia got the boy a glass of water: "Drink this slowly. Do you want me to call your mom?" Tom shook his head. He would have to tell his sister, who was on her way home and then call his mother at work.

When Cara came into the house she was already in tears. Word of her alcoholic father's awful death on Pulaski Avenue had spread like wildfire throughout the neighborhood, and Cara was informed of his demise by the rude teenager, Joy Eggert, as she approached the white stucco house. Hugging his sister, Tom tried to console her by saying their dad "was watching them from heaven." This only served to upset Cara more. Shaking her head and sobbing loudly, Cara yelled frantically. "No! He'll be six feet under with the insects and worms. Don't give me those dumb fairy tales."

Tom then called his mother at work: "Mom, Dad had a heart attack. They found him dead on the street." Claire Haley let out a cry which sounded more like a wail. Tom thought of a poem he had read in school:

"I cry for the lost lonely world.
I cry for the hearts that are broken.
. . . .
So if you cry, cry for the world. There are others crying for it, too."

1950s-1960s Fable

Claire Haley took a few days off from her New York City bookkeeping job to arrange her common law husband's funeral, which was held at Dabinski's Funeral Home on Morningstar Road. Mr. Dabinski was a white-haired man with a penetrating gaze that unnerved people, as if he was sizing them up for a casket.

The kids noticed that their mom started smoking cigarettes—something she had never done before. Unexpectedly, there were many people at the funeral: the neighborhood dads—Mr. Taglia, Mr. Caprino, Mr. Palermo, Mr. Munski, Mr. Coombs, and Harry the Horse, plus the mason Antonio, as well as some shabbily dressed men who had been Thomas Haley's drinking buddies. Looking at these vagrants plus the Elm Park dads, Tom realized that most of them were heavy drinkers—"bar flies."

In an era before the widespread use of drugs, alcohol was truly the scourge of the working class of the 1950s. Family members attending the funeral were their father's hard-luck nephew Rusty, his sister Mary from western Pennsylvania, his common-law wife Claire, and his star-crossed children Tom and Cara. Aunt Mary had told the kids that her brother Tom was a gifted artist and a kind person who never spoke ill of anyone. She did admit that alcoholism was the Haley family curse—afflicting five of her eight siblings. Claire spoke briefly—saying that despite her husband's alcoholism, he was good-natured and generous: "He'd give you the shirt off his back." She went on to blame the local saloons for her husband's death—"Selling a desperate alcoholic booze for blood money—typical businessmen."

Tom wondered what would become of his tiny family — his mother, Cara, and himself — since the option of returning to the Smiths was out of the question. Unlike Cara, Tom had not been allowed to visit the Smith farm in South Jersey during the summer.

A naturalized New York City boy, Tom felt physically and spiritually removed from that rural lifestyle. It reminded him of the Thomas Wolfe novel, *You Can't Go Home Again*. Thinking of his father's sad life, he recalled Charles Dickens famous line, "It is a far, far better place that I go to than I have ever known." The Reverend John Hays from the children's Methodist church in Port Richmond gave the

eulogy — discussing Thomas Haley's artistic talents and personal qualities, as well as the demon of alcoholism which he battled all his life. Despite the deceased man's problems, the preacher did not doubt his devotion and love for his family. "As the children's pastor, I can attest to their Christian values, their strong work ethic, and good character. I am sure that both parents can be commended for raising such nice children. I ask God to take this man — an imperfect soul, like all of us, into his hands."

"Yea, though I walk through the valley of the shadow of death, I will fear no evil, for thou art with me; Thy rod and thy staff they comfort me. Thou preparest a table before me in the presence of mine enemies; Thou anointest my head with oil; my cup runneth over. Surely goodness and mercy shall follow me all the days of my life; And I will dwell in the house of the Lord forever."

1950s-1960s Fable

CHAPTER 27

Port Richmond High School

It was the beginning of a new decade, the 1960s, for the people of Elm Park, Staten Island, and America itself. The new decade was ushered in by a charismatic young President, named John Kennedy, whose administration was called "The New Frontier." In years to come the term "Camelot" would be used to refer to his presidency because of its democratic ideals, service to the country, support of civil rights, and nuclear test ban treaty. Traditional values, beliefs, and customs were questioned by young people who decried the conformity and constraints of the 1950s. Because of his South Jersey farming background, Tom was not enamored with the new freedom. Though hopeful and idealistic, the boy thought that the popular imperative to "do your own thing" was a prescription for anarchy and promiscuity. Some of his mother's Marxist prudery had rubbed off on him—along with her Marxist class biases, opposition to profits, and her authoritarian approach to America's social trends. Tom's bad experience with the Herald Tribune circulation manager—his defrauding the boy by sending him extra newspapers—had left him with a deep distrust of business enterprises, both big and small.

Now a freshman at Port Richmond High School, Tom felt overwhelmed by the sheer size of the school—its multiple floors, long narrow hallways, and the huge student body, totaling more than 2,000 students from a large part of Staten Island's North Shore. He was intimidated by the sophistication and maturity of the upper classmen, who drove to school in fast, noisy cars with their nubile girlfriends. One day, he bumped into Bonnie Rosolio, whom he hadn't seen since he was transferred to P.S. 20. Embarrassed about their past association during the poetry reading fiasco at P.S. 21, Tom didn't know what to say to the pretty curly-haired girl who loved reading poetry. She had matured physically and socially, while the boy was still the skinny paperboy from the wrong side of town. When she started to express her condolences over his father's untimely death, Tom turned abruptly and walked away—fearing he would lose his composure.

A few days later a classmate, Bruce Hatten, needled Tom about a drunken vagrant found dead on Pulaski Avenue: "They said it was your dad," Tom reacted uncharacteristically by knocking him off his chair and pummeling the obnoxious boy until he was pulled off him by his homeroom teacher, Mr. Gento. For that rare display of violence, Tom had to stay after school for a week—missing his autumn afternoon "World Series" fast-pitch stick ball game, which he enjoyed after sitting in school all day long. For the rest of his freshman year at Port Richmond High School, he earned an undeserved reputation as a troublemaker despite his honor roll grades.

Claire Haley was called into the school to confer with the grade advisor, Mrs. Cowan, whom she blasted for lacking empathy towards working-class children: "My son delivers the New York Herald Tribune every morning before school, does his homework, and gets good grades. What more do you want?"

Tom was in the second-tier honors homeroom (designated the "x" class) which included some of his P.S. 20 IGC classmates—Gary Lukovski, Donald Uberow,

1950s-1960s Fable

Bruce Hatten, and Leah Stith, plus new comers Albert Cloots and Tony Aramo. There was also a first-tier honors homeroom (designated the "s" class) which was a cut above the "x" class, representing kids from the affluent North Shore neighborhood of Westerleigh. As luck would have it, the "x" homeroom was located in the school library, which Tom viewed as a godsend. At that stage of his development, the boy had a lot of excess energy and sitting at a desk all day gave him fits. The "x" kids were a raucous, unruly bunch which their homeroom teacher, Mr. Gento, ruled with a firm hand. Many of the "x" students, especially the boys, liked to get out of their seats and browse the library stacks — particularly the sports and science sections.

This drove Mr. Gento crazy — causing him to yell at the wandering "x" kids — mostly the boys. Tom noticed that Mr. Gento had a double standard when it came to infractions against his "stay in your seats" rule. The "x" girls were free to stand in a corner and gossip among themselves, while he herded the boys back to their seats. There was one particular girl, Arlene Patco, for whom the label "teacher's pet" was fitting. About once a week she'd bring a homemade cupcake or cookies for Mr. Gento, who rewarded the cute, chubby freshman with a rare smile. Arlene was his secretary, taking attendance every day, distributing notices and report cards, and collective money for bus passes and lunch tickets during homeroom.

The first-tier honor class, the "s" class, had a condescending attitude towards "x" class counterparts who were beneath them in academic achievement, economic class, and school-wide status. As the years rolled by, this self-assured group of youngsters dominated Port Richmond High School academically, socially, and athletically. Tom was amazed by their genteel manners, good clothes, congenial personalities, social self-esteem, and erudite vocabulary. One day, as a result of Mr. Gento's absence from school, the "x" students were distributed into the other freshmen homerooms, with Tom, Albert Cloots, and Tony Aramo winding up in the "s" class homeroom for the morning. Tom and his two friends looked at each other shaking their heads at the way these superior "s" students tossed around ten-dollar vocabulary words. When his "x" friends got into an argument, usually about baseball, words "bullshit," "scumbag," and "faggot" were thrown back and forth. In the "s" class, the students "refuted" the "fallacious" arguments and "flagrant" viewpoints of their "supercilious" and "impudent" opponent.

The top girl of the "s" homeroom was none other than curly-haired Bonnie Rosolio who presided over the class as homeroom secretary meticulously calling the roll of the students in her class. Returning to her seat, she smiled at Tom who happened to be sitting behind her. "Well hello there, stranger!" Tom, who was tongue-tied, nodded at the pretty freshman and returned to studying his science notes. Now frowning at him, Bonnie whispered "So what do you have to say for yourself, paper boy?" Tom blushed and shrugged his shoulders, wishing he could crawl under his desk. Becoming annoyed, she raised her voice so all could hear "Why don't you wake up and live?"

Tony Aramo tapped Tom on the shoulder, "I think she likes you, Tom."

Port Richmond High School did not turn out to be as formidable a place as it initially appeared to Tom. After all, he made the transition from a corn picking, turkey plucking farm boy to a stick ball playing, newspaper delivering city boy. He had adapted to a new working mom and a hard-drinking dad without any deep-seated scars. And he had endured the widely talked about tragedy of his father dying on the street during his last drinking binge. Consequently, Tom happily adjusted to

1950s-1960s Fable

the all engrossing high school experience. For the most part, his teachers were good at their job—inculcating the standard high school curriculum, as well as fostering the social component—getting along with one's classmates. All public schools talk about imparting democratic values, but it boils down to respecting oneself and respecting others. Of course, teenagers being teenagers, there were days when Tom and his "x" comrades fell short of the respecting others component—especially with regard to their teachers.

Freshman English was taught by a nice middle-aged woman, Mrs. Millman, who had trouble maintaining order over her impudent "x" students. The curriculum included such classic English novels as Walter Scott's *Ivanhoe* and Charles Dickens' *A Tale of Two Cities* to be read by the students and discussed in class. As to be expected, the "x" class wasn't enthralled with these traditional books because they had little to do with their present-day world. Tom actually enjoyed reading these books, but it wasn't going to prevent him from acting bored with the required reading. He would always remember the first line of *A Tale of Two Cities*: "It was the best of times, it was the worst of times, it was the age of wisdom, it was the age of foolishness."

The volatile "x" class student mix was embroiled by the addition of two new students from widely divergent backgrounds. One addition was a boy from Texas, named Ted Donnel, who soon acquired the nickname "Tex"—which he didn't particularly like. The other addition was a six-feet tall big-boned blonde girl from Sweden, named Holly Hawke, who had a high-pitched Swedish accent. Along with Tom, Albert Cloots, and Tony Aramo, these two newcomers constituted a boisterous, unruly group of students that made orderly class discussions of the English novels difficult. The problem with *Ivanhoe* was not so much the complexity of it plot, but the difficult Anglo-Saxon and Norman

(French) names which had to be pronounced during the class discussions. The students got a kick out of the meticulous way Mrs. Millman pronounced the names of the main characters: Brian de Bois Guibert, Baron Front de Boeuf, Desdichado (Ivanhoe), Aethelstane, and the Prior of Jorvaulx. They would deliberately mispronounce them in order to have Mrs. Millman correct them—causing the entire class to burst out laughing. It was apparent that Mrs. Millman's favorite character was Rebecca, who nursed the injured Ivanhoe back to health, because she became offended when Ted Donnel declared that Rebecca was a witch— casting spells on Ivanhoe. "Now Tex, it's clear you haven't read the book carefully." Annoyed, Ted would shout out to the tormented teacher that his name was not "Tex"—it was Ted. This brought on more raucous laughter on the part of the boys.

Then Holly Hawke added to the discord by declaring in her high-pitched voice, "What is all this jousting? In Sweden, they outlawed dueling a long time ago. Not like your Americans Hamilton and Burr." This non sequitur produced another outburst of shrill laughter by the entire class.

At this point, Mrs. Millman was at the end of her rope. In tears, the high-strung teacher walked over to the window, pulled up the sash, and threatened to jump. This freshman "x" English class was located on the third floor. A leap from the window would prove to be fatal for the frail woman. Nevertheless, the cruel response was a loud chorus of "Jump! Jump!" At this point, the next-door teacher stuck his head in the door and told the "x" students to "knock it off" and Mrs. Millman retreated from the window sobbing. One of the girls, an angry Leah Stith looking directly at Ted and Tom, told the boys that they ought to be ashamed of themselves. Coming to their senses, everyone quieted down, opened up their notebooks, and copied the notes that Mrs.

Millman had put on the blackboard earlier in the class. Mercifully, the bell sounded signaling the end of the class and the "x" students filed out of the room—feeling guilty over their cruel classroom antics. Turning to Tom, Tony Aramo remarked quietly, "We're in deep shit now."

The "x" class demonstrated their rebelliousness in another setting—homeroom. The week before midterms, there was an assembly in the school auditorium, in which a police officer was supposed to speak about the dangers of underage drinking. In those days, drinking was legal at age eighteen in New York and many high school students obtained fraudulent ID cards to gain access to Staten Island's many bars and saloons. Since midterm exams were fast approaching, the "x" students asked Mr. Gento if they could be excused from attending assembly in order to study. Arlene Patco, his secretary, went up to him and said "Pretty please, Mr. Gento, let the girls stay here and study. Those jerky boys are too noisy—make them go." And to everyone's surprise, the "x" class homeroom teacher did exactly that. He said the girls could stay but he told the boys to line up and head for the auditorium. But none of the boys moved. Mr. Gento gave the order for the boys to proceed to the auditorium a second time—still the "x" class boys remained seated.

Growing red-faced, Mr. Gento said, "O.K., I will inform your grade adviser, Mrs. Cowan of your insubordination." The "x" boys were called into her office by an angry Mrs. Cowan, where they knew they would be read the riot act for their recent escapades.

"We're in very deep shit now, guys!" exclaimed Tony Aramo to his comrades in arms.

The dozen "x" class boys filed into freshman grade adviser, Mrs. Cowan's tiny office. A gray-haired no-

nonsense thirty-year veteran of New York City public schools, who had moved from the classroom to the guidance office. Mrs. Cowan had a grim demeanor and Tom understood that he and his friends would pay dearly for their adolescent rebelliousness. She spoke deliberately, in a matter-of-fact manner—reciting the indictment against the "gang of twelve." Their first offense was actually a series of offenses committed against their freshmen honors English teacher, Mrs. Millman, over a period of ten days. Not only had they driven the poor woman to tears during this fortnight, but they urged the distracted woman to jump out of the window—to commit suicide.

Mrs. Cowan described their freshman honors English teacher as a "dedicated teacher with twenty-five years of experience, who has certain vulnerabilities, which you kids cruelly exploited. This is the kind of trashy behavior I wouldn't expect from honor students." Moving on, she asserted that the "x" class's refusal to attend the excellent assembly program on underage drinking, was a very serious offense—"sufficient grounds for a three-day suspension from school." Since they were merely "green-horned freshmen," she was offering them clemency—a letter would be sent home for their parents to sign, and then said letters would be placed in their permanent records. If there were no further infractions of school rules, the letter would be removed prior to their graduation from Port Richmond High School. Without further comment, the unsmiling grade advisor dismissed the "x" class boys with a command that they "do not darken my door again for the rest of the school year."

Tom sat in the kitchen while his mother read the letter from his grade adviser, Mrs. Cowan. Cara was pretending to dust the parlor and the middle room while listening to the conversation between her mom and her brother. Whenever a serious infraction was committed by her children, Claire Haley would get out the shoebox of cancelled checks from the Smiths. There were hundreds of cancelled $32 checks—covering the children's monthly board for foster care—extending over eleven years. In addition, there were miscellaneous checks for shoes, clothing, and other expenses. "Do you know how hard I worked to send those checks down to the country? To those people who pretended they were taking care of you and your sister out of the goodness of their hearts?" Claire brought up the moonlighting done at night—"typing addresses on envelopes at five cents apiece until my fingers ached." She declared that if he was a rich kid with a wealthy father, "you could afford to fool around in school, disrespect teachers, and act like a big shot—but you don't have that luxury."

Tom, reaching for straws, attempted to justify his boycott of the assembly by bringing up Mr. Gento's favoritism towards the girls and the assembly topic of underage drinking. "After Dad's heart attack from binge drinking, I didn't want to hear anything about alcohol abuse. Besides, they always start those dumb assembly programs with a Bible reading, which is offensive to non-believers."

But his mom was having none of it: "Don't give me those high-sounding arguments."

What really bothered her was Tom and his friends tormenting his honors English teacher, Mrs. Millman, to the point where she wanted to jump out the window. Tom replied that Mrs. Millman always says that whenever her classes get too noisy. "So you're joining the lynch mob bent on driving her crazy to the point of suicide? Where's your blessed are the meek, the poor, the merciful—etc? Shame on you!"

Leaning into the kitchen, Cara chimed in "I heard that the "x" class kids act like a bunch of juvenile delinquents!"

Her mom told Cara to stick to her dusting and then turned back to Tom, "Cut the crap. My job is to work and put food on the table. Your job is to go to school, do your homework, listen to your teachers, and get good grades." Tom interjected that he also works — delivering the Herald Tribune each morning, rain or shine seven days a week. "You're keeping that paper route! It's good for you and it gives you some spending money."

Sticking her head into the kitchen, Cara said, "Mom can I get a Staten Island Advocate paper route? It's an afternoon paper." Her mom replied that a paper route for a girl was out of the question — her job was to keep the house clean, while her brother was responsible for the backyard, the sidewalk, and the front hedges."

"And taking out the garbage," the boy added. After their little discussion, Claire sent Tom outside to rake the leaves, cut the hedges, and of course take out the garbage

---

June 25, 1962

The U.S. Supreme Court in Engel v. Vitale ruled that prayers, Bible readings, and religious observances in public schools violate the First Amendment of the United States Constitution. The case was brought by parents of public school students in New Hyde Park, New York who complained that prayers to "Almighty God" contradicted their religious beliefs. The case was also supported by Jewish organizations, Ethical Culture groups, and well-known atheist Madalyn Murray O'Hair. The plaintiffs said that opting to have their children excused from the prayers and Bible readings would affect the kids' relationship with their teachers and friends. The New York State Board of Regents had implemented the following prayer to reverse the moral decline of public school students: "Almighty God, we acknowledge our dependence upon Thee and beg Thy blessings upon us, our parents, our teachers, and our country."

The Supreme Court ruled 7 to 1 that it was unconstitutional for a government agency, such as a public school, to require students to recite a prayer or listen to a Bible reading. Justice Hugo Black stated that school prayers violate the "Establishment Clause" of the First Amendment, which stipulates that "Congress shall make no laws respecting the establishment of religion." In siding with the majority, Justice Black declared that government written prayers (no matter how vaguely written so as not to promote any particular religion) still promote a family of religion – recognizing "Almighty God." The New York State Regents prayer represents exactly the type of relationship that early American colonists and our forefathers sought to avoid. This prayer constitutes "a practice wholly inconsistent with the Establishment Clause of the First Amendment." The fact that this Regents prayer was denominationally neutral and voluntary for students, does not distance it from the constitutional proscription of creating an official religion.

In conclusion, Justice Black asserted that it was not anti-religious to say that government "should stay out of writing or sanctioning official prayers and leave that purely religious function to the people themselves." The separation of church and state was fundamental to the formation of the American nation from its earliest days.

Reaction to the Engel v. Vitale ruling forbidding public school prayers was widely unpopular in many locales and states in the years following this 1962 U.S. Supreme Court decision. Subsequent Supreme Court decisions under the "Free Exercise Clause" of the First Amendment have permitted students to pray in public schools as long as such prayers are not officially sponsored by the school and they do not disrupt others from doing their work.

Nevertheless, the unpopularity of any particular U.S. Supreme Court decision does not negate its validity with regard to individual rights guaranteed by the U.S. Constitution.

CHAPTER 28

A Serious Student

After the incidents with his biased homeroom teacher, Mr. Gento, and his troubled freshman English teacher, Mrs. Millman, Tom settled down — earning honor roll grades for his four-year term at Port Richmond High School. His favorite subjects were science, history, and English — though he did quite well in mathematics and fairly well in Latin. Tom did not care for his ninth-year algebra teacher, Mr. Charming, who was anything but charming. He did like his tenth-year geometry, Mr. Gerry, whose patience and kindness was not appreciated by some of his "x" classmates. Ted (Tex) Donnel and Albert Cloots would bring pink paper elephants and tape them to the blackboard. The pink elephants were supposed to represent Mr. Gerry's alcoholism, but Tom never discerned, by his manner or his breath, that his geometry teacher was a drinker — other than Mr. Gerry saying his students were "driving him to drink." Tom didn't appreciate the pink elephant stuff in Mr. Gerry's class, and told his rambunctious classmates to knock it off. In addition to patience, Mr. Gerry had the ability to explain mathematical concepts in a clear, step-by-step manner. Most importantly, Mr. Gerry never characterized a student's question as dumb.

On the other hand, Mr. Charming seemed to know when Tom was having difficulty with a topic — sending him to the board to stumble over a difficult problem.

Tom was adept at simplifying algebraic expressions, handling exponents, and solving algebraic equations, but couldn't quite grasp algebraic word problems. Basically, he could not translate verbal statements into the corresponding algebraic equation in order to solve the word problem. Tom happened to sit directly across from Leah Stith in Mr. Charming's algebra class. The willowy Leah was even more befuddled by algebra than Tom. When either freshman made a mistake in his class, Mr. Charming would link the two classmates together, calling them by the same name—"Leah-Todd"— pronounced to sound like the dancing garment "leotard." Ill at ease in the mean-spirited algebra teacher's class, Tom felt like he wanted to crawl under his desk.

One day in his junior year, Tom suddenly "got word problems." Almost overnight, he developed the ability to solve algebraic word problems of almost any variety— percent problems, number problems, geometric problems, coin problems, motion problems, and mixture problems. As the years rolled by, Tom would have Mr. Charming for intermediate algebra, advanced algebra, and solid geometry—attaining high grades in these subjects. But he never felt fond of, or comfortable with the fast-talking, acid-toned math teacher. Even his vaunted sense of humor did not amuse the ex-farm boy because of its cruel nature.

Once, Mr. Charming told a five-minute joke about Fluffy, the moth, who gained fame and fortune by resisting the temptation to chew on woolen clothes. The sarcastic teacher went on and on, describing the ups and downs of this celebrity moth. After achieving some notoriety, Fluffy went through a period of adjustment to his new-found fame and was discovered crying in a corner at a party. Mr. Charming's punch line was a real let down—"Did you ever see a moth ball?"

Occasionally, Tom and his mother had rarified philosophic discussions on fundamental concepts like truth and morality. As a Marxist, Claire Haley did not believe in objective truth and universal morality. She declared that each economic class has its own truth and its own morality. "A factory worker doesn't look at the world in the same way as the capitalist factory owner." Tom disagreed, taking Plato's view that ideas were real, perfect, and eternal—unlike material objects which were unreal, imperfect, and transient.

Cara, looking at her brother like he was crazy, disagreed, "So, this table and these chairs are not real?" Tom replied that his sister always took her mom's side in their arguments. Tom was a proponent of Immanuel Kant's concept of universal morality—the categorical imperative—a basic principle of right and wrong valid for all people, in all cultures, and for all times. He also disagreed with his mother's view that the Soviet Union provided a better life for its workers, as compared to American workers who were subject to the ups and downs of the capitalist economic cycle. However, when Tom spoke up in his history class, he brought some of his mother's Marxist ideas with him—surprising both his teacher and his classmates.

Over the course of his high school career, Tom had the good fortune to have Miss Forte as his honors "x" history teacher. Young, attractive, knowledgeable, and idealistic in her belief in America's elevated standing in the world, Miss Forte was a harsh critic of the Soviet Union, Red China, and the Eastern European nations under Russian control. She called Russian Premier Khrushchev a warmonger for threatening to bury America with nuclear weapons. She had a dim view of Cuban dictator Fidel Castro because of his suppression of all political opposition, destruction of the Cuban middle class, and his desire to export revolution throughout Latin America.

Their often-heated political arguments amused the "x" class students because it diverted them from the often-boring history curriculum. Occasionally, the Tom Haley-Miss Forte disagreements became so intense that Miss Forte would call the boy a "Red" and he would respond with the epithet "Fascist" — resulting in a trip to his grade advisor, Mrs. Cowan. Tom's reputation as a left-wing rebel, so disturbed Port Richmond's history department that he was interviewed by the department chairman, who grilled him on his political views. "Where do you get your ideas from, Tom?" The boy shrugged his shoulders, "It's just my mom. She never got over the Great Depression."

Tom was occasionally late to his Latin class because it was preceded by lunch recess, during which he participated in quick basketball games with his classmates. Sometimes, a varsity player would tear himself away from his girlfriend to join the pickup game — adding a competitive edge that took the fun out of the game. To his surprise, Tom held his own with these high school stars — after overcoming an initial nervousness. Years of street stickball, sandlot baseball, and schoolyard basketball, plus his early morning paper route — gave the ex-farm boy the strength, endurance, and skills to compete with these gifted athletes pretty much on even terms. Rushing through the narrow hallways to arrive in Miss Galic's Latin class on time — Tom rounded a corner and bumped into the tall, big-boned Holly Hawke, who knocked him to the floor. Laughing at the sprawled teenaged boy, she lifted him to his feet and brushed off his clothes. "So sorry. Did I hurt you, Tex?" Picking up his loose leaf and textbooks, Tom replied, "I'm fine. My name is Tom — not Tex." Scrutinizing the shaken "x" student, Holly said, "Vell, you Americans all look the same — skinny with black hair and brown eyes. Ha! Ha!"

CHAPTER 29

Latin and Science

When Tom was at P.S. 20, his mom had asked Mr. D, his science teacher, what language should her son take in high school. He recommended Latin because many scientific terms have Latin roots and Latin looks good on high school transcripts. Following Mr. D's advice, Tom took four years of Latin in high school. Miss Gallic, a short, wiry, good-natured woman, had been teaching Latin so long that many Port Richmond students claimed that she had taught their parents Latin in the 1940s. The Latin curriculum included the history of the Roman Empire, which at its apex included a big chunk of Western Europe—Italy, Greece, Portugal, Spain, France, and England—as well as sections of North Africa (Carthage). That part of Europe not under the control of Rome's legions—Germany, Switzerland, Holland, and the Scandinavian countries—were ruled by roving bands of barbarians.

The only time the congenial Latin teacher lost her temper was when a fight broke out between senior drama star Roy Rand and sophomore Tony Aramo over Bonnie Rosolio's flirting with the "x" classmate. Apparently, she had been joking with Tony about her wearing a Roman toga, when Roy interjected a comment about her "sweater girl" anatomy—to which Tony objected. The bigger, stronger senior was whacking Tony when Tom tried to get in the middle as a peace-maker—receiving a bloody nose for his efforts.

Todd M. Daley

Then, Miss Galic, wielding her yardstick, cracked it over Roy's noggin—bringing an abrupt end to the fisticuffs. Bonnie's endearing look of sympathy made it all worthwhile to the Herald Tribune paper boy.

Never a gifted language student, Tom found Latin grammar to be daunting with its six cases of nouns—nominative, genitive, dative, accusative, ablative, and vocative; its six tenses of verbs—present, perfect, imperfect, pluperfect, future, and future perfect; and its two voices—active and passive. In addition, the normal word order in English: subject—verb—object, was often reversed in Latin: object—verb—subject. For example, "Omnia vincit amore" is commonly used instead of "Amore vincit omnia" which means—love conquers all. Yet Latin had great benefits for Tom especially in chemistry, where the names and symbols of the elements have Latin roots. Consequently, Tom mastered the chemical symbols of key elements quickly: copper (cuprum)—Cu, gold (aurum)—Au, silver (argentum)—Ag, iron (ferrum)—Fe, lead (plumbum)—Pb, and tin (stannum)—Sn.

Despite his difficulty with Latin grammar and the tedious word-by-word translations, Tom liked ancient Roman history described by the likes of Julius Caesar, Marcus Cicero, and the Roman poet Virgil. Julius Caesar, the great general, had solidified Roman control over Italy and conquered Spain, France, and England, plus parts of North Africa. Caesar's commentaries described the triumphs and set-backs in his European conquests, as well as his crossing of the Rubicon River to seize control of the Roman government from rival military general Pompey. Julius Caesar succinctly described each of his conquests with three words: "Veni vidi vinci"—I came, I saw, I conquered. His military strategy, still used today, was: "Divide et impera"—divide and conquer. And Tom could never forget Julius Caesar's assassination by his unworthy friend, Marcus Brutus: "Et tu, Brute?"

1950s-1960s Fable

From his struggles with the long, twisted sentences of Roman orator, Marcus Cicero, Tom remembered his warnings about Rome's arch enemy—Carthage: "Carthago delenda est"—Carthage must be destroyed. Always the optimist, Cicero's motto was "Dum spiro, spero"—While I breathe, I hope. From the epic Roman poet Virgil, Tom recalled: "Arma virumque cano"—Of arms and of a man I sing. In terms of geography, Tom carried away the concept: "Omnia Gallia in tres partes divisa est"—All Gaul (France) is divided into three parts—courtesy of Julius Caesar.

Tom was also impressed with the Roman Stoics like Seneca and Epictetus, who stressed love and virtue, and living a life of sacrifice, simplicity, austerity, and reason. Epictetus believed that no evil could befall the virtuous person. "I must die. But must I die groaning? I must be imprisoned. But must I whine as well?" The Roman Republic was a pioneer in elected government and Roman jurisprudence provided the foundation for western legal systems. Consequently, Tom felt the western world was indebted to ancient Rome for its language, its literature, its laws, its government, and its ethical philosophy.

Despite his fondness for political issues and historical events, Tom's favorite subject was science—specifically chemistry and physics, which were taught by Mr. Riner, an earnest devotee of science and the scientific method. There was a certitude in science that was lacking in history, where the interpretation of historical events depended on one's economic class, political affiliation, religion, and nationality. Fundamental to science is the concept of causality, in which each physical event can be traced to a specific cause—excepting the randomness which exists in human events and in games of chance like tossing dice.

Mr. Riner stressed the scientific method — the process of hypothesis formation, conducting an experiment, and either rejecting the hypothesis or verifying it as a scientific law. Mr. Riner talked about the four big laws in science: Newton's Law of Gravity, Darwin's Theory of Evolution, Mendeleev's Periodic Law of Elements, and Einstein's Theory of Relativity.

Though history was fascinating to Tom, he realized that historical events were largely determined by human beings and economic forces — and not by deterministic, cause-and-effect laws — as in science. His mom held the Marxist view that history evolved according to a dialectical process in which antagonistic classes, such as peasants vs. landowners and proletariat vs. capitalist, struggled until a new socio-economic equilibrium is established. Marx's dialectical materialism was an optimistic philosophy predicting an ideal, classless society in which each person would be free to benefit from the fruits of his own labor. Although idealistic, Tom did not share his mother's optimism with regard to a future utopian world.

In chemistry, Tom had the advantage of knowing the Latin names of key elements — from which the chemical symbols originated. Mr. Riner had a large chart of Mendeleev's period table of the elements at the front of his room. The arrangement of the hundred known elements on this table fascinated the teenager. A key feature of this table was that each column represented a family of elements with similar chemical and physical properties. Invented by the Russian scientist, Dimitri Mendeleev in the 19th century, the periodic table arranged elements according to increasing atomic weights. Mendeleev postulated that the properties of the elements could be predicted by their location on the table.

1950s-1960s Fable

He even predicted the properties of yet undiscovered elements.

The chemical and physical properties of various elements were demonstrated by Mr. Riner through compelling classroom experiments.

Tom was astonished by the Group IA alkali metals, like sodium and potassium—so different from the typical metals like iron, copper, and aluminum which were shiny, malleable, hard, and strong. Mr. Riner demonstrated the peculiar properties of alkali metals by cutting a small piece of sodium (which had the consistency of clay) and putting it into a beaker of water—resulting in the sodium bursting into flame. The gifted science teacher also showed his class some mercury, the only metal which is liquid at room temperature. He then demonstrated its high density by floating a piece of iron on the liquid mercury to the amazement of his students.

In following the scientific method, Mr. Riner didn't simply state a scientific law as a fact to be recorded by his students in their notebooks. Whenever possible, he conducted experiments in class to illustrate the scientific principle. In addition, Mr. Riner made science come to life through colorful anecdotes, such as Galileo's dropping two rocks from the leaning Tower of Pisa to prove that all objects fall at the same rate of speed due to gravity. He also told the story of Newton sitting under an apple tree, watching it fall to the ground, observing the moon orbiting the earth each month, and postulating the law of gravity. Mr. Riner illustrated the constant rate of free fall under gravity with the feather and penny experiment. A feather and a penny fell at the same rate of speed in a long glass cylinder—once the air was pumped out of the cylinder.

Mr. Riner also demonstrated resonance in which certain objects responded to particular sounds or frequencies.

In the field of nuclear energy, Mr. Riner demonstrated the chain reaction concept by arranging a row of matches and lighting the end match—resulting in an accelerated sequence of burning matches

This experiment reminded Tom of the match head tin can rockets developed in his cellar with his friend Gary Lukovski, who nodded to him during Mr. Riner's experiment. Tom was fascinated by the Heisenberg Uncertainty Principle which stated that there was a limit to the precision with which scientists can measure subatomic particles.

In fact, Mr. Riner indicated that knowledge of subatomic particles like electrons, protons, and neutrons under the quantum theory was a matter of probability, and not certainty as with the mechanics of large bodies. Tom was also captivated by Einstein's famous equation: $E = mc^2$ which Mr. Riner identified as the source of energy in nuclear reactions. A tiny amount of matter can be converted into a tremendous amount of energy because the speed of light, c, is a huge number. Mr. Riner talked about the awesome destructive power of nuclear weapons, which threaten the survival of civilization. He said that the hydrogen bombs developed by the U.S. and Russia are thousands of times more powerful than the first atomic bomb dropped on Hiroshima, which destroyed that Japanese city of a half-million during the second world war

1950s-1960s Fable

CHAPTER 30

John Kennedy at the Ferry

The year 1960 ushered in a new decade—bringing with it a sense of optimism and hope about America's future. Senator John Kennedy and Vice President Richard Nixon were locked in a tight presidential race—capturing the attention of young people throughout the land. Senator Kennedy represented youth, idealism, and the change of the 1960s, while Vice President Nixon represented experience, pragmatism, and the status quo of the 1950s. Growing up under his mother's Marxist influence, Tom naturally favored the Massachusetts senator and he was surprised at the extent of the support for the prosaic Vice President by his classmates and neighbors. In contrast to the witty, articulate, Harvard-educated John Kennedy, the somber, conservative Richard Nixon had the shifty-eyed demeanor of a used-car salesman. Whenever the demagogic Vice President began an anecdote with "Let me make one thing perfectly clear," Tom knew that a half-truth or untruth was surely to follow.

On the other hand, Senator Kennedy spoke about "getting the country moving again" economically, scientifically, educationally, domestically, and internationally—advancing the cause of freedom at home and abroad. John Kennedy was the first presidential candidate to speak in behalf of civil rights for black people—a moral issue that had been neglected by the Eisenhower Administration. Like many of his cohorts, Tom identified with the youthful senator from Massachusetts, who brought the magic of Camelot to the often-sordid world of politics. Talking to his classmates Gary Lukovski and Tony Aramo, Tom convinced them to go with him and see John Kennedy at the Staten Island Ferry, where he was making a campaign speech. Cara joined her brother and his friends, carrying a brightly-colored poster which said:

"Port Richmond students say
Hip Hip Hurray for JFK"

Arriving at the ferry terminal from the Richmond Terrace #1 bus—the most direct route from Elm Park—the foursome disembarked to find a big crowd buzzing in excitement and anticipation for the youthful Democratic candidate for President. Pushing and squeezing through the edge of the crowd by a concrete wall, the youngsters managed to get within twenty feet of the podium, where local Democratic candidates for city council and state assembly were speaking. Fortunately, these boring speeches lasted only a half-hour before the handsome Massachusetts senator took the stage, accompanied by a loud burst of whistles, yells, and applause. Looking tanned, fit, and dazzling, John Kennedy gave his usual stump speech—talking about getting America moving again at home and abroad to advance freedom. He also asked the youth of America to devote their energy, passion, and ideals to make their country, and the world at large, free, prosperous, and peaceful. Senator Kennedy ended his speech by urging everyone to work for the Democratic Party and vote for its candidates on election day.

While he was speaking, Cara had pushed herself so she

1950s-1960s Fable

was right before the platform—waving her poster beneath the youthful presidential candidate. At the end of his speech, the Senator reached down and shook Cara's hand, "That's a delightful poster, my young friend." A newspaper photographer snapped the picture of Cara's fleeting fame, which appeared in the following day's edition of the Staten Island Advocate. The newspaper photograph of the Kennedy-Cara handshake would remain posted on the refrigerator door for many years—an existential moment in the dreamy-eyed artist's life frozen in time forever.

For those years at Port Richmond High School, Tom continued to earn honor roll grades—attaining an academic average that ranged between 95% and 98% in his junior and senior years. His grade adviser, Mrs. Cowan advised him to shoot for membership in the Arista Society, a national honor society for high school students. With his grades reaching the high nineties stratosphere, the newspaper boy thought his election to Arista would be an open-and-shut case. To his dismay, the Elm Park stick ball player was voted down by his honor society peers—many of whom were only 85% merit roll students—well below his near perfect honor roll grades. The reason for Tom's rejection was that he fell short in the area of service credits. He belonged to no clubs, no teams, and had never worked for a teacher during his study period—opting to use that time precisely what it was meant for—to study and do homework.

Furious at the Arista's voting him down, Tom wasn't interested in placating those high school celebrities. "Those Westerleigh faggots can go f_themselves!" he told his friends, Tony Aramo and Gary Lukovski. But his history teacher, Miss Forte, saw the hurt beneath the working-class, street kid's bravado. She asserted that Arista membership would help him win scholarship money and gain acceptance to the best colleges.

The history teacher recommended that the newspaper boy join the UN Club, for which she was the adviser. In addition, she arranged for Tom to work as secretary for the History Department, where that department chairman continually reminded Miss Forte that "history teachers were a-dime-a-dozen." The UN Club consisted of junior and senior honor students who were politically-minded with a keen interest in current events. Along with Tom, Tony Aramo and Gary Lukovski joined the club—transforming it from a sedate discussion club to a raucous group divided into two divergent camps—the conservative majority and the liberal minority—consisting of Tom and his two friends, Tony and Gary. The latter two took Tom's side, not out of any deep-seated convictions—though both were the sons of blue-collar union members—but out of the inclination to stir the pot. A major topic of discussion was Fidel Castro's Cuba—in regard to the Cuban Missile Crisis, in which the Russians attempted to install nuclear-tipped missiles on the Caribbean island nation. Initially, Tom looked upon the bearded Cuban leader as an independent-minded maverick, who refused to bend to American pressure. However, when the Herald Tribune carrier learned about Castro's connivance in bringing Russian personnel, military equipment, and nuclear missiles to his island country—just ninety miles from America—he called the Cuban dictator a "loose cannon who's a menace to world peace."

His Marxist mother, a Castro sympathizer, was dismayed over her son's remarks, but she was equally upset over Castro's Cold War saber rattling. Nevertheless, President Kennedy's nuclear brinkmanship genuinely frightened Tom and his classmates, who went to bed that fateful October doubting they would wake up to the same civilized world, or even wake up at all. Fortunately, Kennedy's naval blockade of Cuba succeeded, as Russian Premier

1950s-1960s Fable

Khrushchev wisely ordered the Russian missile-bearing freighters to turn back—avoiding a nuclear war. Tom had once read in the Herald Tribune that the U.S. had many giant B-52 bombers loaded with nuclear bombs ready to fly over the Artic Circle to the Soviet Union at a moment's notice. During the Cuban Missile Crisis, these B-52 bombers, on heightened readiness status, were continually air-borne—awaiting the presidential order to head towards pre-determined Russian targets. During the early Cold War days of the 1950s, flocks of geese over Northern Canada looked like Russian bombers on American radar screens—occasionally triggering alarms which dispatched nuclear-armed B-52s to fly towards Russia. Fortunately, the American bombers were called back when the blips on the radar screen were correctly identified as feathered, rather than metallic flying objects. From his newspaper reading, Tom was aware of this nuclear hair-trigger scenario and questioned the sanity of world leaders who have permitted this existential threat to mankind's survival to continue. With so many nuclear-armed bombers and nuclear-tipped missiles ready to be launched at a moment's notice, it was a divine miracle that nuclear war had not been unleashed upon the world.

Once the Cuban Missile Crisis receded from the headlines, a new hotspot came into focus for Port Richmond's UN Club—Indo China. After the French were driven from North Vietnam, the Americans took over the role of defending the pro-Western South Vietnamese government from the Communist insurgents—the Viet Cong. President Kennedy had sent military advisers to the beleaguered southeast Asian country, but Tom's mother felt that JFK was too smart to have America drawn into a ground war in Red China's backyard. Tom made a similar assertion at the UN Club, but Miss Forte said the U.S. would never allow South Vietnam to go Communist—under the falling-domino theory. "If Vietnam falls to the Communists, then Laos, Cambodia, Burma, and Thailand would inevitably fall to the Communists," she declared grimly.

Tom replied that President Kennedy had asserted it was "the South Vietnamese's war to win or lose" and we should stay out of their civil war.

"I agree," Tony Aramo chimed in, "make love, not war!" Attempting to soothe the UN club members ruffled feathers,

Gary Lukovski intoned, "It is better to remain silent and be thought a fool, than to speak up and remove all doubt."

Responding to his friend, Tony Aramo sang, "But why do fools fall in love?"

Her forbearance worn thin, Miss Forte ended the UN Club meeting: "It's time to adjourn folks. Good afternoon!"

1950s-1960s Fable

CHAPTER 31

An Offer by the Coach

Gym classes were conducted in a no-nonsense way by the Port Richmond High School physical education department, where all students—boys and girls—were required to participate in separate gymnasiums. Everyone had to line up at their designated spots for attendance and then ten-minutes of warm-up exercises followed. A half-hour free-play period ensued in which students participated in various activities—weight lifting, rope climbing, chaining bar, ping-pong, and basketball. In gym, Tom played basketball with varsity athletes—holding his own and grabbing the attention of basketball coach Lou Trenna, a short, gruff, bespectacled man who reportedly loved height more than talent.

One morning before school, Tom was sitting in the auditorium with his "x" classmates Tony Aramo, Gary Lukovski, and Albert Cloots—studying his chemistry notes. Suddenly the grizzled countenance of Lou Trenna hovered above the "x" class juniors. A blunt, plain-spoken man, Coach Trenna came to the point, "I saw you scrimmaging in gym yesterday. Why don't you come out for the team next year?" The tall, skinny honor student was speechless for a few seconds. He thought about his mom's reaction, his Herald Tribune newspaper, his homework, and the long hours he'd have to devote to basketball practice. He also realized that as a Johnny-come-lately, he would be sitting on the bench while the team veterans started—as it should be.

Tom thanked the coach for his offer but indicated his first priority was to maintain his honor roll grades. Tom had always preferred street stickball, sandlot baseball, touch football and school yard basketball to organized sports — baseball leagues and high school teams — because the pressure to perform during a clutch moment took the fun out of playing the game. He remembered a summer league baseball game when he misplayed a fly ball in the ninth inning — losing the game for his Elm Park team. A mistake in a pickup game was soon forgotten. If he missed a key basket, dropped a fly ball, or struck out in a sandlot game, he didn't have to hear about it for weeks over and over again. Winning vs. losing was not the critical thing for Tom. Playing the game fairly and energetically for the intrinsic joy of sports — was what mattered to the newspaper boy. In any case, his friends Tony, Gary, and Albert were astonished by Tom's calm rejection of Coach Trenna's invitation.

The repercussion of Tom's unusual refusal reinforced his maverick reputation at Port Richmond High School as an oddball — arguing endlessly with his history teachers, refusing to join varsity teams, and not attending school dances. The ex-farm boy, the offspring of an alcoholic father and Marxist mother, raised by hard-working foster parents on a farm in his early years — was not your typical American teenager. He had a strong work ethic, indicated by his stellar scholastic grades and his perseverance as a newspaper boy — getting up at six AM in the morning to deliver theNew York Herald Tribune seven days a week.

Staten Island had an insular conservatism with respect to the rest of New York City. It was least "hip" of the city's five boroughs in terms of street crime, drug use, and gangs.

1950s-1960s Fable

But during the 1960's, there were social and political changes in America at large, which began to seep into the life of Port Richmond High School students. The incipient civil rights movement, which inspired many young people of that era, had its unintended effects on student interactions across racial barriers.

There had been a confrontation at lunch recess between some "s" class students and black students during a pickup basketball game. Tom did not witness it, because he had a different lunch period. Apparently, Tom Spider, one of Tom's P.S. 20 classmates, had been flagrantly fouled driving in for a lay-up by David Stanhoff, an "s" class scholar and varsity basketball player. Usually, such dustups are quickly forgotten and school life resumes with no repercussions. But this time, the hard feelings persisted—escalating into an ethnic turf-war between Westerleigh honors students and mostly black students from the Avenue B section of Port Richmond.

Each morning and afternoon, there were incidents in which some "s" class students were jumped by a motley crew of rough necks, led by Tommy Spider and his cohorts. These ambushes became so frequent that the high school Dean of Boys Mr. Young began escorting some of the "s" class boys from the school bus to the school gate and vice versa—to their everlasting humiliation. Tom knew people from both warring groups and wondered if he and his "x" class friends would be drawn into the skirmishes. As a high-achieving honor student, Tom didn't relish the negative attention his high grades drew from the less scholastically oriented blue-collar students in the school.

Having played with Tommy Spider back in elementary school, Tom was fairly confident that he would not be singled out by the Avenue B kids.

He recalled that at P.S. 20, Tommy had the nickname "Big Boy" because of certain anatomical features that the youngster bragged about. Mr. Spider was an interesting character. A beneficent providence had also endowed the newspaper boy generously—but that was classified information. In any case, the ex-farm boy was an accepted person on Avenue B. Indeed, Tommy and his buddies had often seen him delivering newspapers in their neighborhood over the years.

Perhaps these underprivileged kids sensed that the Herald Tribune paper boy was from the same working-class background. Apparently, the ex-farm boy had earned a grudging respect from these tough Avenue B street kids.

In fact, Tom bumped into Tommy Spider on Avenue B one Sunday morning delivering his voluminous Sunday edition of the Herald Tribune. Straining under the weight of the heavy newspaper-filled canvass knapsack, he stopped his bike when Tommy Spider waved him over to his rickety front stoop. The young street tough smiled at the newspaper carrier. "I see you every morning lugging those dumb papers around. How much do you make?" Tom responded that he earned roughly $10 a week with tips, but he did better on Christmas. Big Boy chuckled, "Shit! That's chump change." Changing the subject, the black teenager indicated that his buddies "had made peace with those Westerleigh punks. I walked past Dave Stanhoff in the hall the other day and he almost shit in his pants—he was so scared! That was enough payoff for me. So I told him things are cool now." Tom replied that he was happy to hear that a truce had been called.

Beneath his street-kid bluster, Tommy Spider wasn't a bad guy, but he had his tough guy reputation to protect. He reminded Tom of those P.S. 20 basketball intramurals

1950s-1960s Fable

so long ago, when those "IGC faggots" beat his 8-1 team, which the black teenager labeled as "pure dumb luck, aided by that long-legged bitch, Leah Stith, who I couldn't take my eyes off of, and the referee Mr. D, who favored you guys." Tommy asked the newspaper boy if he had ever "messed around" with Leah and his scarlet blush told the street-wise teenager that such illicit activity was out of the question for the "x" class honor student.

As Tom peddled away, Big Boy asked him when he was getting a new bike. Tom replied, "If it ain't broke, don't fix it!" The necessity of defending oneself on the streets and playgrounds of Staten Island's North Shore motivated the skinny newspaper boy to build himself physically. With his paper-route money, Tom sent away for a Joe Welder body-building course. Within a few weeks a heavy box came in the mail, which included two ten-pound dumbbells, plus a booklet full of instructions on exercises for a particular part of the body. Every month, Tom received a new booklet that depicted exercises designed to work a different set of muscles — arms, shoulders, chest, legs, stomach, etc. Applying the same diligence that he marshaled for his academic pursuits, Tom devoted thirty minutes everyday to weight-lifting exercises and calisthenics, which included pushups, sit-ups, and knee-bends. Tom recruited his old Elm Park buddy, Mike Palermo, now a varsity baseball pitcher for McKee High School — to join him in his exercise program on weekends.

The two teenagers had bought a fifty-pound barbell from Perry's junk yard — utilizing it in their weight-lifting sessions. When their strength increased to the point where the fifty-pound barbell wasn't sufficiently challenging, they altered the barbell. The two youngsters bought some cement and mixed it with sand and water. Using American ingenuity, they found two large tomato sauce cans, filled them with cement, and attached the cans to each end of the barbell — creating a seventy-five-pound barbell, which brought them to a higher level of strength. Each boy noticed the effects of increased strength on their athletic performance — greater batting power, increased throwing strength, and even better jumping ability. Bigger muscles increased their body weight also — a physical change that the wiry ex-farm boy particularly appreciated.

The added muscle mass gave Tom the appearance of a sturdy street kid, but the appellation "tough customer" could hardly be applied to the Herald Tribune carrier. While working for the History Department, Tom occasionally had to deliver messages to Mr. Young's Office of the Dean. Mr. Young remarked that the "x" honor roll student had never been sent to his office for cutting class, wandering the halls, or fighting in the lunchroom.

"Oh, that brainiac is a goody two-shoes," observed a gum-chewing, tight-skirted coed, who was "serving time" in the Dean's Office for some minor infraction.

Nodding at the provocative teenaged girl, the gruff Mr. Young turned to the honor student, "My job would be a lot easier if there were more students like this young man and fewer cut-ups like you, Missy."

Snapping her gum, the young lady replied, "Mr. Young, you'd be out of a job if everyone was like Mr. Honor Roll!"

The Port Richmond High School students' cafeteria was ruled by a no-nonsense, baritone-voiced history teacher named Mr. McMahon, a crew-cut Korean War veteran who knew how to handle himself. Mr. McMahon insisted on a certain set of rules for the lunchroom: Boys and girls were segregated in separate sections, no one could break into serving lines, all tables had to be cleared

of trays, dishes, utensils, food wrappers, and milk cartons. Smoking was not permitted in the boys' and girls' bathrooms, which were adjacent to the cavernous cafeteria. Mr. McMahon would barge into the boys' room—ousting those students brazen enough to be puffing on cigarettes, which the army veteran would confiscate. A woman teacher performed the same unenviable task for any girls caught smoking in their sanctum. Despite his sternness, Mr. McMahon was a congenial teacher who talked about his war experiences and joked with students in the cafeteria and in the recess

schoolyard. He was aware of Tom's unorthodox political views and often debated with the "x" class honor roll student in the lunchroom. Mr. McMahon was a Cold War warrior and a hawk with regard to the brewing war in Indo-China.

Since boys will always be boys, fights occasionally broke out in the crowded student lunchroom. To yells of "Rumble!" Mr. McMahon would quickly spring into action, breaking up fights by cleverly flipping combatants in opposite directions—sending the offending boys sprawling onto the floor. Occasionally, a muscular teenager would challenge Mr. McMahon to an arm-wrestling contest—which the latter inevitably won with a sudden powerful movement of his right arm. Food fights were the one student indulgence not tolerated by the Korean War veteran. One day "x" class student Bruce Hatten was observed by Mr. McMahon starting a cafeteria food fight by tossing a milk carton at a fellow student. The thrown milk carton triggered a whirlwind of flying milk cartons and food containers that filled the air like a raging snow storm. Without hesitation, Mr. McMahon walked over to the culprit and slapped Bruce in the face so hard that his hand left a red imprint on his cheek for several minutes. Of course, this was the era before parental lawsuits as a result of teacher corporal punishment of offending students.

In fact, it is likely that if Bruce Hatten had told his parents about the cafeteria incident, he would have received a slap on the other cheek for starting the food fight.

May 7, 1954

French troops surrendered at Dien Bien Phu to the Vietminh, North Vietnamese forces, led by Ho Chi Minh. Leader of the fifty-year struggle for Vietnam's independence from the French, Ho Chi Minh was a Communist backed by Red China. The 1954 Geneva Accords resulted in a cease-fire between the French and the Vietminh, and the splitting of Vietnam into two countries – divided at the 17th parallel.

A second Geneva agreement called for free elections to be held throughout Vietnam to unify the country under a single government. Both the United States and the South Vietnamese government, under Ngo Dinh Diem, refused to follow the Geneva Accords – fearing that the popular Ho Chi Minh would be elected president of all of Vietnam.

The U.S. involvement in Vietnam began with President Dwight Eisenhower, who was motivated by the Cold War "Domino Theory." During the 1950s and 1960s, the American government believed that if Vietnam became Communist-ruled, then the other countries of South East Asia – Laos, Cambodia, Thailand, and Burma – would inevitably become Communist like a row of falling dominoes. President Eisenhower sent approximately 1,000 American military advisers to South Vietnam, which were increased to 11,000 by President John Kennedy in 1963. These military personnel were mostly U.S. Special Forces (Green Berets), who trained the South Vietnamese to fight the Viet Cong – Communist-trained guerrilla fighters operating in the South.

1950s-1960s Fable

However, President Kennedy realized that it was South Vietnam's war to win or lose, and America's role should be limited to providing equipment and advisers to the beleaguered third-world country. After President Kennedy's assassination in November 1963, President Lyndon Johnson began to escalate the war — sending thousands of American combat troops to Vietnam. By 1965 there were 170,000 American troops, by 1966 there were 320,000 American troops, and by 1967 there were a total of 464,000 American troops in South Vietnam. The U.S. relied on search and destroy missions, along with jet bombers, missiles, helicopters, napalm (incendiary), and chemical defoliants to clear the Vietnamese jungles and flush out the Viet Cong guerrilla fighters. But the Viet Cong was a resourceful enemy who employed hit-and-run tactics, knew the terrain, used underground tunnels, and gained the support of the Vietnamese peasants.

When North Vietnam started sending regular North Vietnamese Army troops to back up the Viet Cong, President Johnson and his successor, President Richard Nixon, resorted to extensive bombing campaigns against the North. Between March 1965 and November 1968, the U.S. dropped one million tons of rockets, missiles, and bombs on North Vietnam. President Nixon expanded the bombing campaign to Laos and Cambodia — pounding the Ho Chi Minh Trail, an 800-mile network of foot paths and dirt roads, though which men and material were sent from the North to the South. In January 1968 during the Tet Offensive, North Vietnamese forces launched major attacks throughout South Vietnam — including American military bases and runways. The American base at Tan Son Nhut, where General William Westmoreland resided, along with the South Vietnamese presidential palace in Saigon, were also attacked by the North Vietnamese troops and their Viet Cong allies.

The growing opposition to the war by the American people, already widespread among college students, became so great that President Johnson put an end to escalation and opted not to run again for the presidency in 1968. His successor, President Nixon talked about Vietnamization — having the South Vietnamese take over the fighting.

By the late 1960's, the war had become a bloody stalemate and peace talks between the North Vietnamese and the U.S. had commenced in Paris. In January 1973, a peace treaty was signed — calling for the withdrawal of all American troops from Vietnam and an exchange of POWs. Within two years, the South Vietnamese Army suffered a series of defeats and disorderly retreats — culminating in a North Vietnamese victory over all of Vietnam. The 17-year long Vietnam War resulted in 58,282 American battle deaths and approximately 100 American POWs dying in captivity. Another outcome of the Vietnam War was the realization by the American people that overwhelming military might does not guarantee victory in impoverished third-world countries.

CHAPTER 32

The Scholarship Class

Port Richmond High School offered a scholarship preparation course for junior honors students. The course provided enrichment material to help students on both the New York State Regents Scholarship exam and the SAT exam. The class was taught mainly by Mr. Stavros, known for his extensive knowledge of classic American and English novels and for his occasional outbursts of temper. He also had a peculiar habit of referring to his students by their surnames—Mr. Stanhoff or Miss Rosolio. The prep course had an enrollment of fifty students—mostly "s" and "x" class students, plus some other motivated students. Tom was in the class with the elite "s" class students, whom he didn't know very well or even felt comfortable with, but he made up his mind to get the most out of the course. The course syllabus ranged over enrichment topics in mathematics, physics, chemistry, biology, history, literature, and vocabulary—which were not part of the regular high school curriculum.

The students were given a list of one thousand vocabulary words to memorize—broken down into chunks of fifty words to be learned each week. Tom was one of the few students to make an effort to study the words each week—many of the "s" students appeared to know the words already.

Mr. Stavros quickly became aware of the newspaper boy's diligence and would call on him often during his oral vocabulary drills, to the annoyance of some of the "s" class students. The vocabulary words, which Tom would remember for years, included such arcane words as abate, aberration, abstain, besmirch, capacious, deleterious, ephemeral, fallacious, flagrant, fraught, heinous, impetuous, impute, intrepid, mendicant, meretricious, miscreant, nonchalant, obstreperous, perfidious, philanthropy, prosaic, querulous, recluse, sophistry, spurious, surreptitious, tawdry, truculent, ubiquitous, unctuous, venal, venerable, and wary.

Each student in the class was assigned a book report from a list of such notable authors as Mark Twain, Herman Melville, Washington Irving, Nathaniel Hawthorne, Charles Dickens, Leo Tolstoy, Feodor Dostoevski, Thomas Hardy, George Eliot, Louisa Alcott, Emily Bronte, Thomas Mann, Honore de Balzac, Alexandre Dumas, Sinclair Lewis, John Steinbeck, F. Scott Fitzgerald, Ernest Hemingway, and Thomas Wolfe. In particular three novels made a big impression on Tom: *1984*, which was assigned to Bonnie Rosolio, *The Magic Mountain*, which was assigned to David Stanhoff, and *Look Homeward Angel*, which was assigned to Tom himself. Mr. Stavros asserted that good novels constitute a perfect blending of form and content, and great novels depict universal truths about the human condition.

George Orwell's *1984* was a bleak futuristic novel about a totalitarian society in which rebels and nonconformists were imprisoned, tortured, brain-washed, and even put to death. Oceania was an authoritarian society ruled by a mythical leader, Big Brother, whose pronouncements and predictions were infallible. There was a perpetual state of war in Oceania—creating a climate of fear, hysteria, fanaticism, and hatred throughout the society.

The true ruling body in Oceania was the Party, which controlled all behavior, speech, and thought. The Party had instituted "newspeak"—a language stripped of most words in order to restrict the range of thought—making "thoughtcrime" impossible. The protagonist of *1984*— Winston Smith—a writer, whose job was to rewrite history, had rebelled against the Party. He had begun keeping a diary, and he had committed the ultimate folly—falling in love with Julia and renting a room as a hideaway for himself and his girlfriend.

Love affairs were strictly forbidden by the Party, which sanctioned marriage for the sole purpose of begetting children. As a result, Winston was imprisoned, interrogated, and repeatedly beaten—until he became a hollow shell of a man. Emerging from prison, the protagonist had been squeezed empty of feelings and ideas—filled instead with love for Big Brother. Bonnie Rosolio concluded that the worst thing about *1984* was that people were forbidden to have lovers: "How inhuman!" she exclaimed.

Thomas Mann's *The Magic Mountain* was about an early 20th century tuberculosis sanatorium in the Swiss Alps. The protagonist was Hans Castorp, a maritime engineer who was forced to "take the cure" when a moist spot was found in his lungs. The attitude of the TB patients in the Berghof Sanatorium was care-free, ill-mannered, and frivolous. The moribund (near death) patients were isolated from the relatively healthy ones, and the dead were brought out in the early morning when the others were sleeping. The subjective nature of time was a continual motif in the novel. The conventional notion that time passes slowly when one is bedridden is incorrect—time speeds up during monotony and slows down with activity.

The Magic Mountain also dealt with the subjective nature of one's beliefs, values, and attitudes. From the perspective of the Swiss mountain top, Castorp evolves from a conventional German engineer to a cosmopolitan person with enlightened views.

Much was made of Hans Castorp's love affair with an older Russian woman, Clavdia Chauchat, who was incurably ill with tuberculosis. During Carnival Night, the shy Castorp was emboldened to speak with the Russian woman—not in his native German but in French. Their conversation took on a surreal quality as they discussed illness, sensuality, morality, freedom, and death. In a philosophic vein, Castorp linked the paired opposites in life—disease and pleasure, terror and magic, love and death—all expressions of the flesh which ennoble life. After Clavdia left the Berghof Sanatorium, Castorp decided to help the desperately ill patients at the sanatorium—visiting them, talking to them, and comforting them as a "sympathetic fellow sufferer." His work with these "children of death" allowed Castorp to free himself from the obsession with death that dominated his thoughts. Hans Castorp went beyond the plastic phrases of humanism and the pious words of religion to put his principles and ideals into concrete actions and kind deeds. David Stanhoff said he liked Castorp's dream on the snowy mountain when the protagonist declared "For the sake of goodness and love, man shall let death have no sovereignty over his thoughts." Tom was so impressed by David's presentation that he read *The Magic Mountain* during the summer.

1950s-1960s Fable

Thomas Wolfe's *Look Homeward Angel* had a powerful impact on Tom, not only because of its beautiful writing and its bigger-than-life characters, but because he identified with the novel's protagonist, Eugene Gant.

The story was centered on the North Carolina town of Altamont, which was surrounded by big mountains—isolating the southern town from the outside world. Eugene's parents had divergent temperaments, habits, and backgrounds.

The boy's mother, Eliza, was a hard-working, thrifty, brooding southerner who ran a boarding house and invested in the town's real estate. The boy's father, Oliver Gant, was a generous, turbulent, hard-drinking man who had migrated to the South from Pennsylvania. He worked as a stonecutter, shaping slabs of marble and limestone into gravestones and statues. Mr. Gant, a libertine, had gargantuan appetites for food, liquor, and women—fathering ten children, six of whom survived into adulthood. Oliver Gant would go on wild drinking binges every six weeks or so, becoming verbally and physically abusive towards his wife, Eliza. There was little affection or warmth between the boy's parents. Whenever Mr. Gant would put an arm around his long-suffering wife, she would rebuff him with "Get away from me! It's too late for that now." Consequently, Eugene's parents were separated: Mr. Gant live in his stonecutter's shop, while Eliza lived at Dixieland, her large boarding house filled with transient guests.

Like Tom, Eugene Gant was a paper boy, delivering papers in the poor side of town—earning two cents a copy for weekly deliveries and ten percent of his weekly collections—amounting to four to five dollars per week. Eugene was very close to his older brother Ben who worked as a circulation manager for the town's local newspaper and had no opportunity for schooling or travel. Ben would stick up for Eugene when his tight-fisted mother, Eliza, forced the boy to wear hand-me-down clothes and shoes that did not fit him. When he was annoyed with his parents' hypocrisy, Ben would

turn to his guardian angel saying, "Oh for God's sake! Listen to this will you?" His miserly mother made

Eugene feel guilty over the sacrifices she was making to send him to the state university. But Ben would have none of it—urging his younger brother to take whatever his parents offered him and get out of Altamont. Unlike his loquacious brother, Luke, and his bombastic father, Mr. Gant, Ben was quiet—a stranger in the Gant household. Ben would buy Eugene gifts for his amusement, admonishing and cuffing him occasionally, but defending his younger brother before the other family members.

Eugene was grief stricken by the untimely death of his beloved brother, Ben, from emphysema. The entire family recalled the young man, strangely alone and quiet throughout his short life—"walking through their lives like a shadow." On Ben's death bed, Eugene prayed for his brother—though "he did not believe in God, nor in Heaven or Hell." Near the end of *Look Homeward Angel*, Eugene had a dream in which Ben came to him as a ghost and asked

Eugene why he was wandering the streets of Altamont. The protagonist replied that he was searching for something—an artifact from the past to remember and keep throughout his life: "a stone, a leaf, an unfound door . . . And of all the forgotten faces." Like all of us, Eugene Gant was haunted by the lost faces of the past and "by the grief of time and sorrowful hauntings of brief days."

As with Thomas Mann's *The Magic Mountain*, Tom would reread Thomas Wolfe's *Look Homeward Angel* — getting new perspectives and insights over the years. With regard to George Orwell's *1984*, Tom saw a parallel between Big Brother and the authoritarian regimes of Russia and China.

There was a fundamental difference between the Communists' distortion of Marxism and pure Marxist theory in terms of class struggles, surplus value, capitalist profit, and the fair distribution of goods and services in society. Mr. Stavros stated that fiction in the form of novels offers a window on to reality that nonfiction cannot offer, because fiction is fact shaped and organized for a purpose — to depict man's existence in the world and his struggles to make sense of the world. In any case, Mr. Stavros's scholarship class paid rich dividends to Port Richmond High School.

That year, Port Richmond lead all Staten Island schools in the number of Regents Scholarships won. In addition, Tom had the highest score on the New York State Regents Scholarship exam among his classmates — topping the more gifted "s" class students.

CHAPTER 33

Union Issues

During the spring term of Tom's final year at Port Richmond High School, he got a job at the A & P supermarket in Port Richmond. His mom had shopped there for years—hiring a cab to bring the groceries home every Saturday with Cara often coming along to help out with the grocery bags. Upon their arrival at the white stucco house on Pulaski Avenue, Tom would run outside to carry the four or five grocery bags into the house from the cab. In those days, before the appearance of the ubiquitous plastic shopping bag, there was the big, brown paper shopping bag which was used as garbage bags and to cover school books. Over the years, Claire Haley had gotten to know the A & P store manager, Jimmy Severian, a preoccupied, ill-tempered man who rarely smiled and had little to say to the part-timers—except to give them their work duties for the day. She had bragged to the manager about her hard-working son, the senior honors student at Port Richmond High School. The New York City bookkeeper felt that her son was too old to be delivering the New York Herald Tribune, which only brought him between $8 and $10 a week—except for Christmas and Easter, when tips boosted his wages to as much as $50.

So after five years as an early-morning paper carrier, Tom gave up the Herald Tribune paper route for the A & P grocery store on Richmond Avenue.

1950s-1960s Fable

His hours were three afternoons a week from 3 PM to 9 PM, plus an eight-hour Saturday shift for a total of 26 hours per week.

The eight-hour long Saturday took some getting used to because it cut into Tom's stick ball and basketball playing time. For the first month, it was Tom's job to fetch the shopping carts from the A & P parking lot and the nearby streets. Manager Jimmy Severian grimly told him to scour the neighborhood for the carts because some customers took the shopping carts home to carry their groceries and never returned them.

Then, Tom got a promotion to the dairy department, where he handled returning milk and soda bottles, grinded the coffee for customers, stacked the dairy shelves with milk, butter, and cheese, and swept the area—clearing wood shavings, paper, cigarette butts, and food wrappings from the floor. He was so good at sweeping that Jimmy solemnly bestowed on Tom the important job of sweeping the entire store, plus the front sidewalk. One of his coworkers, a woman cashier, said to Tom, "You're the sweepinest boy I've ever seen!" One day, Cara, now a pretty teenager, came into the A & P store with Elena Taglia and Doris Schmidt to visit her brother at work in his new job. After that, Tom became very popular with the other high school part-timers at the A & P.

There was a definite demarcation between the full-time and part-time A & P workers, the latter of whom were mostly high school and college students. There was much worker-to-worker bickering within the store, which surprised Tom until he realized that these people were stuck in dead-end low-paying jobs—with little hope of promotion. Tom never hassled with either the full-time or part-time workers. One middle-aged man said of Tom: "He's just a big easygoing kid."

This A & P full-timer gave Tom some useful advice: "No matter where you work or what you do—always look busy. Apparently, the A & P workers' union was not a strong one, hence compensation and benefits were quite meager.

Tom received the minimum wage, which was $1.25 per hour at that time. After tax deductions, his pay check averaged around $30 a week—a relatively large amount for the ex-newspaper boy. He gave half of it to his mother to help her with the household expenses and saved most of the remainder. He had opened up a passbook account at a Port Richmond saving bank when he first began his Herald Tribune paper route years ago, accumulating over $250 in savings. Benjamin Franklin's dictum—"A penny saved is a penny earned."—was a categorical imperative in the Haley family.

Port Richmond High School was a stir in rumors about the formation of a teacher's union, referred to as the United Federation of Teachers. The goals of the UFT was to improve public school teachers' working conditions—in terms of working hours, classes taught per day, and preparation periods—plus compensation—in terms of salary, benefits, and pension. During the late 1950s and early 1960s, public school teachers, who were well educated, hard working, and deeply committed towards their students, received meager compensation throughout the country. One morning in May as Tom approached the high school front gate, he noticed several teachers picketing in front of the school—holding "Teachers on Strike" signs. He went over to his "x" classmates, Tony Aramo, Gary Lukovski, and Albert Cloots, telling them not to cross the picket line. They disagreed with their idealistic friend and went inside as soon as the homeroom buzzer sounded.

1950s-1960s Fable

Tom turned around and walked home to the astonishment of his friends and teachers. When his mother found out from Cara about his idealistic hooky-playing, she hit the roof.: "Strike or no strike, you're going to school. Don't give me any crap about not crossing the picket line!" So the next day, Tom obediently crossed the picket line, stopping to tell the striking teachers he sympathized with them. His Marxist mom told him about Lenin's pragmatic rule: "Sometimes the proletariat has to take one step backwards in order to take two steps forward." The boy realized sadly that there were bread and butter limits to Marxist idealism.

After doing quite well at P.S. 21 in Elm Park, Cara had a tough time adjusting to Port Richmond High School. A habitual chatterbox, she had trouble focusing on what the teacher said—especially in classes she had little interest in—such as math and science. In subjects like English, Spanish, and art, where her interest was keen, Cara got good grades. In fact, she could have attained an 85% merit roll average, were it not for her failing grades in mathematics. Part of the problem was Cara's grade adviser placing her in the regents math courses, algebra and geometry—subjects that the dreamy-eyed teenager could not grasp. After a couple of years of frustration, Cara implored her mother to visit the school and change her program to the commercial track—enabling her to take business math. In the commercial program, Cara took business math, bookkeeping, steno, typing, English, and Spanish, which were more suited to her interests and needs. Yet she barely maintained a C+ average of 75%, which was not reflective of her true ability.

Occasionally, Cara would play hooky and Tom would find a postcard from the school stating she was absent. Taking Cara aside, he warned her not to do it again or he would inform their no-nonsense mother. To make matters worse, Cara was occasionally badgered by disingenuous teachers who couldn't believe she was Tom's sister. The oft-repeated query was, "Isn't Tom Haley, the honor-roll student, your brother? What happened to you?"

But it is not an uncommon phenomenon that two individuals raised in the same family have different childhood experiences. When Tom looked back on their childhood on the Smith, he understood that Cara didn't have it quite as good as he did. He remembered reading a quote by philosopher Karl Popper: "Success in life is largely a matter of luck. It has little correlation with merit."

1950s-1960s Fable

CHAPTER 34

Nervous Breakdown

During her teenaged years, Cara seemed to lose interest in sketching and painting. Her pencils, paint brushes, sketch pads, and portable easel remained in her clothes closet, where they lay dormant, along with her artistic endeavors. One plausible explanation resided in Cara's new-found interest in boys. In the vernacular of the times, Cara had become "boy-crazy." Tom had learned through the grapevine that Cara was "going steady" with a Port Richmond High School senior, named Larry Adamo. Larry was a husky, leather-jacketed greaser who lived in Mariners Harbor and drove a bright red Chevy hard-top with a Hollywood muffler. Tom knew exactly where the teenage Romeo resided because he had once delivered the New York Herald Tribune to the house next door. One morning, the newspaper boy observed the swarthy teenager peering through the front window—making sure his shiny red Chevy had been unharmed the night before. Tom always knew when Larry was on his way to an assignation with Cara because he could hear the loud rumbling of his big Chevrolet's engine from the other end of Pulaski Avenue.

To his credit and Cara's insistence, Larry always came to the front door of the white stucco house whenever he was taking her out. And he always nodded affably to Tom and spoke politely to Claire Haley, who fixed him with an unblinking stare—similar to a lion eye-balling an antelope. There were certain benefits to Tom in this unlikely adolescent romance: It was good to have one of the school's reputed tough guys as an ally, and whenever Larry passed Tom on the street, he'd give him a ride in his notorious red Chevy, which boosted Tom's standing with the neighborhood kids and his "x" classmates at the high school.

Initially, Cara seemed to be on cloud-nine as a result of her romance with one of Port Richmond High School's "bad boys." Her mom set a strict 10:30 PM curfew and she was permitted to go out only on Friday and Saturday nights. Cara always entered the house aglow with joyful spirits, laughter, and hugs for her befuddled brother and mom. Then one night, she returned home in a gloomy mood, barely acknowledging her startled family before entering her room and slamming the door.

Sadly, she did not emerge from her bed for a week. Initially, it appeared that Cara was suffering from the flu, with the usual symptoms of fever, weakness, nausea, dizziness, and fretful sleeping patterns. Then, there was a change in her condition—there was bed-wetting and recurring nightmares from which she woke up screaming and babbling unintelligibly. In the middle of the night, she would call out Larry's name—telling him to touch her breasts. This wasn't the Cara that Tom had grown up with—there was a frightening change in the teenager's personality.

When Claire Haley tried to take her daughter's temperature, Cara cried out, "Help!" Her mom called the family physician, Dr. Atlas, an old-fashioned medical bag toting doctor who still made house calls. After a brief examination, Dr. Atlas diagnosed her condition: There was nothing physically wrong with Cara—she was having a nervous breakdown. Dr. Atlas made some phone calls and the next morning, Cara was sent to Creedmore Hospital, which was a large state-run mental hospital located in Queens Village, Queens. Tom and his mother visited Cara on Sunday afternoons, leaving around 9 AM for a grueling 2 ½ hour trip which included the #3 Castleton Avenue bus, the Staten Island Ferry, a subway ride to midtown, another subway ride to Queens, and finally a bus ride to Queens Village. Tom was struck by the imposing height of the 20-story Creedmore buildings, of which there were fifty units housing approximately seven thousand patients with varying mental disorders—depression, schizophrenia, manic delirium, and catatonia. After a long walk over the extensive grounds of the state hospital, they located building "E" and tool the elevator up to the 17th floor, where Cara was staying. There was a large visiting room filled with threadbare sofas and chairs, plus long wooden tables and folding metal chairs. Large windows fronted by steel bars provided a panoramic view of the 300 acres of sprawling park-like grounds of Creedmore Hospital, which were threaded by paved walkways and wooden benches. The visiting room was occupied by people in civilian clothes, plus white-uniformed orderlies and nurses who kept their eyes on the female inmates, who wore pale-green dresses.

The wards of Creedmore were segregated with regard to the gender and the severity of the cases. The 20th floor had the most severely disturbed patients—people who had little chance of ever returning to society as "normal" functioning human beings. It was astonishing to Tom and his mother that except for severe cases, they could hardly discern inmates from visitors—were it not for the pale-green patient uniforms. After registering at the reception desk, a nurse called for Cara in her microphone: "Bring out Cara Haley. Cara Haley, please." Tom was shocked to hear his sister's name resounding over the public address system.

What happened to the dreamy-eyed artist that she had wound up at Creedmore Hospital, so far from the farming area of Bloomington, South Jersey?

The crowded, noisy reception room filled with somber families talking nervously to their zombie-like inmate relatives, under surveillance by the white-garbed orderlies, was a nightmare straight out of a Kafka novel.

Cara shuffled out, escorted by a nurse, looking wan, haggard, drowsy, and barely aware of her environment. Her mom, followed by Tom, rushed to Cara—kissing and hugging her tightly with the teenager looking surprised at their display of affection. She responded to her family with some recognition, but with little emotion or joy. When Tom asked his sister about how she was doing and how she was treated, Cara began to sob quietly—the tears streaming down her face. Tom and his mother struggles to maintain their composure, trying to maintain an upbeat tone to the interview. They had brought Cara some clothes, slippers, and some snack items like potato chips, pretzels, and chocolates. But Cara exhibited little interest in anything offered to her. Tom removed the hospital-issued cardboard slippers and put new pink velvet slippers on her feet, which hardly elicited a response by the placid teenager.

Her mother filled the awkward quiet by carrying on a stream of idle chatter about the run-down state of the house, the gossip at her bookkeeper's job in Manhattan, the customers at the A & P who asked Tom in which aisle were the pickles, the doings of her neighborhood friends Elena Taglia and Doris Schmidt, and the unusually hot spring they've been experiencing. Awakening from her lethargy, Cara asked if she would be going down to the Smith farm. Taken aback, Claire Haley said, "I should never have let you go back there! Your brother had his paper route to attend to, but you went down there and this (pointing to the noisy reception room) was the result." After visiting hours were finished, Tom and his mother had a meeting with Dr. Reuben, the supervising psychiatrist of the 17th floor patients. Sitting at his desk in his book-filled office, Dr. Reuben was the stereotypical shrink, wearing a gray business suit and adorned in a neat mustache and goatee. Holding Cara's folder, the middle-aged psychiatrist took down detailed biographical information on Cara's childhood—including the early years spent with her foster parents in the South Jersey farming area, and the turbulent years on Staten Island when Thomas Haley was carrying on with drinking binges, alternating with periods of sobriety—culminating in his untimely death from a heart attack on the street. Dr. Reuben learned that Cara had her father's gift for art, but was an underachieving student in elementary school and high school. Abruptly changing the nature of their conversation, the psychiatrist asked them if Cara ever talked about something inappropriate happening to her as a child.

"You mean she was molested by those people in on the farm? I'll sue those bastards and put them in jail!" Dr. Reuben asserted that she mustn't jump to any conclusions, but incest could not be ruled out. Dr. Reuben diagnosed Cara's condition as severe depression with psychotic features such as schizophrenia. Surprised, Tom interjected, "Does that mean she has a split personality?" The psychiatrist responded that schizophrenia means that the personality splits or separates from reality. Moving on, Dr. Reuben said present-day psychiatry has moved away from these imprecise labels—opting instead to describe aberrant behavior in terms of specific behaviors.

Her mother was defensive about Cara's recent years on Staten Island, declaring that her father was a generous, well-meaning man but an incurable alcoholic. She said that she'd kick him out when he was drinking, but she allowed him back into the house because he swore he was going to stay on the wagon and become a good father to the children. Turning to Tom, "You and your

sister were always campaigning to bring him back into the fold." Tom agreed, admitting that "naïve optimism" is a universal trait of all children. Claire Haley returned to her original thesis that the source of Cara's troubles resided with her early childhood experiences: "That foster family didn't treat her so well and something tells me that there was some funny things going on there. When she first got sick, Cara said that a Jersey City relative, Uncle Eddie had once done something to her."

Tom recalled this peculiar Smith family relative, who also made him feel funny. He acknowledged that he was favored by the Smiths over Cara because of his good school work and because he was very helpful to Mr. Smith, who was hampered by polio. "But Helen and Harry were very good to both of us. Helen taught us about God and right and wrong. She showed me the books in the cellar and she encouraged Cara to sketch things on the farm. She turned chores into games, and told us about God and talked about Jesus's Sermon on the Mount—that the meek shall inherit the earth. Harry would play baseball with us and rescued me from my wooden shack during a thunder storm. We never felt like we were foster kids. The Smiths treated us like we were their own children. We never lacked for anything," said Tom.

"Well, they didn't do it for nothing. I paid them $32 a month. And that ain't hay!" observed Claire Haley bitterly. "All those years working in the city and typing up envelopes at night. And my daughter was mistreated by those half-wits. There's no justice in this world."

1950s-1960s Fable

Dr. Reuben observed that such childhood experiences were not unusual, but different individuals react differently to them. Some people have a genetic disposition to mental breakdowns because of certain experiences in childhood, and others emerge from

traumatic experiences unscathed. "It boils down a combination of negative environment and a genetic predisposition towards a mental breakdown." The psychiatrist indicated that Cara's youth was a plus towards her attaining a full recovery. He proposed a treatment that combined "psychotherapy and electroconvulsive therapy — in other words, electroshock therapy." Both Claire Haley and her son were stunned by the term electroshock therapy. Tom recalled the Mary Shelley novel *Frankenstein*, in which the corpse of a criminal was brought to life by a passing a strong electric current through his brain. It appeared to be a very cruel and inhumane way of healing people who were suffering from mental illness. Dr. Reuben said that ECT "jumpstarts the brain" — boosting neural transmissions. He asserted that electroshock therapy has been quite effective for severe depression and catatonia. The psychiatrist also declared that there was "no long-term cognitive impairment with ECT and memory losses were only temporary." He explained that the patient was put to sleep with an injection of a mild anesthetic, like sodium pentothal, which relaxes their muscles, because the electric current triggers a seizure in the patient. Both Tom and his mother shivered at the thought of Cara undergoing such gruesome shock treatments.

"It sounds horrible to me," observed Claire Haley. "Can't they just give Cara some medication to get her back on her feet?" Dr. Reuben said that once the prescribed regime of electroconvulsive therapy was completed, she would be given some medication, but there were "no magic pills."

As mother and son made the long journey by bus, two subways, the Staten Island Ferry, and the #3 Castleton Avenue bus to the white stucco house on Pulaski Avenue, Tom wondered about the peculiar twists of fate that forced an innocent person to undergo ECT therapy as a result of a nervous breakdown.

It could happen to anyone, he thought, even me.

Tom and his mom continued to make their Sunday 2 ½ hour trek to Creedmore State Hospital from Staten Island, with the visit taking up most of the day. Since Tom was working at the A & P in Port Richmond three afternoons and Saturdays, he brought his high school books and loose-leaf notebook to get some homework done on the lengthy public transit commute. The ability to use productively, otherwise wasted travel time, through reading and studying was a habit that would prove useful in future years when the ex-farm boy attended City College of New York, a commuter college. Somehow, despite the distractions and the stress of his sister's illness, Tom was able to maintain his high honor roll average of 98% in that final semester at Port Richmond High School.

A continual annoyance was the inquiries by Cara's teachers about the reasons for Cara's prolonged absence from school. Tom merely replied that she was hospitalized with an illness and wasn't sure exactly when she would be returning to Port Richmond. His homeroom teacher, Mr. Gento, who was Cara's Spanish teacher, was particularly inquisitive about the cause of Cara's absence. From his questions, Tom got the impression that this nosy teacher (who still resented the "x" class boys for their refusal to attend assembly years ago) believed that Cara had gotten pregnant. But Tom refused to provide any information about the nature of Cara's illness.

1950s-1960s Fable

In the late 1950s and early 1960s, both mental illness and teenage pregnancy were considered terrible afflictions which families never spoke about.

One Sunday afternoon, Cara's neighborhood friends Elena Taglia and Doris Schmidt, went with Tom and Claire Haley to visit Cara at Creedmore. Dr. Reuben encouraged the visit because he felt it would aid in Cara's recovery to see her friends and readjust to life

outside the hospital. The shock treatments had helped Cara emerge from her depression, but she occasionally behaved erratically — demonstrating outbursts of temper which were unlike the old Cara. The past week, she had gotten into a fist fight with another patient because of an alleged insult made by the young woman towards Cara. Upon the arrival of her two friends, Cara was beside herself with joy — rushing to hug Elena and Doris and hardly acknowledging her brother and mom. Tom assured his miffed mother that it's normal for teenagers to favor their friends over their family. The visit went quite well as the teenaged girls talked about the latest doings, mainly who was going with whom from Elm Park, until Elena mentioned that their neighbor, Antonio the mason, was quite ill with emphysema.

At this unexpected bad news Cara broke into tears sobbing that she wanted to go home and nurse their beloved neighbor back to good health: "I'm tired of this place, Mom. You railroaded me because I was dating that boy, Larry Adamo!" Her mom tried to calm Cara down, but to no avail. Finally, a nurse came out and took Cara back to her room. Despite Cara's emotional up and downs, Dr. Reuben said that after the series of electroshock treatments were completed, she would be released from Creedmore within six weeks. Once back on Staten Island, Cara would join a therapy group for continued counseling and rehabilitation.

Tom continued working at the A & P in Port Richmond and studying hard at Port Richmond High School in the spring semester of his senior year in which he opted to take only four majors—English, Latin, solid geometry, and physics. He wanted to get out early so he could start work at the A & P supermarket at 2 PM weekdays—skipping the social studies elective "Problems of Democracy." No longer the argumentive history buff, the ex-newspaper boy focused on mathematics and science, especially physics.

He enjoyed Newtonian classical physics, in which most of the observable phenomena of the world could be described by algebraic equations. His physics teacher, Mr. Riner, sensed that Tom was stressed by his sister's illness, yet never questioned him about the nature of her illness. Once he asked the teenager, "What are you going to do when you get out of here?" Tom replied that he was heading for the A & P where he worked afternoons. His science teacher said he meant when he graduated.

"Oh," replied the ex-farm boy, "I'll be going to C.C.N.Y. to study science." Yet, the idea of attending college seemed a remote and scary prospect to the teenager—he wanted to remain at Port Richmond High School where he had found a home for himself. But most of all, he wished he could see his sister passing him in the halls with her shy little wave to her studious brother. And he wished he could spend summer afternoons playing stick ball, and winter afternoons playing basketball forever. Like Peter Pan, he didn't cherish the idea of growing up and spending most of his day working at a boring job in order to pay his bills.

CHAPTER 35

Prom Night

In this final winter before college, Tom would go with Mike Palermo to Cromwell Center in St. George to play basketball. As a varsity pitcher at McKee High School, Mike was well known throughout Staten Island for his athletic prowess in all sports. As his Elm Park buddy, everybody assumed that Tom was also a varsity athlete, so the ex-farm boy was chosen to play with the top Staten Island high school basketball players—participating in fierce pickup games with these high-caliber players. The Cromwell Center basketball games provided an opportunity for Tom to blow off steam and forget about his family problems—especially his concerns about the well-being of his sister, Cara.

After a 10-inch snowfall covered Staten Island, Tom and his Elm Park friends, driven by cabin fever, brought shovels to the P. S. 21 schoolyard and cleared the basketball court so they could play basketball. They were abuzz about Wilt Chamberlain's 100-point game against the New York Knicks. The 7-foot 1-inch 260-pound center played the entire 48 minutes of the game, shot 36 for 63 from the field, and made 28 of 32 free throws. As the cold, snowy days of winter gave way to the balmy days of spring, Tom spent his free time playing soft ball and stick ball at the P. S. 21 schoolyard.

At 17 ½ years of age, Tom had attained his full height of 6 feet 2 ½ inches and a weight of 170 pounds, plus the added strength from his regimen of calisthenics and weight lifting. The ex-newspaper boy had become almost unhittable as stick ball pitcher—throwing a moving fast ball that rose or sunk and darted left or right—depending on the way the ball was gripped and on surface irregularities of the spalding. Even the formidable stick ball hitter, Mike Palermo had trouble hitting Tom's elusive pitches, but Tom had couldn't hit his friend's dazzling fast ball either. Thus, their games were extremely low-scoring matches—often ending in scoreless ties.

One day in June, Tom and Mike were playing Harry the Horse and Mr. Taglia, two of the men from their Elm Park neighborhood, a challenge stick ball game for a $5 winner's pot at the Port Richmond school yard. The game was scoreless with Tom and Mike sharing the pitching duty for their team, while Harry the Horse went the distance on the mound for the grownups. In the bottom of the ninth inning, Mike connected on one of Harry's fast pitches and sent the ball over the fence 250 feet away—to win the game. As the two youngsters, cheered and celebrated, someone was observing the boys from the high school entrance. Coincidentally, it was Prom Night at the high school and Bonnie Rosolio was leaving the formal dance with her date. She stopped momentarily to observe her old P. S. 21 classmate, feeling melancholy about this boy whom she once knew so well but now was remote from her and her friends at the school. "So this is what turns him on—how strange!" Her date, Roy Rand, asked the pretty curly-haired teenager what had she said, but Bonnie merely shook her head and said nothing.

In June, Cara returned to the white stucco house on Pulaski Avenue in a somewhat impaired state. Tom noticed a fragility in his sister's personality—an extreme sensitivity to environmental disturbances such as loud noises, bright lights, traffic or commotion. There was a definite antagonism on Cara's part towards her mother, whom she blamed for "railroading" her to Creedmore. If Claire Haley made her some soup for lunch, the dreamy-eyed artist hardly touched it. A half-hour later, Cara would make herself a peanut butter-and-jelly sandwich—eating it ravenously as if she had been starving for weeks. For the duration of the summer, Cara had to attend weekly group therapy sessions at St. Vincent's Hospital in West Brighton. One positive sign noticed by Tom and his mother was that Cara had taken out her easel, drawing pad, and pencils from the closet, and was starting to sketch again. Happening to notice one of her drawings, Tom was surprised to observe a compelling sketch of a semi-nude sensual couple engaged in a passionate embrace.

One day at the supper table, Claire Haley broached the subject of Cara's future: What would she be doing in the fall? Cara responded quickly, "I'm going back to Port Richmond to finish high school."

Tom concurred, "A high school diploma is a necessity in this day and age."

But the kids' mother vehemently disagreed, "No. You'll have to make up part of your junior year, plus your senior year—1 ½ years of schooling, Missy."

Flushing with anger, Cara raised her voice, "So what? I'm not a 50-year old yenta like some people!" Furious, her mom reached over and slapped Cara's face —surprising herself and her family with an unwarranted display of anger. Cara emitted a blood-curdling scream and ran out of the kitchen.

Tom yelled at his mother: "Why did you do that?" Her son left the small kitchen also.

Their mom sat at the table—feeling ostracized and melancholy—wondering what happened to the pure joy she felt when she hugged her children on the Smith farm after a long bus trip from Staten Island years ago. The trouble with lovable children was that they grew up to become cantankerous, willful teenagers.

1950s-1960s Fable

CHAPTER 36

Rites of Spring

It was Tom's favorite season—the trees bursting with leaves, the flowers blooming with bright colors, and gentle breezes carrying honey-suckle fragrance along Staten Island's North Shore. Tom thought of Tennyson's famous line: "In the spring, a young man's fancy lightly turns to thoughts of love." Notwithstanding these romantic ruminations, Tom got out his well-worn baseball glove and his heavy 42-ounce baseball bat, from which he had sawed off an inch from the fat end. The bat's bottle-neck shape—the heavy fat end tapering into a thin handle—enabled him to swing hard with good bat speed and get "good wood" on the ball. Mike Palermo had gathered a bunch of his Elm Park buddies—Tom, Joey Caprino, Gene Munski, Neil Coombs, along with Tom's classmates, Tony Aramo, Gary Lukovski, and Alfred Cloots—to play some Graniteville fellows in a game of softball at a fenced-in little league field near Forest Avenue. Many of the players knew each other from Port Richmond and McKee high schools, which made the game less competitive and more fun. There was much good-natured bench jockeying on both sides. In such a relaxed setting, Tom always played well—participating in the pure joy of the game.

Under agreed upon rules, the pitcher would lob the ball underhanded—with no windmill-style fast pitching—making it easier for everybody to hit the ball. As it turned out, the game was an exciting, run-filled contest with lots of hits, many homeruns, and several dazzling defensive plays. Mike Palermo and Gene Munski made some great stops on hard-bit balls at third base and shortstop respectively.

Tony Aramo was a solid catcher, blocking the plate well on opposing runners attempting to score. Tom excelled in the outfield—leaping high against the center field fence to rob opponents of homeruns and throwing out a couple of runners from deep in the outfield with his rifle arm. Offensively, both teams hit lots of homeruns with Mike topping everyone with three huge homeruns that cleared the fence by more than 100 feet. Neil Coombs took advantage of his vaunted foot speed by beating out two bunts and stealing four bases. Gene Munski, an ambidextrous switch-hitter, amazed everybody by throwing both right-handed and left-handed and hitting homeruns from the left and right side of the plate.

The game was made more interesting by a sizeable group of spectators from the Graniteville area—including some pretty teenaged girls that Tom and his Elm Park buddies had never seen before. One girl in particular continually called out to Tom whenever he did something noteworthy in the game, "Way to go, you big Guinea!" Her repeated singling him out got to the point where his teammates were teasing the ex-newspaper boy about his vocal fan. This short, dark-complexioned girl with a sleek pony tail, a pert expression, a ready smile, and a strong New York City accent has caught Tom's eye. In fact, near the end of the game, he became so distracted by the girl's continual stream of remarks directed at him that he collided with Joey Caprino in the outfield while chasing a fly ball. Both outfielders fell down as if shot by gun, with Tom, the taller of the two teenagers sustaining the greater damage—a badly split lip. Instantly, the girl, who was called Joanie, ran out to the field and held a perfume-

1950s-1960s Fable

filled hanky to his bleeding lip, making sweet cooing sounds all the while. Looking up at the cutie's face, Tom smiled, "I think I must have died and gone to heaven."

Joanie giggled, "Oh shut up you big Guinea. Why don't you look where you're going?"

Coming to his senses, the ex-farm boy replied, "By the way, I'm not Italian."

Eyeing him intently, she asked, "So what are you?"

Shrugging his shoulders, he replied, "A little bit of this and a little bit of that."

Quick with her repartee, Joanie cracked, "Well, I like your this and your that!"

At this point, Mike walked over to the prone centerfielder and helped him get up and walk off the field to the exaggerated cheers and applause of both teammates and opponents. Nodding at his old Elm Park buddy, Mike observed, "You got yourself a nurse, so let's finish the frigging game!" And the memorable Elm Park vs Graniteville softball game resumed, while Tom and Joanie talked on the sidelines — enjoying one time-honored rite of spring memorialized by Tennyson.

CHAPTER 37

Friendly Competition

One afternoon in the middle of June, Tom found himself sitting in the high school auditorium with the top senior class honor roll students. These high achieving students included David Stanhoff, Linda Henderson, Stuart Miller, Holly Hawke, and Tom himself—all "s" class students except the latter two individuals, whose overall averages at Port Richmond High School were slightly lower than those of David, Linda, and Stuart. Tom, had a cumulative high school average of around 93%, but for his junior and senior years it ranged between 96% and 98%. Since these five candidates were close to a statistical dead heat for top scholastic honors, Mrs. Cowan, the senior class grade adviser had decided that the person with the best speech would be valedictorian and the second-best speaker would be salutatorian.

Tom wouldn't have been in the running for top honors were it not for the big jump in his grades during his junior and senior years—barely making the honor roll by the skin of his teeth as a freshman and sophomore. His "x" class homeroom teacher, Mr. Gento, never one of Tom's fans, once asked him the reason for his surge in grades. Tom responded that he had "found religion" in his junior year. The temperamental homeroom teacher observed that Tom was "one of a kind—thank God." As the ex-newspaper boy looked at the select group conversing in the auditorium, Tom realized that he had come along way since he first began reading the books in the cellar book case on the Smith farm. In a melancholy mood, he realized that his high school career, with its many ups and downs, would soon be over. Holly Hawke had also progressed from an underachieving, thick-accented class cut-up to one of the top students in her class. Yet the six-feet tall Swedish immigrant still maintained her droll sense of humor—combining serious inquiry with heightened awareness of the absurdity of everyday life. Holly glanced admiringly at David Stanhoff, who at six feet four inches, was one of the few boys taller than the big-boned Swede. "Vell, good luck on your speech, Mr. Davidhoff. May the best man vin."

Frowning, the scholar-athlete replied, "My name is David Stanhoff, Miss Hawke. Nevertheless, best wishes to you on your address." Tom understood that Holly tended to morph into her thick Swedish accent for the sake of laughs. She wouldn't have been among "the top five" if Holly didn't speak and write English fluently. The studious Stuart Miller smiled at his neighbors, but continued writing and editing his speech. Tom remembered quizzing Stuart on his biology notes during lunch room, while the other students gabbed and horsed around. Stuart was a whiz in biology and chemistry—hoping to become a physician someday. Linda Henderson, always organized and efficient, studied a stack of index cards upon which she had written her speech—memorizing her address line by line. Always the serious student, Linda struck Tom as a future scientist who would peer tirelessly into arrayed test tubes until she arrived at a cure for some dreaded disease. At this point, the irrepressible Tommy Spider bounced into the auditorium—inquiring about the nature of the doings at the assembly. He accosted the group, shaking hands with everybody and congratulating them on their high grades. "

Book learning is fine and dandy, but there's no substitute for being street smart." When Tommy shook Holly Hawke's big paw, he winced as if she had hurt him "Wow, you're one big mama! Do you play basketball, Holly?"

Smiling wryly, Holly said, "No, Big Boy. In Sweden, we don't play ball games. We ice skate and ski on mountains." Peering down at him intently, she inquired: "Why do they call you Big Boy?"

Tommy winked at the tall Swede and said, "Come out with me some night and I'll show you why." Holly responded with a friendly shove that sent the short Avenue B resident flying.

Recovering quickly, Tommy turned to his old nemesis, David Stanhoff, "You could have used that big Swede under the boards this year. None of you guys could block shots or rebound." Looking at Tom, Tommy remarked, "And you were too busy on that rickety red bike of yours, selling newspapers to join the basketball team and grab some rebounds."

Tom shook his head, "My game is stick ball, Big Boy." Laughing derisively, Tommy rejoined, "Well come over to Avenue B and I'll show you bookworms how we play stick ball."

The Dean of Boys, Mr. Young entered the auditorium and noticed Tommy Spider hanging around the honor students. He asked Tommy what he was doing in the auditorium. The Avenue B resident replied that he was preparing his valedictory speech: "Ladies and gentlemen, I come to you as the number one street-smart student at Port Richmond—bar none." Then Tommy dashed through an auditorium exit door before the Dean could question him further.

1950s-1960s Fable

Mrs. Cowan emerged from the curtains on the stage and told the students to get ready to speak. The speeches were as unique as the honors students giving them. There were the usual remarks expressing appreciation for their parents and teachers, who had devoted themselves in behalf of the students. Stuart Miller talked about his teachers' efforts and his hard work, which would prepare him for college and ultimately medical school to realize his life-long dream of becoming a doctor. Linda Henderson talked about the pursuit of knowledge as a noble pastime which would eventually benefit mankind though scientific research. Holly Hawke was uncharacteristically serious, as she compared Swedish and American education—choosing the later because it stresses problem solving and creativity. Tom was the most nervous of the five speakers, but overcame initial jitters to speak convincingly about the need to fight economic injustice and worker exploitation. The ex-farm boy declared that enlightened people should work for an ideal world where there would be no rich or poor—everybody would be equal, politically and economically.

However, the best speaker was David Stanhoff, who talked about our wonderful high school memories, as well as the debt we owe to our parents and teachers. He said that success was not measured in dollars and cents, but instead from the individual deriving satisfaction from his work. David reminded the students that they should never lose sight of their obligations to their fellow man. Citing John Donne, David Stanhoff asserted that all men are connected to all other men. He concluded by urging each Port Richmond High School graduate to do their share "to help make America an even greater nation than it is today."

David was given the honor of delivering the valedictory address, and Tom agreed with the senior grade adviser's decision. It was an awesome speech that reflected the youthful idealism of the 1960s.

Linda Henderson was chosen to give the salutatorian address, which surprised Tom because he was captivated by Holly's interesting speech, but the noble idea of scientific research benefiting mankind was compelling. He wondered how that concept fit in with the invention of the atomic bomb which threatened the very survival of the human race.

1950s-1960s Fable

CHAPTER 38

Joanie Gardello

In the late spring, Tom began seeing Joanie Gardello, the perky Graniteville teenager, who had taken a fancy to him during the softball game with his Elm Park buddies. Tom couldn't believe his good fortune that someone so kind, so pretty, and so easy going was his girlfriend. Their romance was undertaken secretly without the consent of his mom, who had made it clear that Tom should concentrate on his studies and his A & P job—and not waste his time on frivolous dating. Claire Haley was unsuccessful in imposing such a restriction on her more rebellious daughter after her nervous breakdown. After their argument about Cara's future, the dreamy-eyed artist changed her mind about returning to high school and got a clerk-typist job in the Manhattan—working for an insurance company. She told her mom that she would go to night school to get her diploma, but wanted to work because she was tired of wearing her mother's hand-me-down clothes and living like a pauper. With her typist's salary, Cara began buying herself a nice wardrobe and started a whirlwind social life, in which she dated a new fellow every weekend. She was also supposed to participate in a group-therapy sessions one night a week and on alternate Saturday afternoons. It became clear as time passed that she had begun to skip these sessions, as her social life took greater priority.

Tom used his past weekend night basketball playing at Cromwell center as his cover for dating Joanie, who assumed that there was nothing amiss in the Haley household with regard to his social life. Using his portion of his A & P paycheck, Tom paid for his secret dates with his good natured, brown-eyed girlfriend, who didn't seem to mind Tom's lack of a car. The two happy teenagers went to the Ritz movie theater on Richmond Avenue, Central Diner on Forest Avenue, and the Staten Island Zoo via public transit buses, which at that time were punctual, reliable, and inexpensive. Tom's favorite animal was the monkeys, which he called "our second cousins, once removed." Joanie disagreed, asserting that humans could not be related to monkeys because the latter lack a soul. Changing the subject, he pointed to the petting zoo.

At one point, Joanie asked Tom, "What ever happened to your old red bicycle?" Tom asked her if she wanted a ride on his beat up old bike, which was stored in his cellar—rusted, fender less, with bald tires, but still working.

Giving him a coy look, "Yea, I'll sit on the bar while you peddle, but don't touch my butt!" Tom was surprised that the McKee junior knew about bike because, he seldom rode it lately. Joanie replied that she used to see him delivering newspapers to her Graniteville neighbors, off Forest Avenue, years ago. "I felt sorry for you, seeing you delivering that newspaper that nobody ever reads every morning—rain or shine. I had a crush on you even then, you big brainiac!"

Tom did a double take, "What do you mean by brainiac?" She smiled knowingly, "I got the low-down about you from some of your buddies—you're one of those brainy honor-roll students. You can't put anything past Joanie—I have my sources." Tom looked away, as

1950s-1960s Fable

his eyes filled with tears. He hugged the cute nursing student—not quite believing his good fortune in finding such a clever, warm-hearted, and high-spirited girl. One Sunday in late June, Tom and Joanie went to South Beach together, getting a ride from her 20-year old cousin, Rosie and her boyfriend, Robert, a Port Richmond High School graduate who remembered Tom as a free-spirited freshman, whose class drove Mrs. Millman to the verge of jumping out of a window. Joanie was surprised, "I thought you were always the gentlemen—so you have your evil side, Mr. Honor Roll!" Tom replied that everyone has a dark side, eyeing his pretty girlfriend in her blue, tight-fitting, one-piece bathing suit. The blue-green waves, relentlessly breaking against the shore, were free of the flotsam and pollutants that in subsequent years would make swimming unsafe. Grabbing the ex-paper boy's hand, she headed for the water, "Come on, let's take a dip." Like everything else about her, Joanie was a good swimmer, while Tom, who had never learned to swim, just waded in low water. Joanie was incredulous, "You mean the stick ball champ doesn't know how to swim? I'll teach you. Come here."

After thrashing about in the waves, Tom gave up and the two went for a walk along the beach. Walking in a southerly direction where there were fewer swimmers, they noticed a motley group of people, who appeared different from the other swimmers and sun bathers on the beach. They were dressed casually in shorts and dungarees, but did not wear bathing suits and they appeared to be led by a bespectacled young man, who appeared to be a counselor of some sort. There was a tentative quality about many of the members of the group, as if they had never been to the beach before. A few of them waded into the water, carrying their shoes—their conversation muffled by the dull roar of the breaking waves against the shore. Tom noticed one member of the group, a pretty teenager sketching the seashore on to a large sketch pad she held on her lap.

Suddenly, at the moment he recognized his sister, Cara turned towards Tom and Joanie, smiling, "Well, look whose here! Don't worry, I won't tell Mom you got a girlfriend. We both know how to keep secrets." Before Tom could respond, Cara was introducing her "smart brother and his pretty girlfriend" to her cohorts, as well as the group leader, Eric Evans. As they made small talk for a few minutes, Tom realized that psychiatric outpatients were no different from anybody else. Joanie had less problems with the therapy group than the fact that her boyfriend was keeping their friendship secret from his mother. But tolerance was one of the pretty Graniteville teenager's special qualities, which was why Tom adored her.

One day, Tom took Joanie for a long walk down Morningstar Road towards Richmond Terrace and the choppy Kill Van Kull, with its busy water traffic of tugboats, barges, and freighters. Turning west on Richmond Terrace, the couple walked towards the Bethlehem Steel shipyards of Mariners Harbor. Tom never tired of looking at the abandoned shipyards, ramshackle warehouses, immobile cranes, rotting docks, and corroded ships with their rusty anchors. Joanie observed, "Well, Mariners Harbor has seen better days. It's not would you'd call picturesque."

Tom agreed, but remarked that "the place, despite its squalor has an aesthetic appeal." Then he showed his girlfriend the old apartment building where he and Cara stayed with their mother in her one-bedroom cold water flat, when they first came to Staten Island years ago. Tom remarked "the waterfront illustrates the third law of thermodynamics: Everything in the universe runs down to random disorder — what scientists call entropy."

Shaking her head, Joanie observed, "Only you would know something like that, Mr. Pessimist."

1950s-1960s Fable

Smiling, Tom thought of T. S. Eliot's poem, "The Waste Land," from which he recited a few lines, "A rat crept softly though the vegetables, dragging its slimy belly on the bank. While I was fishing in the dull canal, on a winter evening behind the gashouse." Not quite

understanding Tom's sentimental attachment to this run-down neighborhood, Joanie said little, but held his hand tightly. She was puzzled by her melancholy boyfriend, who dazzled her with his wide-ranging, but obscure knowledge.

As the two teenagers walked back up the long sloping incline of Morningstar Road, they encountered a shabbily-dressed, grizzled old man, who looked like a vagrant. The man asked Tom if he had some change to spare because he was hungry. Joanie held Tom's hand tightly and moved a bit away from the red-faced man, who reeked of alcohol. Tom's reached into his pocket for his wallet and gave the man a dollar plus some change. Then peering closely at the old man's face, the ex-farm boy recognized him as his father's companion in the ramshackle house at the end of Pulaski Avenue. Looking much the worse for wear, Tom could see that he was on his last legs.

Scrutinizing the tall teenager closely, the old man exclaimed, "Why your Thomas Haley's son! You look just like him too. I remember your dad introducing you to me. He was so proud of you—a hard-working newspaper boy, good student, and stick ball champ."

Tom could feel Joanie tugging at him to end the conversation and walk away from the vagrant, but he ignored her. "I knew Thomas Haley for many years. He used to talk about you and your sister often. He once said something about the two of you living on a farm with some people in South Jersey. It bothered him a lot." Tom indicated that the old man's memory was accurate.

"And how's your mom doing? She didn't care for me — not that I blame her. It seems so long ago that me and your dad were drinking buddies. This area has seen better days, hasn't it, Tom?" The teenager agreed. Responding to Joanie's nudges, he shook the old man's

hand, wished him luck, and moved on with his girlfriend—realizing she knew some things about himself he'd have to explain. Fortunately, her tolerance and acceptance of her boyfriend's unusual past was virtually unlimited. He was one lucky guy.

The two teenagers went back to Elm Park, where Tom showed Joanie his house on Pulaski Avenue, the white stucco house fronted by the six-foot high hedge. His mom had gone to New York City to see a play by Tennesee Williams, "The Glass Managerie"—but Cara was home to welcome the two of them and make them some ice tea, along with her homemade cupcakes. Cara showed Joanie her art work and Tom got out a blank verse poem, he had written in his English class as a sophomore about the Mariners Harbor waterfront. She was enthusiastic in her praise for the works of both siblings and happy to see her boyfriend's shabby, but quaint home. Tom also showed Joanie photos of his foster family, the Smiths and their children Helen and Harry, who introduced Tom to books, encouraged Cara to draw, taught them how to ride bicycles and play baseball, and inculcated the moral values epitomized by Jesus's Sermon on the Mount.

Mariners Harbor

"Richmond Terrace bends, winds, and twists as if unsure of its way to the harbor; Beyond the Terrace lies the choppy gray-blue waters of the Kill Van Kull. The run-down waterfront tells us of past glory days long gone by; Long ago the shipyards were abuzz with important work and activity.

1950s-1960s Fable

The name "Bethlehem Steel" stood for war-time ship building;

But today the shipyards lie silent—occupied by gray rats and stray cats. Old docks, decaying shacks, and rotting hulks washed by the oily water;

Rusty ships dragging iron anchors on long clanging chains swaying in place; A once mighty warship armed with rusty cannons that will never fire, joined by ghostly vessels that creak and groan with the restless waves. These corroded iron hulks of ancient ships that once plowed the seven seas; The waterfront is filled with barges, cranes, and shacks locked in eerie silence, Rust, dirt, oil slicks, debris, flotsam and jetsam paint a picture of awful decay. An old sailor walks slowly along a rotting wooden wharf—avoiding its holes, this abandoned, lonely graveyard of ships— reminds us of the cruel march of time."

CHAPTER 39

PRHS Graduation

Near the end of June was the magical day anticipated by nearly 500 Port Richmond High School seniors — graduation day. The graduation ceremonies were held at the Ritz Theater on Richmond Avenue, where the stage was decked with a plethora of pink, white, and yellow flowers. The Ritz Theater marker had changed its inscription from "To Kill a Mockingbird" to "Closed Today PRHS Graduation." The boys wore white jackets with black trousers, while the girls were adorned in white graduation dresses sewn in their sewing classes. The elements cooperated in orchestrating a mild evening — rare for a late June night. Using his high honor roll status, Tom was able to obtain a ticket for Joanie, in addition to tickets for his mom and sister. Claire Haley was unexpectedly receptive with regard to Joanie's attendance at her son's graduation. After all, Tom was no longer a high school student, so her prohibition against dating in high school was no longer operative. His mother's perception of their relationship was that it was a short-lived summer romance that would wither at the vine — once Tom started going to City College of New York.

David Stanhoff gave a superb valedictory address speaking of the "essential tripod of the complete man — character, mind and body." Quoting John Donne's famous line that "no man is an Island, entire of itself," David reminded the graduates of their obligations to their fellow human beings as members of the human

1950s-1960s Fable

race. Tom went up to the stage to receive awards for highest honors in history, plus an honorable mention in science. Then near the end of the graduation ceremony, Tom was unexpectedly called up for the William Halloran Scholarship awarded to the highest achieving senior attending a public college. He and his mom were stunned to learn it was a $2,000 scholarship, which along with his $2,500 New York State Regents Scholarship — amounted to $4,500 — a significant amount of money for that time. Cara and Joanie wanted to know what he was going to do with that money. Would he buy a car?

"Over my dead body!" responded his mom, who kept the money in her bank account — doling it out to her son over the next four years. Her lack of trust in her son's ability to handle his scholarship money would irk Tom for many years.

After graduation, Tom and Joanie decided to walk down Richmond Avenue — passing Kresge's and Woolworth's — stopping at the latter five-and-dime store where Tom bought his girlfriend a charm bracelet. Joanie was ecstatic, "I'll never take it off!" He also bought her a bright red ribbon, with which she tied her glossy black hair into a bouncing pony tail. Standing on the sidewalk, they embraced and kissed — stopping to catch their breath. Tom had never been so happy in his life — thinking it doesn't get any better than this.

Walking back on Richmond Avenue towards Castleton Avenue, they stopped in front of Stechmann's, which was packed with the new graduates celebrating their recent status as Port Richmond High School alumni. In four years at Port Richmond — whether from lack of funds, or lack of free time, or simply from shyness — Tom had never ventured into this legendary ice-cream-parlor teenage hangout. So it was with a certain amount of trepidation that he entered the crowded establishment.

There was a break in the noise as the patrons took in the unusual spectacle of the high school's most notorious loner hand-in-hand with the tawny brunette, whose exotic beauty drew everyone's attention. As a McKee student, Joanie was a stranger to virtually all the regulars at Stechmann's. Sensing that all eyes were on them, Tom and Joanie felt very nervous. Fortunately, Tommy Spider, sitting at a table with his Avenue B friends, called the two teenagers over and they plunked down at his table—grateful for the feisty street kid's invitation. Coincidentally, one of Tommy's friends, Carlton, went to McKee, so the conversation got off to a good start. Joanie and Carlton talked about classmates and teachers they knew at their school.

Tommy leaned over towards the ex-newspaper boy, "She's a fine looking girl. You got good taste my man. So what happened to your paper route? I don't see you around the neighborhood anymore." Tom replied that he was now working at the A & P on Richmond Avenue. Tommy said that he was now driving a truck for Farr's furniture store—delivering televisions, sofas, dining room tables, and bedroom sets for $6 an hour plus tips. Tom was impressed, since he was getting less than half that amount working for the A & P.

The class valedictorian, David Stanhoff, came over to congratulate Tom on his $2,000 Halloran scholarship. The tall scholar-athlete, who led Port Richmond's basketball team in scoring, shook hands with Tommy Spider and his friends. "We had our ups and downs, but I have to admit, Tommy, you're one of a kind."

The latter snickered, "Well, you white dudes all look alike and talk alike to me. But if you want to learn something—come over to Avenue "B" and I'll show you how to play hoops." Pointing to Tom, "Let this guy show you the way, because I doubt you've ever been to my neck of the woods."

Sensing that someone was looking at him, Tom looked across the room to see Bonnie Rosolio staring at Joanie and himself. The pretty curly-haired young woman, whom Tom knew when he was a sixth-grader at P. S. 21 in Elm Park was with her long-time boyfriend, Roy Rand. The muscular matinee idol, who along with Bonnie had starred in many of the high school's stage productions, was also staring at Tom and Joanie. Leaning over to Bonnie, he remarked: "Well, I see our boy has found himself a girlfriend. And you thought he was a hopeless case of repressed sexual impulses. Mr. Honor Roll has good taste. She's a cutie!"

Frowning, the curly-haired dramatics star said, "Oh, shut up." Then smiling wistfully, she murmured, "Good for him. He's been through a lot."

Todd M. Daley

CHAPTER 40

Fun City

One sultry summer night, Tom and Joanie went to New York City to take in the sights and see a movie. They walked around the honky-tonk Times Square area with bright neon lights, theater markees, and the hustle and bustle of its crowded sidewalks—touted as "the cross road of the world." There were other sights that shocked the naïve adolescents—beggars, hustlers, prostitutes, vagrants, drunks, and drug addicts—interspersed with foot-patrolmen who kept their eyes on these petty criminals. Tom told his wide-eyed girlfriend that his mother referred to those street people as the "lumpen proletariat." Puzzled, the pretty brunette inquired as to the meaning of "that peculiar expression." Hesitating momentarily, the ex-newspaper boy replied, "Well my mother has unorthodox political views about which the less said, the better off we'll be."

Stopping and peering up at him with her big brown eyes, Joanie inquired, "What sort of ideas, Tom?" Tom indicated that she was a "self-styled Marxist." Joanie responded that "nobody is perfect"—as if leftist ideas were an affliction. Tom thought that the old aphorism that opposites attract was quite true—at least in the case of their teenage romance. As she fixed him an adoring look, Tom realized her unconditional love was one of the greatest gifts of his entire life. They decided to see a movie—wavering between

1950s-1960s Fable

"Whatever Happened to Baby Jane" and "The Manchurian Candidate" — opting for the latter because Joanie disliked horror movies.

She also sensed that Tom preferred movies with a political message. "The Manchurian Candidate" was about some American soldiers brainwashed by the Chinese Communists who would return to America for the purpose of committing a political assassination. The complicated conspiracy was conceived in order to elect a presidential candidate that would further the Communists' political objectives.

Emerging from the darkened movie theater, the two teenagers walked around until they found a Horn and Hardock's restaurant in the area. This legendary restaurant featured menu items like sandwiches, hamburgers, macaroni and cheese, bowls of soup, slices of cake and pie in little glass enclosed shelves with the price displayed — 15, 25, 35, 50 cents — amazingly inexpensive even for those low-priced times. Customers simply put the necessary coins into the corresponding slots, turned the handle, and the glass door opened for the particular food item.

Tom told Joanie about the time he went to Horn and Hardock's with his sister, his mom, and his Aunt Dorothy and Uncle Mel, who treated them to their first restaurant meal ever. He was struck by the kindness of his two relatives, particularly Uncle Mel whom he had never met before and who was not a blood relative. Having the same large shoe size as Tom (size 12 ½), this successful owner of a shoe outlet on Long Island sent him expensive Florsheim shoes and socks every few months for many years. From family folklore, Tom knew that Aunt Dorothy had given Claire Haley part of her own inheritance from her parents, which provided the down payment for the white stucco house on Pulaski

Avenue. The aphorism that we are all dependent on the kindness of friends, family, and sometimes strangers — was clear to the ex-newspaper boy.

As Tom and Joanie walked towards Broadway heading for the downtown bus, they saw a middle-aged man in a black suit standing on a wooden soapbox and holding a Bible— proclaiming that the world was coming to an end. He urged the passing pedestrians to "repent and change your sinful ways for the apocalypse is at hand. The Messiah is coming!"

Tom started to laugh but he saw Joanie's face darken with dread. Hugging his petite girlfriend, Tom whispered in her ear, "Don't worry Joanie, I'll be with you until the end of time."

Distracted by the two teenagers, the self-styled preacher told them to "beware of godless leaders who lead this country astray — Kennedy, Johnson, Nixon, Rockefeller, Reverend King, and the devil incarnate himself — John Lindsay.

Irked by the street preacher's random list of politicians, Tom exclaimed, "John Lindsay happens to be a great mayor. He cares about poor people and the minorities."

"Minorities?" responded the street-corner reverend, "As a man of God, I am the only true minority in America. Look at the filth and squalor in this modern-day Sodom and Gomorrah! See the hookers and pimps, the winos and junkies, the crooks and creeps that abound! Behold the motley crew walking the streets from the four corners of the earth. All are welcomed here with open arms and given welfare by that Hollywood movie star — John Lindsay."

Defending the liberal mayor, Tom asserted that "the streets have never been cleaner.

1950s-1960s Fable

People come here because it's a Mecca—a beacon of hope for the entire world."

Looking up at her tall boyfriend with admiration, Joanie chimed in: "Yeah, Mayor Lindsay is cool.

He's made New York City a fun place—Fun City! Where else in the world would you'd rather be? Look at the bright lights, hustle-bustle, and all the people walking around. It's the crossroad of the world!"

Shaking his head, the urban prophet growled at the pretty teenager, "Get thee to a nunnery, my pretty wench!" With

that rejoinder ringing in her ears, Joanie grabbed Tom's hand and pulled him away from the nutty soapbox preacher.

"Well, you meet all kinds of people in New York," her boyfriend remarked as they continued their tour of Fun City.

November 8, 19 58

John Vliet Lindsay was elected to the United States Congress in 1958, representing Manhattan's upper East Side for four terms. John Lindsay was a native New Yorker, born on West End Avenue to an upper-middle class family of English and Dutch ancestry. Lindsay attended prep school at St. Paul's and Yale University in New Haven, Connecticut. Completing his college studies in 1943, Lindsay joined the U. S. Navy as a gunnery officer. Obtaining the rank of lieutenant, John Lindsay earned five battle stars through action in Sicily and several landings in the Pacific during World War II. After the war he worked as a bank clerk, before entering Yale Law School — receiving his law degree in 1948, ahead of schedule.

After marrying Mary Anne Harrison, a distant relative of U. S. presidents in 1949, John Lindsay was admitted to the bar. In 1952, he became the president of the New York Young Republican Club and was active in New York City politics. In 1958 with the backing of prominent Republicans, John Lindsay was nominated and then elected to Congress as the representative of "the Silk Stocking" district of upper Manhattan. In Congress, Lindsay established a liberal voting record that put him at odds with the Republican Party. He was a staunch supporter of federal aid to education, Medicare, and the federal department of Urban Affairs. Lindsay earned a reputation as a maverick – opposing federal interception of communist literature and obscene material. John Lindsay justified his votes by asserting that communism and pornography were the two major industries of his "silk stocking" district. A strong supporter of civil rights, John Lindsay was the leader of a group of liberal Republicans in the House of Representatives that voted for President Johnson's Civil Rights Act of 1964.

In 1965, John Lindsay was elected mayor of New York City on the Republican ticket – defeating Democrat Abraham Beame, the City Controller. One newspaper columnist described Lindsay as "fresh, where everyone else is tired." Lindsay inherited a city with serious fiscal woes – in the face of declining manufacturing jobs and a dwindling middle class. In addition, municipal workers – including teachers, police, fire, sanitation, subway conductors and bus drivers – demanded higher pay and increased benefits. During the 12-day transit workers strike, Mayor Lindsay jailed TWU leader Mike Quill, who referred to the youthful mayor as "Mr. Lindsley" asserting that "The judge can drop dead in his black robes because I would sooner rot in jail than call off the subway and bus strike." Consequently, the Lindsay Administration was besieged with a series of municipal strikes, including transit, sanitation, and teacher strikes – forcing the mayor to walk four miles from his apartment to City Hall each day. Mayor Lindsay remarked, "I still think it's a fun city" – from which the sarcastic term "Fun City" was derived.

In 1968, the United Federation of Teachers, under Albert Shanker, initiated a strike that lasted until the middle of October – protested the decentralization of the New York City school system into 33

1950s-1960s Fable

separate school boards. That same year, there was also a nine-day sanitation strike and a three-day Broadway shows strike.

The quality of life in New York reached a low point as mounds of garbage caught fire, strong winds blew refuse through the streets, and the rat population of Manhattan exploded. With the schools shut down, the police involved in a slowdown, the firefighters threatening job actions, the city accumulating uncollected garbage, and racial tensions beginning to explode – the city teetered on the brink of anarchy. Somehow the unlucky mayor weathered the urban storm – settling the strikes with sizeable increases in labor contracts for New York's municipal workers.

After the assassination of civil rights leader Martin Luther King, John Lindsay was one of the few white politicians (besides Robert Kennedy) who could walk into black neighborhoods and talk to the disenfranchised and gain their trust. As a result of his early opposition to the Vietnam War, John Lindsay was called "the red mayor" and "a traitor." After criticism for alleged neglect of the outer boroughs, the Lindsay administration became more pragmatic and efficient in delivering vital services to the entire city. In addition, the Lindsay administration brought 225,000 more jobs to the city, put 6,000 more cops on the street, and hired hundreds of new teachers and para-professionals for the classroom. And unlike cities like Detroit, Los Angeles, and Newark, New York City did not experience devastating urban riots and widespread looting.

John Lindsay was also credited with rejuvenating the city's parks, as well as the arts and culture, particularly Broadway – transforming New York into an international tourist attraction. Under Mayor Lindsay, New York City did become more prosperous, more just, and more diverse. Indeed, despite the social unrest of that era – New York really was Fun City!

Todd M. Daley

CHAPTER 41

Summer of Love

Tom and Joanie spent so much time together that summer following his graduation from high school that the fetching teenager was his first thought in the morning before embarking for his A & P job, and his last thought before falling asleep at night in his sun-porch bedroom. They covered the entire city together — taking buses, subways, and ferries to Staten Island beaches and parks, New York City museums and movie theaters. They went to Central Park to walk through its tree-shaded pathways and to see the zoo nestled amidst its sloping hills and valleys. They took a bus that went across the Bayonne Bridge, which spanned the Kill Van Kull, to an amusement park in Bayonne, where Tom knocked over a statue with a baseball to win a teddy bear for Joanie. One Saturday night, Tom took Joanie to DeNinno's Pizzaria on Richmond Avenue where they shared a pizza and Tom had his first alcoholic drink — a bottle of Rhinegold beer. Though it tasted bitter, Tom felt obliged to finish it and not waste his 50 cents. Joanie ordered a soda, but took several sips of the beer — becoming giggly and tipsy after a while. John Sebastian's words blared from the jukebox:

"You didn't have to be so nice I would have liked you anyway. If you just looked once or twice and gone your quiet way. You came upon a quiet day You simply seemed to take your place. I knew that it would be that way the minute I saw your face." Looking at his adorable heart-throb, Tom sighed, "Joanie, what am I gonna do with you?"

1950s–1960s Fable

Gazing at him with her big brown eyes, she responded in a whisper, "Anything you want to."

Overcome with emotion to the point of tears, Tom said, "No, I wouldn't do anything that would tarnish your reputation, Joanie. You are too special for that sort of thing. I want to do the right thing by you and protect you from harm."

As the place filled up with people and became noisy, Joanie told Tom to take her home. Strolling up Walker Street towards Elm Park, the two teenagers decided to walk through the cemetery that faced P. S. 21, which Tom had attended when he first came to Staten Island from South Jersey so many years ago. He recalled the schoolyard games and the poetry recital when his inebriated father distracted him by calling out from the audience.

He remembered the afternoon when Mr. Taglia told him that Thomas Haley had collapsed and died on Pulaski Avenue from a massive heart attack during one of his drinking binges. From Thomas Mann's *The Magic Mountain*, Tom recalled that when a person is consumed with the life force of love, there are opposing thoughts of sickness and death. Mann had linked love, sickness, and death as mystical expressions of the flesh which ennoble life.

They sat down on a bench surrounded by tombstones, shrubs, and evergreen trees in the small cemetery. It was a crystal clear midsummer night with a half-moon providing good illumination. The nighttime sky was alit with hundreds of twinkling stars
Looking into the heavens, Tom observed, "That's a waning moon. Each night it will get smaller and smaller."

Poking him with her elbow, Joanie replied, "How do you know? Do you watch the moon every night?"

Tom responded, "No, I'd rather look at you, Joanie." He indicated that a waning moon has the illuminated part on the left, while a waxing moon has the illuminated part on the right.

"Only you would know a ridiculous fact like that," Joanie remarked — feigning annoyance.

Adding insult to injury, the ex-newspaper boy continued, "Half-Moon was the name of Henry Hudson's ship that first entered New York Harbor and sailed up the Hudson River in 1609."

Sitting on his lap and pinching his face, she snickered, "There you go again with one of your ridiculous facts. Say something else stupid like George Washington sat on this bench 200 years ago and screwed Pocahontas."

Laughing, he corrected her, "No, that was the old Dutchman Peter Stuyvesant who did that after he bought Manhattan from the Lenape Indians for $24."

While this historical discussion occurred, Joanie had changed her position on Tom's lap so she was facing him — slowly rocking back and forth. "You know what? I think you spend too much time with your nose buried in books. But I love you, Mr. Honor Roll."

Responding, he covered her face, arms, shoulders, neck, and chest with kisses. Barely audible, Tom murmured that he loved her too.

Joanie unbuttoned her blouse, exposing her delicate bra. For the first time, Tom felt the wonderfully soft swelling flesh of her breasts.

1950s-1960s Fable

Then Joanie shuddered and whispered in his ear, "I think we better stop before we reach the point of no return." Tom, besides himself with pent-up sexual feelings, restrained himself, putting his arms around Joanie—hugging her tightly. Their rapid panting subsided as the intensity of their passion receded and they moved away from that dangerous sexual precipice.

"I'm so tired now, I could fall asleep. Take me home, Tom." He agreed and they stood up slowly and walked out of the cemetery arm-in-arm, down Walker Street, past his old school P. S. 21, towards Morningstar Road — under the twinkling stars and the shining half-moon, which had shone on young lovers since the beginning of time.

It was business as usual at the white stucco house on Pulaski Avenue, where Cara and her mother commuted to work in Manhattan each day via the # 3 Castleton Avenue bus. Claire Haley had described the # 3 bus route on meandering Castleton Avenue as the grand tour of Staten Island's North Shore. The bus passed many Catholic churches on its circuitous journey to the St. George Ferry. It was one of their mom's pet peeves that the mostly Catholic commuters would repeatedly cross themselves each time the bus passed a Catholic church.

Tom inquired, "How do they know it's a Catholic church and not a Protestant church?"

Cara, the keen-eyed artist said, "Well, Protestant churches don't have stained-glass windows and they are smaller, less ornate and there is no statue of Mary in front."

Religious issues no longer interested Tom, who never discussed them with his Catholic girlfriend, Joanie

Gardello Claire Haley had been promoted to office manager at the Royal Canadian Bank on Wall Street, where she had been working since Tom entered high school. And Cara was working for an insurance company during the day, while she studied stenography and office procedures at night, hoping to advance from her clerk-typist job to a secretarial position. With extra money flowing into the house from Cara's and Tom's jobs, their mom had begun to fix up the old house — making some long-overdue repairs of the antiquated plumbing. In the kitchen, the dripping sink and the erratic gas stove were replaced. In the bathroom, the slow-draining sink was replaced by a new pink porcelain sink, the old-fashioned iron-legged bathtub was replaced by a modern bath-shower combination, and the noisy, leaky toilet was replaced by a modern fast-flushing toilet. Shaking her finger at her son, Claire Haley warned him not to hammer any two-by-fours between the toilet and the wall — as he had done in the past in an attempt to fix a leaky toilet.

Admiring her new bathroom, their mom asserted, "Indoor plumbing is without a doubt man's greatest invention!"

Smiling, Cara interjected "What about toilet paper? I would say it's right up there with John Crapper's invention."

Tom disagreed with both of them, declaring that the outhouse was the greatest commode ever invented. Musing, he said "I always enjoyed the Smith's outhouse, even with the horseflies, bees, and hornets buzzing around near the ceiling. You could do your business at a leisurely pace, listening to the birds chirping outside while reading the newspaper or a good book."

1950s-1960s Fable

Cara disagreed, "I hated that place, the bugs were awful, and the stench was unbearable. The simple joys of the country life are not for me!" On his way to Joanie's house, Tom thought about his childhood experiences on the Smith's South Jersey farm—building that wooden shack by himself, chasing the pigs when they got loose, feeding the chickens and ducks, plucking the feathers from the scolding-hot turkeys, weeding Mom Smith's vegetable garden, and picking corn in the fall. Spending much of the summers roaming barefoot over twelve acres of fields was an idyllic childhood that ended abruptly when his biological parents took Cara and himself up to Staten Island. The early years were rough— adjusting to new friends in a new neighborhood with unfamiliar parents and his father's fierce drinking binges— ending in his untimely death on the street. He had so much to tell Joanie about these childhood experiences—which undoubtedly left some scars on the psyches of his sister and himself.

Walking towards her house along Morningstar Road, Tom passed youngsters he barely knew, who played the same street games of punch ball and stick ball that he had played a few years ago. He seldom saw his old Elm Park buddies, Mike Palermo, Joey Caprino, and Gene Munski, who were playing American Legion baseball during the summer. Rumors had it that Mike Palermo would be signed by the Yankees to pitch for their class "C" minor league baseball team. Busy with his A & P job and dating Joanie during his free time, Tom no longer played organized baseball. To be young and in love represented the greatest blessings that life could bestow on a person. He was particularly fortunate that her parents were fond of him—dubbing Tom "the all-American boy."

Todd M. Daley

CHAPTER 42

The Worst News

When Tom rang Joanie's doorbell, she quickly emerged from her house—slamming the front door and looking upset. Her big brown eyes were reddish and tear-filled and her shiny black hair was uncharacteristically disheveled. Even her clothes lacked their usual freshly laundered and ironed appearance. Feeling that something was terribly wrong, Tom was gripped by fear and dread. Sobbing, the pretty teenager took his hand and said, "Let's go for a walk. I have something to tell you." The last time Tom had heard a similar message was when Mom Smith told him that he and his sister would be leaving the farm to live with his birth parents on Staten Island. The same hollow feeling in the pit of his stomach wrenched the ex-farm boy. At a loss as to where to go, the two teenaged lovers walked aimlessly along Forest Avenue—towards Morningstar Road.

Stopping at a diner on the corner, they found a booth in a corner. Neither of them had an appetite, but Tom felt obliged to order some coffee and apple pie, which were left untouched. Sobbing convulsively, Joanie summoned the strength to explain the reason for her sorrow: Her father, a middle-level manager for a big pharmaceutical company, was being transferred to the new corporate headquarters in Indiana. Forgetting himself momentarily, Tom declared, "Indiana was one of the three states that Lincoln grew up in—Kentucky, Indiana, and Illinois."

1950s-1960s Fable

Joanie reached across and stroked the ex-newspaper boy's cheek: "You will always be my honor-roll boy.

I love you, Tom. I'll write to you and visit you. I have cousins here." The boy shook his head — vainly trying to deny the reality of their unhappy situation. "Just like when you lived on that farm in South Jersey. Your parents moved you up here without asking you."

The tears streaming down his cheeks, Tom was inconsolable. He recalled John Kennedy's words, "Life is unfair." The two star-crossed lovers sat there in the booth holding hands and crying. Tom began shivering. Joanie sat next to him, hugging him and rubbing his hands and arms — vainly trying to quell Tom's shivers. After sitting in the diner for hours, they walked home. At one point, Tom crossed the busy Forest Avenue-Morningstar Road intersection shambling blindly — narrowly missed by a car, which alarmed Joanie.

All he said to her was, "It's all right." She realized immediately that her boyfriend was in trouble — he was a broken young man. They returned to her house, where he collapsed on her front porch. Her father drove Tom home, where he was put to bed in his summer sun-porch bedroom by Joanie herself. After that, Tom did not leave his bed for two weeks.

His mom was frantic with her son's physical and mental state — so unlike the spirited, upbeat, energetic adolescent. It was frightenly similar to his sister's nervous breakdown just six months prior. The same symptoms exhibited by Cara — apathy, inertia, torpidity, and the overwhelming despair of depression. However, there was one difference between brother and sister. When Tom spoke, which was seldom, he never said anything inappropriate of irrational. When questioned about how he felt or when he was getting out of bed, his response was: ""It's all right."

With little more than a month left before classes began at C.C.N.Y., the ex-newspaper boy's condition could cause him to forfeit the $2,500 Regents Scholarship and the $2,000 Halloran Scholarship. Cara took one look at her brother and proclaimed, "Nervous breakdown! Just like me. He needs help right away. Mom, call Dr. Atlas." Spurred Cara's assessment of her brother's mental condition, Claire Haley called Dr. Atlas, the reliable family physician, who still made house calls—carrying his black doctor's bag and a charging a mere $10 for home visits. After examining the teenager, Dr. Atlas made his diagnosis—acute depression caused by a broken heart.

Wailing uncontrollably, his mother exclaimed, "I knew it. Both of my children carry bad genes from their alcoholic father and his crazy family. Half of them were drunks and the other half were dim-wits and misfits. He used to call them mountain men, but they were just ignorant hill-billies—the lowest of the low."

Cara hugged her distraught mother, "You don't really mean that, Mom. I have an idea. Let's call the Smiths. It might help Tom overcome his melancholia, which is really a broken heart."

Shaking her head, Claire Haley declared, "And that's why I was against his going steady with that McKee girl. He needed that like a hole in the head!" Suddenly overwrought with sadness and fatigue herself, Claire Haley consented to the Smiths' visit. She would agree to anything that could help her son at this point.

CHAPTER 43

Helen to the Rescue

Mom Smith and her daughter, Helen, now a married woman with two of her own children, stood over Tom's bed in the small sun-porch bedroom — peering down at the sleepy ex-farm boy who was once part of their family. The blinds were pulled down in the stifling hot room, which contained his metal desk and an old bureau. There was a big Philco radio with which he had listened to Phillies night games. He had fixed the old radio himself by replacing burnt-out vacuum tubes.

The lanky teenager sensed their presence and opened his eyes. "It's all right." Then getting a better look at Helen, he smiled for the first time in a fortnight.

Helen signaled to the others to leave the room a few minutes, pulling up a chair next to Tom's bed, leaned over, and kissed the boy's feverish cheek. "Do you recall how hard it was for you and your sister when you first moved up to Staten Island? Remember how Mom and Dad visited you? And we're all so proud of you and Cara. You're both so grown up now. Remember Jesus's Sermon on the Mount? Blessed are the meek, the merciful, the poor, the pure in heart, and the broken hearted — like you, Tom."

Breaking his silence, Tom said he would abide by those words but it was so hard think about anything but his girlfriend, Joanie.

Stroking the teenager's sweaty forehead, Helen said, "St. Paul talked about faith, hope, charity, and love.
Love bears all things, believes all things, and hopes all things." Sobbing quietly, Tom whispered, "All I can think of is Joanie and the nice times we had together. The worst thing about it is the way time drags on. You're haunted by the past and trapped by the present and afraid of the future."

Nodding, Helen replied, "Yes, time will pass very slowly at first. It will be your enemy, but then time will be your friend. It has been said that time heals all wounds. As it will with you, Tom." Then, reaching into her handbag, Helen presented Tom with a musty old book, a biography of Alexander Hamilton. I found this book behind the old bookcase in Mom's cellar. It must have fallen off the bookcase, so you never got the chance to read it."

In spite of his profound melancholia, Tom was intrigued—taking the book from Helen and leafing through it. "It looks interesting. After science, history is my favorite subject."

Grasping the ex-newspaper boy's hand, Helen made him promise that he would read the book—to which the teenager readily agreed. "He started out as an orphan and rose to become one of our Founding Fathers," Helen declared.

Mom Smith had brought some steak sandwiches on rye bread—an old favorite of Tom and Cara as youngsters when they returned to the small clapboard house after roaming the twelve-acre Smith farm. Using a mother's intuition, his foster mother insisted that Tom get up and go into the kitchen for lunch. Weakened, emaciated, and pale, Tom gathered himself slowly and shuffled onto the front porch and down the long narrow hallway to the middle room and kitchen.

1950s–1960s Fable

In the bright, sunny kitchen Claire Haley, Mom Smith, Helen, and Cara were seated at the small wrought iron table discussing safe subjects like the hot, dry summer which had curtailed the Smiths' corn and vegetable crops. Claire Haley was uncharacteristically quiet during this unremarkable conversation. Tom was somewhat taken aback by this unlikely congregation—as if he was unable to connect his bedroom visitors with the persons sitting at the table. It amazed Tom that his natural mother and foster mother were sitting quietly at the same table. After all, this was the first meeting between his birth mother and his foster family since he and his sister had moved to Staten Island more than seven years ago.

Was this strange meeting really happening or was he dreaming? Maybe his ill-fated teenage romance with Joanie Gardello was just a dream—a dream with a nightmare ending.

As if reading his mind, Claire Haley piped up with her often-repeated adage: "Life must be lived on the basis of reality."

Frowning, Cara replied, "Not another one of your silly axioms Mom. It's like saying—if you step in dog shit then you are unlucky."

For the first time in two weeks Tom laughed, "Cara, that's very funny!"

Reddening with anger, Claire Haley said, "Yeah, your sister's a scream."

Trying to change the subject Mom Smith asked Tom when he would be starting college—to which Tom replied, "Soon. In fact, I want to buy some notebooks, pens, and pencils."

Placing her arm around the teenager's narrow shoulders, Helen responded, "That's the spirit, Tom. Now eat something, you look like a skeleton." Smirking, Cara said—"Yeah, food must be eaten on the basis of taste."

CHAPTER 44

A Game of Stick Ball

After the Smiths had left the white stucco house onPulaski Avenue, Tom returned to his sun-porch bedroom feeling a void that could not be filled. Time had never weighed so heavily on the active teenager. Heretofore, there never seemed to be enough time to do all the things that came to mind. He tried to think of the days before Joanie had come into his life. Just the thought of his girlfriend caused him to shudder. In those halcyon days, his time was divided between school, work, and sports. He also devoted part of his spare time to reading. Turning on his lamp, the ex-newspaper boy picked up the Alexander Hamilton biography given to him by Helen.

Like himself, Alexander Hamilton had humble origins, was a voracious reader and copious note-taker — compiling notebooks on literature, history, geography, and the books of the Bible. Coincidentally, Hamilton's parents lived as common-law husband and wife on the Caribbean island of St. Croix. Throughout his political career, Alexander Hamilton was tarred with the epithet "Creole Bastard" by such political opponents as John Adams, Thomas Jefferson, and Aaron Burr (who killed Hamilton in a duel in 1804). Unlike Jefferson, who was a slave owner, Hamilton was a true believer in the equality of the races.

And unlike Jefferson, Hamilton actually fought in the American Revolution, demonstrating bravery under fire. Like many of America's "Founding

Fathers" — Alexander Hamilton was a deist — believing that God did not interfere in human affairs. As the first Secretary of Treasury, Hamilton conceived of the idea of financing America's war debts through tariffs on foreign goods. This policy also encouraged the development of American manufacturing. As a Federalist, Hamilton worked hard to establish a strong federal government — rather than a loose union of states, as favored by Jefferson. Hamilton also started the U.S. Postal service and the Coast Guard. Alexander Hamilton's greatest contribution was his work, along with James Madison, in writing the United States Constitution. He also was instrumental in getting the Constitution adopted by the states with his Federalist Papers, which were also written by Madison and John Jay. Once questioned why "God" was not mentioned in the U.S. Constitution, Alexander Hamilton responded, "We forgot."

The morning sunlight filled the six-windowed sun porch with a brightness that awakened Tom. A ray of sunlight edging through a slit in the blinds fell on his eyes — causing the ex-newspaper boy to squint. He had spent most of the night reading the musty Alexander Hamilton biography given to him by Helen. Outside, there were the pleasant sounds of some youngsters playing the running bases, bounce pitch form of stick ball in the street. With Mike Palermo, Joey Caprino, and Gene Munski playing American Legion baseball and gone from Pulaski Avenue, a new generation of kids had taken over the Elm Park neighborhood.

1950s-1960s Fable

Donning his dungarees, T-shirt, and worn sneakers, and grabbing his old baseball glove, Tom ran out to join the group. In typical New York City street kid custom, the ex-farm boy was quickly accepted into their stick ball game — running, throwing, catching, and hitting the high-bouncing spaldeen.

Coming to bat in the next inning, Tom got a hold of the elusive spaldeen with the broomstick bat and sent it 250 feet on to the roof of a distant house — to the "oohs" and "ahs" of his younger teammates. The pure joy and physical exertion of the stick ball game made Tom feel alive for the first time in the last few weeks.

After all, he was a New Yorker and he had his whole life ahead of him in the optimistic 1960s era of this eternally hopeful country. As Thomas Wolfe had once said: "America is a fabulous country, the only fabulous country. It is the only place where miracles not only happen, but where they happen all the time."

THE END

Todd M. Daley

ABOUT THE AUTHOR

The author has taught science and mathematics for 47 years on the high school and college levels. He has bachelor's and master's degrees from C.C.N.Y. and a Ph.D from New York University. Over the years he has written a textbook on arithmetic — Mathematical Concepts (Copley) and a short book on western philosophy — A Brief Guide to Philosophy (AuthorHouse).

www.ingramcontent.com/pod-product-compliance
Lightning Source LLC
Chambersburg PA
CBHW071428070526
44578CB00001B/33